PERIPHcRAL VISIONS

PERIPHERAL VISIONS

THE HIDDEN STAGES OF WEIMAR CINEMA

EDITED BY KENNETH S. CALHOON

WAYNE STATE UNIVERSITY PRESS   DETROIT

KRITIK: GERMAN LITERARY THEORY AND CULTURAL STUDIES

Liliane Weissberg, EDITOR

A complete listing of the books in this series can be found at the back of this volume.

Copyright 2001 © by Wayne State University Press,
Detroit, Michigan 48201. All rights are reserved.
No part of this book may be reproduced without formal permission.
Manufactured in the United States of America.
05 04 03 02 01   5 4 3 2 1

Library of Congress Cataloging-in-Publication Data

Peripheral visions : the hidden stages of Weimar cinema / edited by
Kenneth S. Calhoon.
    p. cm.—(Kritik)
    Includes bibliographical references and index.
    ISBN 0-8143-2927-6—ISBN 0-8143-2928-4 (pbk.)
    1. Motion pictures—Germany—History. 2. Kracauer, Siegfried,
1889–1966—Criticism and interpretation. I. Calhoon, Kenneth Scott,
1956– II. Title. III. Kritik (Detroit, Mich.)
PN1993.5.G3 P39 2001
791.43'75'0943—dc21   00-012283

CONTENTS

5

ACKNOWLEDGMENTS

I am indebted to Liliane Weissberg for her ongoing support and to Anton Kaes for his abiding encouragement and confraternity. A fellowship from the Alexander von Humboldt Foundation facilitated much of the editorial work on this volume, and the National Endowment for the Humanities made it possible for certain of the contributors to meet and exchange preliminary ideas. The University of California Press has graciously consented to the inclusion of a chapter from Janet Ward's *Weimar Surfaces: Urban Visual Culture in 1920s Germany* (copyright 2000 by The Regents of the University of California). Film stills were provided by the Stiftung Deutsche Kinemathek, the Bundesarchiv-Filmarchiv (Berlin), and the Filmmuseum Frankfurt. The following museums granted permission to reproduce works from their collections: the Art Institute of Chicago, Musée National du Chateau de Versailles, and the Staatliche Museen zu Berlin. I am especially grateful to the contributors themselves, who watched with patience as this project lumbered toward completion.

K. S. C.

KENNETH S. CALHOON

Introduction

Among the holdings of London's National Gallery is a "perspective box"
by the seventeenth-century painter Samuel Van Hoogstraten. Less than ninety
centimeters at its widest dimension, this five-sided wooden case invites visitors
to peer through two peepholes into an intricately rendered Dutch interior whose
furnishings, decorations, tiled floors, and mere size suggest altogether comfortable
circumstances. Rooms and hallways appear in perfect geometrical perspective—
an illusion made possible by painted distortions, which the carefully placed
apertures are calculated to correct. A sixth, open side was originally covered with
a translucent material that admitted light while concealing the artifice behind the
deception.[1] The trompe l'oeil effect is reminiscent of such famous earlier creations
as Palladio's Olympic Theater, where corridors, inclining up from the stage and
fitted with foreshortened models of Renaissance palazzi, give the impression of
streets extending off toward distant vanishing points.

Yet, while Palladio's theater was intended for festive, costume-rich productions (it was inaugurated in 1585 with a "vulgarized" interpretation of *Oedipus Rex*),
Van Hoogstraten's device looks ahead to a modern dramatic tradition that affords
views onto private domestic scenes. Clearly, Van Hoogstraten's optical experiment
predates modern theater by more than a century. Nonetheless, its particular mise-
en-scène, which absorbs the spectator while excluding him corporeally, is consistent
with the convention of the "fourth wall," which guaranteed a certain realism and
made of the theatergoer a clandestine observer. The perspective box and modern
theater are separate though related moments in the consolidation of an interiority,
its autonomy synonymous with spatial closure. Whereas Van Hoogstraten employed the same anamorphic projections that enabled Baroque ceiling painters to
extend architectural space into the heavens, his singular achievement was to make
a very small space appear life-sized.[2]

Common to the Olympic Theater and the perspective box are principles
of design that were eventually brought to bear on the construction of movie sets,
which themselves waver between the gigantic and the miniature. The futuristic
cityscape of Fritz Lang's *Metropolis*, for example, was created with wooden models
of skyscrapers not much taller than the workers who built them.[3] These facades,

like those on Palladio's stage, were distorted to suggest height and extension. Such illusions of monumentality, as well as the illusionist thrust of the German film industry overall, provoked Siegfried Kracauer to impugn a mass ornamentalism—a disarticulation of meaning and form that resulted in a virtuosity of marvelous but empty visual conjuring. What bothered Kracauer was not simply the profusion of disconnected and hollow effects but the ability of the cinematic apparatus to reassemble the fragments into a coherent and believable whole. By posing as nature, the machinery of cinema recreated the fourth wall, and with it a physical and emotional interior premised on the exclusion of the socio-technical world—a world of which that same machinery was a supreme expression. Van Hoogstraten's invention represents an intermediate and ambiguous juncture in the establishment of monocular perspective, which secured the appearance of an integral space by concealing outside forces, making the illusion at once optical and ideological.

The eclipse of the world at large has its cinematic equivalent in the suppression of offscreen space, as exemplified by a shot from Arnold Fanck's *The Sacred Mountain* (1926). The scene is of a rustically appointed Swiss interior, at the far end of which a female figure (Leni Riefenstahl) is seated on the sill of a large window, contemplating the Alpine view beyond. Absorbed, she personifies the self-containment of the space she occupies, suggesting a concentration, or *Sammlung*, that occludes the periphery and its attendant distractions. The window's beveled casing accentuates the perspective that frames the distant mountain. Light entering from a side window adds a painterly touch, as does a checkered tablecloth, which recalls the alternating black and white tiles that, in Dutch painting, typically helped foster the illusion of depth. Here, angular shafts of sunlight on a bare floor both lead the eye into the picture and draw it back to a lamp burning in the foreground. This "still" is in every respect a "still life." The spare but carefully tended furnishings are markers of a wished-for domesticity. The mountain, situated at the geometrical vanishing point, naturalizes the construction, which the film itself, in its persistent disruption of spatial coherence, disintegrates.

At stake is a space whose integrity depends on the successful effacement of the mechanisms that create and maintain it. Van Hoogstraten and his contemporaries reveled in the interplay of artifice and illusion. This can also be said of many early films, such as those by Méliès, which tended to foreground their own "magical" capacity for effect.[4] Yet film worked increasingly to hide its devices, even while the "equipment," to quote Christian Metz, "has its discursive imprints . . . in the very text of the film."[5] The movement toward naturalism effectively contradicts Walter Benjamin's belief that the cinema, because of its inexorably mechanical character, could not ultimately pass itself off as nature. Therein lay its radical potential. Benjamin cites—as reactionary—Franz Werfel's praise of Max Reinhardt's *A Midsummer Night's Dream* (1935); Werfel claimed that Reinhardt, by using "natural means" to create "supernatural effects," realized an artistry otherwise thwarted in

Der heilige Berg (1926), directed by Arnold Fanck.

film by the intrusion of the "outside world," with its streets, interiors, railroad stations, restaurants, automobiles, and the like.[6]

This juxtaposition of dream to external forces confines the latter to the realm of the repressed while inscribing the former as a locus of the "purposeless efficacy" (*Zweckmäßigkeit ohne Zweck*) that for Kant conditioned the experience of beauty. Tantamount to an absence of content, this aestheticism, Kracauer thought, was nowhere more abundantly manifest than in the lobbies of metropolitan hotels. A place where atomized individuals commingled anonymously, the *Hotelhalle* was an inverted image of the church, a "space in itself" (*Raum an sich*) in which decoration, dislodged from its sacred context, had become decoration for its own sake.[7] Likewise, the new movie palaces of Berlin were lavishly adorned, exhibiting a "surface splendor" (*Prunk der Oberfläche*) worthy of Baroque theaters.[8] The consequence of this dazzling multiplicity of effect, paradoxically, was to reenforce the illusion of depth on the screen—an illusion that could be sustained only if everything else were perceived as flat. Distraction, in and of itself a reflection of an increasingly fractured and alienated world, was enlisted as a means of redoubling concentration. In a formulation that hints of Odysseus and the Sirens and as such invokes a separation of spectator and spectacle that insures the autonomy of both,

Kracauer proposed that the decorative excess of the movie theater had one aim: "to bind the public to the periphery in order that it not sink into the abyss" (*das Publikum an die Peripherie zu fesseln, damit es nicht ins Bodenlose versinke*).[9]

The object of Kracauer's discontent was less the mass ornament per se than its incorporation as a bulwark against the fragmentation of modern life: "Distraction [*Zerstreuung*], meaningful only as . . . a copy of the uncontrolled chaos of our world . . . , is forced back into a unity that no longer exists."[10] Implied here is the regression behind what for Werfel was an ideal: the hallucinatory recovery of a lost wholeness and the concomitant absence of an *outside*. This isolation of the film-vision from the social matrix parallels the mechanism by which the dream, following Freud, feigns meaninglessness by disfiguring the associations that guide the search for sense. Kracauer reserved praise for the "street film," specifically Karl Grune's *The Street* (1923), in which the technique of associations, disburdened of the teleology of plot, supports an incoherence that mirrors the heterogeneous topography of the modern city. In a poem from 1911, T. S. Eliot evokes the street as avenue of epic descent into the seedy, liminal reaches of the urban milieu, where an excess of the social coincides with the inability "to say just what I mean":

> Let us go then, you and I,
> When the evening is spread out against the sky
> Like a patient etherised upon a table;
> Let us go, through certain half-deserted streets,
> The muttering retreats
> Of restless nights in one-night cheap hotels
> And sawdust restaurants with oyster-shells:
> Streets that follow like a tedious argument
> Of insidious intent . . .[11]

Under the aegis of twilight, Eliot's poem exposes the "remains of the day," those *Tagesreste* that are the raw material of dreams. Voices pass in and out of consciousness as if overheard on a streetcar, in a museum, or perhaps over the radio. Such pronounced intersectioning, characteristic of both Modernist writing and the city itself, enables the street film to register the very ruptures that the methods of filming and editing typically work to close.

The city, then, presents a seemingly infinite reserve of interstices, of hidden and marginal spaces whose liminality corresponds to the gaps undone by the filmmaking process. Opposite the "reality" that these spaces embody is the cinematic dream-work, which in Weimar Germany culminated in the construction of alternative, artificial cities—projections, *pace* Kracauer, of an illusory totality. Perspective boxes on a grand scale, these virtual cities, which were built to be seen but not entered into, were enveloped by the monumental interiority of the

Ufa film sets.[12] In the massive indoor studios of Neubabelsberg, the *souterrains* and *Hinterhöfe* of Berlin found their expressionist/gothic counterparts in the catacombs of Lang's *Metropolis* and the ghetto of Wegener's *Golem*. The liminal thus yields to the subliminal, which in turn serves a cinematic sublime defined by the complete absence of outside forces.

In consideration of questions concerning spatial practices and transformations in and around Weimar cinema, the essays in this volume, though some more explicitly than others, have Kracauer as their interlocutor. Perhaps more than Benjamin, Kracauer is patron of the optics that looks for insight on the periphery, inviting the investigation of those other spaces that are implicated, if not present, in the films themselves. Michel Foucault would later speak of heterotopias—other places of utopian character that nonetheless occupy real space and help define the world from which they are set apart.[13] Kracauer's hotel lobby, a space in itself, is one such place; kindred topoi, many of which are discussed in these essays, include amusement parks, department stores, train compartments, cemeteries, museums, the chamber (*Kammer*), bordellos, gardens, ships, sideshows, and ultimately Neubabelsberg itself, the film-city where so many of these other spaces came to be simulated. His realist predilections notwithstanding, Kracauer's engagement with the film-city and the city proper nurtured an awareness that the reality of modern life lay precisely in its irreality.

Birthplace of such gargantuan productions as *The Golem, The Nibelungs,* and *Metropolis*, Neubabelsberg realized the technological paradise foreseen by such utopian visionaries as R. N. Coudenhove-Kalergi. A controlled environment consisting of some eighty acres of semipermanent sets, this playground par excellence embodied the "organized happiness" (*organisiertes Glück*) for which Kracauer criticized the *Lunapark*, whose crisscrossing searchlights and military bands simulated the effects of war. With a particular view to the architectural culture behind the Weimar film sets (as well as the new cinema palaces), Janet Ward follows Kracauer as he endeavors to expose the illusion of monumentality and remind the viewer of the atomistic, technical sleights of hand that both create and disappear behind the appearance of seamless unity. That Benjamin shared these concerns suggests a neo-Hegelian element, for Kracauer's displeasure extends beyond the illusory facades to the professional skills that produced them, skills that, emptied of social relevance, "slide over, by default, into a misplaced art of seduction." Kracauer's aim, as Ward points out, is not to eliminate film but to "de-auratize its monumentalist posturing in the name of social(ist) enlightenment." Ward clarifies Kracauer's critique by comparing him to his rival, Béla Balázs, celebrant of expressionist atmosphere (*Stimmung*), for whom "the 'monumentality of milieu' is simply a positive term in the infinitely expanding field of fabrication and experience of film." Balázs had no quarrel with what Kracauer viewed as the "disrespectful impersonation of the macrocosmos," and this is what troubled Kracauer above all: that the film industry gave architects license "to create visual architectural effect for its own sake."

Ward ventures that while Neubabelsberg was "perhaps . . . the most truly modern or protopostmodern aspect of Weimar film," Kracauer's fascination with the culture of overproduced, self-interfering images was reserved for the actual city of Berlin. This postmodern strain is amplified by Courtney Federle, who, with respect to Kracauer's writings on Berlin, demonstrates how Kracauer "reads the metropolis as a dishomogenous space not only filled by the mythologizing sites of representational and institutional architecture but also formed by a spatial practice that recognizes spontaneous and accidental formations." In the accidental and asynchronic spaces of the modern city Kracauer locates an "urban unconscious," in which the intended meanings of monumental architecture break down and recombine with truths at once repressed and safeguarded by city planning. Thus the Kaiser Wilhelm Memorial Church, by day a weighty reminder of imperial stability, came by night to reflect the glow of advertising lights and movie marquees, becoming "a chance and fleeting monument to the new world-historical formation of the double injunction to work and enjoy, to produce and consume." Much as Neubabelsberg celebrated the work of designers whose skills had lost their social significance, so Berlin's most famous church reflected an order that had rendered it—and all monuments—essentially hollow.

The city as spatial aggregate of unplanned and unmastered coincidence finds expression in Ludwig Berger's *Ich bei Tag und du bei Nacht* (1932), analyzed here by Sabine Hake. The title (literally: I by Day and You by Night) suggests an analogue to the vacillation between the diurnal and nocturnal spectacles of the Kaiser Wilhelm Memorial Church, though unlike Kracauer, Berger sides with the pleasure industry and its power of reenchantment. A story of chance encounter and mistaken identity, *Day and Night* features a young man and woman who, unbeknownst to each other, share a bed in a furnished room that he rents by day and she by night. Their names, Hans and Grete, point to an affinity between film and fairy tale consistent with Berger's investment in "the reality of desire." Berger, who published several books of fairy tales, believed the cinema and fairy tale to be ideally complementary; his incorporation of music was meant to enhance the fantastical elements of cinema and to foster "pleasure traditionally identified with regression and dream." Focusing on the formal innovations facilitated by the advent of sound, Hake details the ways in which Berger uses nondiegetic, "disembodied" song to subvert the realism/escapism dyad in order to create a cinema based on the reality of fantasy. He exposes in the process the arbitrariness of realistic conventions, all the more deceptive for their verisimilitude ("precisely in its function as a marker of the real, the big city betrays its status as a construction"). Hake demonstrates how song, with its ability to orchestrate imaginary moves, took over the function of associative and conceptual montage, which cinema abandoned in its quest for ever greater naturalism. Indeed, if the continuity editing of postexpressionist cinema parallels the narrative current of monumentalist urban design, the expanded auditory field of sound cinema may correspond to the asynchronic, transgressive

14

spaces of which that narrative is not master: "As placeholders of desire, the songs . . . become floating signifiers in the sound film's new scenarios of sensory deception and critical illumination." Careful to point out the feminizing thrust of Kracauer's criticism of the passivity ostensibly cultivated by the pleasure industry, Hake stresses Berger's resistance to the model that pits pleasure against reflection and makes women (Kracauer's "little shopgirls") responsible for the "enduring appeal of escapist entertainment."

With its register of fulfilled wishes, the fairy tale projects discursively the cinema's capacity for restoring pleasure in the face of lack, suggesting an affinity between the cinematic apparatus and visions of a better society. In a footnote to her essay Mary Brodnax cites Coudenhove-Kalergi's vision of a pan-European state transformed by superior engineering into a "single garden of Eden." This utopian figure is rhetorically consistent with the conciliatory ending of Fritz Lang's *Metropolis,* whose action proceeds from the disruption of eternal pleasure by the spectacle of unending labor, much as Eden itself is disturbed by the prospect of perpetual toil ("By the sweat of thy brow shalt thou eat bread" [Genesis 3:19]). Maria's introduction of the heart as mediator between capital and labor indicates the means by which economic history works to conceal the opposition between its own materialism and the teleology of redemption. Yet *Metropolis,* Brodnax maintains, "is preoccupied with arguments which elide radical distinctions between body and soul and deflate salvation models of history." La Mettrie's *L'homme machine* (1748), which describes the human soul as the product of sensation, is the forerunner of the materialism personified by the robot Maria, to which the true Maria's anima is ideologically counterposed. Whereas in *Metropolis* the deidealized soul survives as a foil and object of ridicule, the principles the robot embodies are embraced by Walter Ruttmann, whose film *Berlin, Symphony of a City* portrays humans as "relays" in a modern world premised on "the carefully regulated flow of information." Ruttmann's experiment serves as the prototype of a cinema ideally suited to providing metropolitan individuals with a soul (=sensorium) adapted to a world they were not otherwise equipped to comprehend. Using references that range widely from the works of John Donne and Jacques Louis David to The Who's *Tommy,* and including a reappraisal of La Mettrie, Brodnax develops a trajectory along which the robotic Maria, creation of the sinister Rotwang, reappears as the animated cinemagoer, endowed by the filmmaker with a material soul: "Ruttmann proposed to merge the body with the cinematic apparatus to induce the birth of an adequate, cybernetic person."

Ruttmann's self-characterization as a "mechanically enhanced father" with the capacity to "impregnate" the city of Berlin with "organic cyborgs" confirms the notion of the "male womb," by means of which Anne Leblans locates *Metropolis* within a modern patriarchal tradition that sought to imitate the female ability to give life, yet neutralize the contingency of natural childbirth. The fairy tales popularized by the Brothers Grimm bear witness to this attempt. These tales enabled the child to journey into the depths of the forest while remaining under the shelter of a home provided by caring parents. Likewise, the entertainment industry made it possible for the public to submit playfully to the dangers it feared most deeply. Lang's film both exhibits a fairy-tale logic and thematizes the problem of male birth. Rotwang's archaic home, in which the real Maria is held captive and the mechanical Maria is "born," mimics the witch's cottage in "Hänsel and Gretel." Moreover, much as the witch displaces evil away from the natural mother, so Rotwang's robot replaces a woman—Freder's mother—who died in childbirth, making Freder the counterpart to the fairy-tale hero abandoned to the wild. Freder's journey begins when he leaves the eternal gardens of pleasure, the quintessential male womb, and descends into the workers' underground city, where, following Leblans, "the workers' labor resembles that of a mother 'in labor,' taxing their organisms to the extreme and leaving them utterly exhausted." Freder leaves one male womb for another, and even the logic that brings *Metropolis* to the brink of cataclysm is the rationale of domination: "Why not protect oneself against the arbitrariness of technological disasters by provoking them?" There is something here of the carnival, which defuses social tensions by ritualizing them, much as the fairy tale, following Leblans, "brought the monstrous parent into the home only to exclude him more effectively." Other "male wombs" discussed by Leblans include such commonplace institutions as the Christmas celebration, in which the home replaces the mother as the source of gifts; Macy's Christmas parades, through which a department store casts customers as eternal children; the amusement park, where visitors regain control through voluntary submission; and "pleasure palaces" such as the Haus Gourmenia, whose rooftop garden transformed nature into "a more perfect version of its former self." Finally, there is Neubabelsberg, where 750 of Berlin's poorest children, who in *Metropolis* correspond to the worker-instigated deluge (and thus attest to the threat of uncontrolled procreation), were pampered and entertained with a generosity worthy of Christmas itself.

Aligned with the carnival is the pronounced theatricality of early cinema. The subversive potential of its excessive gesture and dress contrasts with the naturalistic paradigm of nineteenth-century drama and its attempt, ultimately, "to force 'theater' out of the theater" (Arno Holz).[14] The modern (as opposed to modernist) stage was co-extensive with bourgeois intimacy, devoid of play and increasingly isolated from the social world, an interior space whose programmatic claustrophobia duplicates the restrictions of the closet itself. Transformations in fin de siècle dramatic practices set the scene for Ellen Risholm's reading of Leopold Jessner's *Backstairs* (1921), a film that indeed culminates in a murder committed in a closet. A so-called *Kammerspielfilm, Backstairs* exemplifies a cinematic genre derived from the *Kammerspiel* theater, arguably the fullest realization of bourgeois intimacy. *Kammerspiele* reenacted the control already firmly exercised over the domestic sphere, leaving the *Kammer* (chamber), like the home, bereft of dynamism (another "male womb," to use Leblans's formulation). Yet *Backstairs,* Risholm maintains, resists the naturalization of "home" by dissecting space and mobilizing the periphery. (The backstairs themselves are one of several hidden stages the camera probes.) By exposing the invisible mechanisms of control and revealing the spatial dominance of agents who are bodily absent, Jessner's film blocks the narrative movement from the spatial (historical) to the psychological (eternal). If but momentarily, the *Kammerspielfilm* restores to the *Kammer* the liberating potential once endemic to chamber music (*Kammermusik*), in which space was malleable, constructed and ever reconstituted by the free play of performance. Even this musical practice would grow rigid with time, much as the *Kammerspiel* itself, in seeking a kind of specular sameness of performer and spectator, achieved a "purposeless efficacy" consistent with the exclusion of the historical world. In citing one scholar's characterization of chamber music as "one of those happy lands without a history," Risholm demonstrates how perfectly the fairy tale accords with the ideal of effortless and innocuous domination.

The post-Enlightenment dramatic tradition also helps form the context of my own essay, which begins by considering Rilke's "Panther" in light of the prohibition, prevalent in the theater after Diderot and Lessing, against the reciprocated gaze. The panther's inability to see beyond the bars passing before its eyes immediately suggests a kinship to the early railway passenger, reportedly unable to look out of the window of a speeding train. The shock that attended the rise of railway travel has been linked to the cinema, whose apocryphal beginnings are tethered to an approaching locomotive (Lumière's *L'Arriveè d'un train*) but also to Freud's *Beyond the Pleasure Principle,* invoked by Benjamin to explain how the cinema worked to rehearse and thus neutralize the excessive stimuli of industrial modernity. Benjamin's influential essay has had the effect of preserving a deterministic moment in Freud, with certain recent studies tending to regard the train (and kindred phenomena) as a cause rather than a projection. Yet, a full century before Lumière's purportedly traumatic screening a critical vocabulary was in place that defined fright as the explicit Other of aesthetic experience. The advent of film, which entailed a threat of visual reciprocity, contradicted the antibaroque sensibilities of (to cite a prominent example) Lessing's *Laokoon,* undermining the spatial boundaries defended by an aesthetics struggling with a fear of the void. This *horror vacui* finds a highly equivocal personification in Murnau's vampire (*Nosferatu,* 1922), whose movements toward the camera articulate a disconcerting depth of field, but whose renunciations and fear of daylight brand him the ultimate aesthete. The same ambivalence is germane to the window itself, which in Murnau's film coincides with the abyss, and which combines the pleasant prospect of illumination with the agoraphobic exposure to the outside.

Appropriately, Carsten Strathausen begins his discussion of the mountain film (*Bergfilm*) with reference to a famous photograph of Hitler standing before a massive window and contemplating an Alpine vista. The image cites such famous Romantic paintings as C. D. Friedrich's *Wanderer above the Sea of Mist* and suggests a lineage along which Strathausen follows the modern vicissitudes of the sublime. The similarities are not merely topical, for the chasms and crevasses depicted in the mountain film are diegetic extensions of ruptures in the imagery itself that prevent the spectator from suturing the film into a coherent whole. In this respect, the mountain films of Arnold Fanck (for example, *The Sacred Mountain* and *S.O.S. Iceberg*) regress to a more primitive stage in filmmaking, what Tom Gunning has called the "cinema of attractions," which sustained a tension between pleasure and apprehension and thus toyed more explicitly with the prospect of danger: "The destruction of cinematic space in Fanck's films is usually 'framed' by coherent narrative elements meant to reassure the audience . . . , a practice which naturally highlights the subsequent shock of losing 'perspective' as nature destroys the space provided by the camera." This interplay between the destruction and confirmation of cinematic space seems intended to recreate or rehearse the narcissistic loss that preconditions the sublime moment that, following Thomas Weiskel, occurs when a conscious metarelation between mind and *image* is erected in the place of a lost harmony of mind and *object*. Noting that Weiskel's account of sublime substitution accurately describes the process wherein the spectator's imaginary builds continuity into the gaps, Strathausen urges that suture *is* the cinematic sublime.

When a contemporary critic, quoted by Strathausen, relegates Weimar film to "a means of tickling the senses, an accumulation of sensations,"[15] he names what for Ruttmann (*Berlin, Symphony of a City*) was a technological virtue. Brodnax has already proposed that "suture" describes an operation similar to Ruttmann's program of endowing spectators with self-consciousness, enabling them to comprehend their surroundings. This mechanical ideal is reversed in *Metropolis* when the robot is burned—an act that has the effect of "reassuring the frightened masses that a common biology allies them with [their] masters." If this foretells a darker hour to come, it also delineates an appropriation of the sublime that allowed the masses to identify with their leader, to find in him (the sign of) the object they had lost. Kracauer, who criticized the pleasure industry for its ability to pass technology off as nature, that is, to install the illusion of wholeness in place of fragmented technique, impugns an aesthetic ideology at work in the mountain film, which "naturalizes" technical ruptures by projecting them as breaks in the terrain. Borrowing Romantic imagery only to undo Romantic utopias, the mountain film banishes its protagonist in order to prepare him for entry into a paradise defined by a "carefully regulated flow." This contest renews a more archaic scene, which inaugurated human toil and wed it to the labor of painful birth ("In sorrow thou shalt bring forth children" [Genesis 3:16]). The fairy tale, of which the mountain film now seems merely the most explicit incarnation, replaces the womb with "home" but confers on the latter the semblance of nature, situating the source of modern horror at the heart—and hearth—of the commonplace.

18

Notes

1. John Nash, *Vermeer* (London: Scala, 1991), 38–40.
2. Celeste Brusati, *Artifice and Illusion: The Art and Writings of Samuel Van Hoogstraten* (Chicago: University of Chicago Press, 1995), 181, 198.
3. A photograph of this set is reproduced in the essay by Janet Ward.
4. See the essays collected in the volume *Georges Méliès—Magier der Filmkunst,* ed. Klaus Kreimeier (Frankfurt am Main: Stroemfeld/Roter Stern, 1993), as well as Erik Barnouw, *The Magician and the Cinema* (New York: Oxford University Press, 1981).
5. Christian Metz, *The Imaginary Signifier: Psychoanalysis and the Cinema,* trans. Celia Britton, Annwyl Williams, Ben Brewster, and Alfred Guzzetti (Bloomington: Indiana University Press, 1982), 76.
6. Walter Benjamin, *Illuminationen* (Frankfurt am Main: Suhrkamp, 1977), 150.
7. Siegfried Kracauer, *Das Ornament der Masse: Essays,* afterword by Karsten Witte (Frankfurt am Main: Suhrkamp, 1977), 157.
8. Ibid., 311.
9. Ibid., 314.
10. Ibid., 316.
11. "The Love Song of J. Alfred Prufrock," in T. S. Eliot, *The Waste Land and Other Poems* (New York: Harcourt Brace Jovanovich, 1988), 3.
12. Helmut Färber, "Architektur, Dekoration, Zerstörung: Etliches über Kinematographie und äußere Wirklichkeit," in Klaus Kreimeier, ed., *Die Metaphysik des Dekors: Raum, Architektur und Licht im klassischen deutschen Stummfilm* (Marburg: Schüren, 1994), 102–3.
13. Michel Foucault, "Of Other Spaces," trans. Jan Miskoviec, *Diacritics* 16 (1986): 22–27
14. Quoted in *Geschichte der deutschen Literatur vom 18. Jahrhundert bis zur Gegenwart. Band III/I: 1848–1918,* ed. Victor Zmegac (Königstein: Athenäum, 1980), 201.
15. Quoted in Jürgen Keiper, "Alpträume in Weiß," *Film und Kritik* 1 (1992): 57.

1

JANET WARD

Kracauer versus the Weimar Film-City

Beyond the projected images of early German cinema is a three-dimensional, socioeconomic dimension manifest in the architecture of the Weimar film industry. The massive and elaborate studios built just outside Berlin by the Universum Film Aktiengesellschaft (Ufa) had by 1925 come to represent something as important and fascinating as the films themselves. Ufa's semipermanent, vast film sets bespoke the new, utterly concrete presence of film-as-apparatus, as societal engine—or, at the very least, as instantaneous and inflammatory reflector of modernity's racing motor.[1] The huge "film-city" (*Filmstadt*) at Neubabelsberg was certainly Babelesque, consisting of towers and tunnels over eighty-odd acres of artificially lit outdoor and indoor playgrounds.[2] Its remote location outside Berlin and guaranteed financial backing offered limitless opportunities for the continued expansion of outside scenes.[3] As a result of Ufa's tradition of recreating entire cities within controlled lighting environments, the former "glass houses" of prewar film production at Neubabelsberg were replaced during 1925 and 1926 with what was reputed to be the largest film atelier in Europe.[4] In this last decade of silent film, the sets did far more than "speak for" the actors. The "high" experienced by visitors to the Ufa city evidently provided a surrogate feeling of filmic omnipotence—here in the words of a journalist who in 1925 accompanied director Fritz Lang onto the famed set for *Metropolis* and experienced his own Babel-sublime by stepping momentarily into the shoes of the projectionists: "We walk further, and climb up a high tower made of powerful beams, to the position of the [camera] operators, from where Babelsberg lies deep down at our feet like a small city. To the point from where incredible optical effects are to be captured for the film."[5] The site of Neubabelsberg itself (and to a lesser degree the other fifteen or so film ateliers in Berlin) became a cinematic fetish for the public imagination—a concoction of film-cities within the film-city of Berlin proper.[6]

Ufa was founded during the First World War essentially as part of the German propaganda machine—a legacy that is visible in the following quotation from an *Ufa-Programm* of 1925–26, which effectively introduces (or advertises) the self-sufficiency of the studios as no less than a national powerhouse:

The Neubabelsberg concern at Ufa is specifically made for outdoor shots. Here the skyscrapers and the lines of streets from *Metropolis,* city of the future, reach high up into the sky. . . . An amusement fair with carousels, swings and roller coasters—one of the sets for a scene in the film *Variété*—stretches far into the distance. . . . In addition to the detached buildings there are two large ateliers on the lot. Administration buildings and workshops are located in 22 massive structures. Neubabelsberg is an industrial concern that can produce its entire needs on site. A power plant translates a high-tension current of 10,000 volts in three transformers into normal direct current, and delivers enough power for about 15,000 amperes of light consumption. . . . Of special interest are the underground film chambers that provide special protection against any explosions caused by spontaneous ignition. The best known super-films have been made in Babelsberg, from *The Golem* to *The Nibelungs* to *The Last Laugh,* and there are always new works being made here that create respect and status for German work far beyond Germany's borders.[7]

The site of cinematic production was thus glorified into a cradle of creative life force for the national collective. With such pragmatic sentiments about filmmaking technologies, the Weimar film industry took up the tools of expressionist yearnings for a mythological rebirth for Germany in the wake of the defeat of World War I, and created thereby a neo-expressionist monumentalism. The rebuilding of Germany via film took place quite literally, since film offered the most lucrative and creative opportunities to underemployed architects—both in set design and in constructing the new movie palaces. The need for employment dovetailed with the theoretical desires of one such expressionist architect, Bruno Taut, who in a 1918 text, "A Program for Architecture," had already urgently requested an outdoor studio as a playground for architecture (and, by implication, for film production): "a well-situated experimental site (e.g., in Berlin: the Tempelhofer Feld), on which architects can erect large-scale models of their ideas. Here . . . architectural effects (e.g., glass as a building material) shall be tried out, perfected, and exhibited to the masses in full-scale temporary constructions or individual parts of a building."[8] This wish was indirectly granted architects by the German film industry, but as part of a commercial-cum-nationalistic design.

Only the voice of the Weimar cultural critic Siegfried Kracauer resonates during the 1920s with a certain angst about all of the intoxicating architectural benefits and spectacles induced by the German film industry. A former architect himself, but now thoroughly disillusioned with monument-building, Kracauer complains about the monumental film sets used by Ufa.[9] His disengagement from the architectural profession is on a par with Robert Musil's similar repugnance for his own training as an engineer. Kracauer had worked from 1909 to 1917 for Theodor Fischer, one of the most renowned architects of the day. Wolfgang Pehnt comments that Fischer's name was associated with "picturesque impressiveness" and monumentality[10]—no doubt a factor in Kracauer's subsequent low tolerance for the same, whether on the street or on the screen.

In an article entitled "Calico-World: The Ufa City in Neubabelsberg" which was first broadcast as a Frankfurt radio speech on January 24, 1926, then published in the *Frankfurter Zeitung* a few days later, Kracauer asserts his retaliatory stance toward the Weimar film-city. Assigning to its fake (namely "calico," "material") facades a degree of worn-out metaphoricity in a manner akin to that of Friedrich Nietzsche's (as yet unknown) extramoral diagnosis of language,[11] or even more akin to the longing expressed by Maeterlinck for the irretrievable treasures below the surface,[12] Kracauer complains: "Architectural constructions jut upward as if meant to be inhabited. But they represent only the external aspects of the prototypes, much the way language maintains facades of words whose original meaning has vanished" (MO 282). Not coincidentally does he refer to F. W. Murnau's (and Ufa's) *Faust* of 1926 as a literally "mammoth film" (*Riesenfilm*),[13] for it is the filmic enterprise itself, with its foundations of capitalism and nationalism, that has become exaggeratedly Faustian and overblown. Neubabelsberg is, he warns, a disrespectful impersonation of the macrocosmos, a "Noah's ark" of apparently realistic things made of "paper-mâché" that "rendezvous" here in a haphazard fashion, such as the "monstrous dragon" from Lang's epic, *The Nibelungs* (OM 281, 282).[14] Its fault is not that it is not nature, but that it *poses* as nature: things here are but "copies and distortions" (*Abbilder und Fratzen*) (MO 281; OM 271). The industry has, in Kracauer's eyes, re-created the very thing Walter Benjamin more naively hopes that film, as avant-gardistic art form, can and will destroy: namely the mimetically imbued aura, the voyeuristic-cinematic "fourth wall" in which absolute faith is invested (MO 288).

Kracauer's evident discomfort amidst the "calico-world" is hence not merely due to the extravagance of the film sets, but also and moreover due to "the things projected onto the screen" (MO 284)—that is, the camera's intrinsic power to transform this (of itself senseless) jumble of artifacts into an alternative, highly believable reality. For his readers, Kracauer repeatedly endeavors to dispel the apparatus' uncanny effect which visitors to Ufa (as to Universal Studios today) try to re-create first hand. Against this, he plays the role of cool, detached detective, a product of the antiornamental New Objectivity,[15] exposing the representational "crime" of the pro-filmic condition of the film sets and mercilessly exposing the technical sleights of hand involved in any mise-en-scène, but especially those effects that are fantastic and "supernatural" (MO 284). He likes to undo the work of the camera and re-create the distance between actor and filmed environment. In a Brechtian manner he calls attention to the film-city's components as ahistorical and nondevelopmental, as new ruins that are not naturally fallen but a lawless set of artificial metamorphoses, a fragmented mixture of anorganic things soon to be dismantled. Only through what is for Kracauer a brigade of pointillistic, disconnected, cellular processes inherent in the entire filmmaking process (e.g., invisible mechanics, lighting, camera angle, editing) is the appearance of a unified whole created, and it is of this he would like to remind his readers.

What the spectator-subject of film *does not see* is revealed and derided by Kracauer as a manufactured, patently false, and potentially harmful art (or industry) of manipulation. The illusion of monumentality, as told in *Metropolis* by the allegory of the Tower of Babel or the dizzy shots of the skyscraper-city itself, is effectively cut down by Kracauer's critique to its miniature model size. Many of the Weimar film sets were indeed gigantic, but some, like the workers' tower-blocks underground in *Metropolis,* were just a partial base, the height of which was artificially reflected upward using Schüfftan's famous mirror technique (a method that was, it is rumored, occasionally sabotaged by screen architects fearing for their future employment).[16] In point of fact, the forest in Lang's *Siegfried* was a collection of huge cement trees. The rooftops in *Faust* were models, while the Castle of Worms in *Siegfried* was truly massive. Kracauer's point is that the viewers—as merely passive recipients of the artistry of "cinematic special effects" (*Filmtricks*)—cannot know this (MO 284; OM 274).

What Kracauer appears to be conflating in his analysis here are some distinct stylistic differences between the actual film-architects: while it was Erich Kettelhut, Otto Hunte, and Karl Vollbrecht who were essentially behind the gigantic stasis of the Lang sets, Robert Herlth, Walter Röhrig, and Hermann Warm, among others, worked in tandem to effect a more sensually flowing, "milieu"-based style for Murnau, and even for Lang's most expressionist early film, *Destiny* (*Der müde Tod,* 1921).[17] However, Kracauer's attack has certain merits with respect to *Metropolis*. In 1927, the year of *Metropolis'* premiere and Kracauer's ensuing "Calico-World" article, the degree to which Ufa's posturing via Lang had become exaggerated would become even more apparent—not only in the mise-en-scène of *Metropolis,* or in the allegorical tale of the tower of Babel, or even in the Harbouesque plot of the film, but also in the fact that the film that had been fervently promoted for the entire previous year cost more than five million Reichsmark, lasted seven hours, and recovered only one-seventh of its production costs.[18] Since *Metropolis* only compounded Ufa's already rising debt and was not a success abroad, Ufa's most monumental effort to outdo Hollywood was a definitive failure. In this sense, then, Kracauer's attack on the Ufa artifice was vindicated.

But how are we to account for Kracauer's distrust and derision of architectural cinematics per se, of filmic staging in all its three-dimensionality? Remaining paramount is of course his socialist concern for the mass urban viewing public that is at the mercy of the new entertainment medium. It is estimated that three and a half million Germans went to the movies every night. For Kracauer, Weimar film gives cultish status to (that is, regressively impacts upon) modernity's prime product of commodification and technologized Taylorism: namely the "mass ornament" that turns the holistic entities of community and individual personality

24

Set design, *Metropolis* (1925/26), directed by Fritz Lang. Courtesy of the Stiftung Deutsche Kinemathek, Photo-Archive.

into a merely functioning "tiny piece of the mass" (MO 78). Kracauer's comments in "The Mass Ornament" essay of 1927 evidently anticipate Horkheimer and Adorno's argument, in their *Dialectic of Enlightenment* (1944), against modern architecture's mass urban planning, for committing, like the Hollywood culture industry, a "mass deception" of its inhabitants/viewers.[19] Film—with its massifying production line, monumental film sets, and manipulated spectators—constitutes for Kracauer only the most recent and striking phenomenon arising out of the ultimate irrationality underlying the capitalist system of infinitely self-reproducing, self-perpetuating rationality. This irrational base of filmic production is also noted by another Weimar journalist, Alfred Polgar, who, writing for the *Berliner Tageblatt* in 1928, was similarly struck by the stark "incongruity" or gap between the huge expenditure in human, mechanical, and monetary terms needed to make a film, on the one hand, and the apparently seamless filmic product, on the other: "The misunderstanding between the enormous expenditure of toil, money, nerves and muscle strength, of people, machines, skills and stupidity, patience, passion, energy of every kind, sweat from every source—and that which this effort brings forth. . . .

It all looks grand, and small, too. Charming, and pathetic. Freshly built, and yet already there for a long time. A fossilized today! Spirits of millions of Rentenmarks hover around it, complaining" (B 143, 44). Kracauer finds that the rationale of capitalism, like the mass ornament that is its "aesthetic reflex," knows no inner sense except to be an "end in itself" (MO 79, 78). The mass ornament of film and other forms of Weimar popular entertainment arise as surface protrusions mirroring the functioning and fragmented subjectivities of a mechanized city in modern capitalism. Despite his warning cry, Kracauer is nonetheless the first to point out that the mass ornament remains more of a genuine artistic production than any outdated high art form. Kracauer remains ambiguous: neither a reactionary Luddite nor a leftist technophobe, he is simply highly suspicious of the state of homogeneity for the working classes induced and encouraged by the German and American film industries' rival ambitions. His goal is not to smash the camera apparatus itself for being (as Jean-Louis Baudry would say[20]) a fatalistically predetermined instrument of Platonism or a regressive recreator of the Lacanian mirror-stage, but rather, to deauratize its monumentalist posturing in the name of social(ist) enlightenment.[21]

Kracauer's second—and equally crucial—major target in the Weimar film industry, in the essay "Cult of Distraction" (appearing one month after "Calico-World" in the *Frankfurter Zeitung* in 1926), is the actual cinematic event staged by the newly built premiere movie palaces, particularly in Berlin.[22] For never before or since in the history of cinema has there existed such a joint offensive of, as Kracauer so aptly phrases it, "atmospheric bombardment" (*Stimmungs-Kanonaden*, OM 311),[23] launched by the movie palace's architecture at the unsuspecting viewing public.[24] Hence we see that the philosophy of "surface splendor" (*Prunk der Oberfläche*) informed and designed both the Babelsberg film sets and the cinema buildings' exteriors and interiors (MO 323; OM 311). This was the "cult of distraction" that the new urban masses of modernity demanded and enjoyed nightly. The Ufa "film palaces" (*Filmpaläste*) or "light-play houses" (*Lichtspielhäuser*) were the Weimar mass equivalent of the elitist structure of the Wilhelmine Bayreuth opera house, with such corresponding, often neoclassical names as *Marmorhaus, Universum-Filmpalast, Titania-Palast, Gloria-Palast, Mercedes-Palast, Capitol,* or *Babylon*.[25] Indeed, the *Gloria-Palast,* opened in 1926, was publicly heralded as Germany's post-Bayreuth *Festspielhaus* for the modern age, and unlike most of the Weimar premiere film palaces, which were done in the New Objectivity style, the auditorium of the *Gloria* was remodeled in full baroque splendor in order to be less offensive to the important building directly opposite it, namely the neo-Gothic *Kaiser Wilhelm Gedächtniskirche.* The largest cinema was eventually built not in Berlin but in Hamburg. The *Ufa-Palast,* which opened with a mountain film in the midst of 1929's depression blues, offered the public 2,667 seats, as well as restaurants, bars, and fifteen thousand square meters of office space. With such gargantuan dimensions, it is not surprising that it was marketed as an object fit to inspire national confidence.[26]

Interior, Gloria-Palast (1926).

These movie palaces helped create a unified, essentially Teutonic mythology of cinema-going experience that was for Kracauer but a schematized "effect-ridden total work of art" (*Gesamtkunstwerk der Effekte*) (MO 324; OM 312) or "pseudo-totality" (*Scheintotalität*) (MO 328; OM 317). Increasingly, Kracauer sounds like Nietzsche attacking the nationalistic, feminizing,[27] theatrical art inherent in the Wagner cult;[28] both share a repugnance at the downside to the effects of mass art. Kracauer is indicating here just how easily architectural effects may take over from function and structure, which were the components of the Bauhaus's parallel credo for a building as a "total work of art." The single feature film showing, along with its varieté acts during the silent film era, was thus couched in a setting that was equally and vitally a part of its production and distribution; indeed, as Kracauer complains, the film-text itself was but part of a "larger whole" (MO 324). The whole was a multimedia event incorporating strobe lighting and a literally "orchestrated" musical anticipation of emotional response. Beyond the actual architectural event of the film's presentation were yet more features aimed at enhancing the illusion but occluding self-awareness: the movie palaces' advertising facades on the building exteriors and further gimmicks in the foyers, the film

27

industry's star cult (promoted by gimmicks such as the stars' photos on stamps for fans to collect and arrange in albums), souvenir film programs which laboriously explained the entire narrative of the films and much of what went into the making of them, pre-release press hype in film trade magazines, and the mass distribution of film stills in the popular illustrated magazines for mostly female readers.[29] The age of the blockbuster feature film (*Großfilm*) had thus given birth to its three-dimensional equivalent, the systematic and rival presentation of the same by the movie theater as a *Großkino*. It is precisely this systemization of mass entertainment that alarms Kracauer. His comments on the Berlin pre-Disney Lunapark, for example, another Babelesque site of organized entertainment for the masses, go so far as to invoke military motifs of crowd control; the Lunapark is where search lights are aimed—luckily—"not at enemy aeroplanes" but at the attractions; the marching rhythm of the military music accompanying the light shows "inwardly illuminates" the audience; and the trapeze artist is "caught in the crossfire" of the white beams of the searchlight.[30]

Kracauer is specifically impatient with expressionist architects for crossing over to the film industry; he writes scathingly of Taut and Hans Poelzig for their desire to build great monumental projects—a visionary enterprise rather than a real one, since in the immediate post-World War I years actual building projects were denied them.[31] In a 1921 article, "Über Turmhäuser," Kracauer states:

> The involuntary idleness that has been imposed for years now on German architects has not been able to stifle their desire for grand building projects. The impossibility of building in reality has driven artists like Poelzig to create Expressionist movie palace architecture, while fanatics like Taut are dreaming up hazardous glass palaces and a utopian alpine architecture. But in the end even the most ingenious Rabitz[32] fantasies will not suffice for the architect; he is driven to construct buildings and to invent works of permanence. . . .[33]

Kracauer has in mind here Poelzig's film set of the Gothic-stylized Jewish quarter of Prague for Paul Wegener's *Der Golem* (1920) as constructed life-size on the Tempelhofer Feld in Berlin. (Poelzig's original color designs for the film were in fact far more tower-oriented than the eventual film set of labyrinthine streets and passages.) The origins of Kracauer's extreme realist stance vis-à-vis film after World War II are already clearly visible in such reports as this from the 1920s—they inform his subsequent, somewhat obsessively psychologizing, character-based reading (in *From Caligari to Hitler* [1946][34]) of the expressionist film decade as the dreamlike, early "symptom" of a "disease" of which Nazism was a more advanced stage. Here in 1921 he sees the fantastical immortalities achieved in the monumentalist architectural substitutes of stage and screen as essentially *unreal*, as arising from an inability to build otherwise: in short, as born of a loss of societal applicability of professional skills that thus slide over, by default, into a misplaced art of seduction. The vogue of lavish film set design by German architects during the silent film era

28

is indicative, for Kracauer, of their frustrated desire to create "towers" for posterity. Thus he was delighted when Taut was appointed Magdeburg's city planner in 1922—for this would, he accurately predicted, enable Taut to move from his utopian paper designs and on to functionalist suburban housing projects.[35]

Hence while Kracauer favors an authentic, posthumanist representation of modernity's distracted, uncontrolled "display of pure externality" (MO 326)[36]—rather like Irmgard Keun's Doris in her desire to become what Berlin is, that is, sheer luster (*Glanz*)[37]—he protests the film industry's regressive face mask over the same: "[T]he architectural setting tends to emphasize a dignity that used to inhabit the institutions of high culture. It favors the lofty and the *sacred* as if designed to accommodate works of eternal significance—just one step short of burning votive candles. . . . Distraction—which is meaningful only as improvisation, as a reflection of the uncontrolled anarchy of our world—is festooned with drapery and forced back into a unity that no longer exists" (MO 327–28). For this, then, one does not even require the ostentatiously monumentalist scenarios of Lang's silent films with their architecturally static, symmetrical mass scenes.[38] For the "*reactionary* tendencies" of the film product are a side effect of the parent industry's preexisting ambitions and techniques (MO 327; emphasis original).

There is, however, an important subtext to Kracauer's noble attack (in addition, that is, to the irony of his own self-distancing from the mass film audiences toward whom he is supposedly sympathetic, both in his tone and in the implied bourgeois readership of the *Frankfurter Zeitung*)—namely his own rivalry with a contemporary cinematic hermeneut, Austria's most well known film critic of the time, Béla Balázs. In *Der sichtbare Mensch* (1924), the Hungarian Balázs theorized on the notion of "atmosphere" (*Stimmung*) as inherited from nineteenth-century art theory, suggesting that without the application of such atmospheric qualities, silent film would produce only a bare, neutral description of an event or object and actors would be made mute.[39] This enthusiastic validation by Balázs of *Stimmung* as an "objectified lyricism" directly supports filmic expressionism for producing a totalized environment (SM 91). *Stimmung,* according to Balázs, can be produced via intimate close-ups of the actors, but also by channeling audience perspective into the hero's own point of view. The methodology of producing this "subjective image of the world" via the camera lens is crucial (SM 91): he wants to invest as much organic status as possible in mass scenes,[40] and of course also in such mammoth structures as the Eiffel tower, warehouses, factories, and railway stations, as well as in the photographic illusions of gigantic size, space, or height. These images of sublime, auratic "pathos" deserve more than just supporting roles in the all-important "reality-effect of greatness" (SM 86, 89). For Balázs there are rightly monumentalist scenes in film because of preexisting monumentalist scenes in our urban industrial lives. In Balázs's view, the "monumentality of milieu" is simply a positive term in the infinitely expanding field of fabrication and experience of film (SM 90). It is certainly true that over the course of the twentieth century, the Hollywood film industry has followed this advice rather than Kracauer's more agonistic line.

Evidently Balázs's advocacy of the pictorial, sheer viewability or non-use inherent in an architecturalized cinema—whether on location in the city, at Neubabelsberg's terrain, or inside the Ufa movie palaces—is not dependent on any actual socioeconomic "culture" of film, and therefore runs counter to Kracauer's major concerns.[41] Citing Kracauer's 1927 review, *Visible Man,* Miriam Hansen states that Balázs's "denial of verbal (i.e. written) language, according to Kracauer a 'serious blunder' (*schlimme Entgleisung*), leads him to a romantic conflation of physiognomy and class struggle, a confusion of mere visibility with genuine concreteness."[42] On the other hand, Kracauer's critique cannot account for the filmic-psychic notions of dream, distortion, and vision—indisputably important levels of expressivity in film and first explored by Balázs. Moreover, Balázs is more at ease with stylizing techniques such as camera angles, the art of the cameraman, lighting, location, and actors' physiognomy; in other words, cinematic *Stimmung* deserves to be read as more artful and metaphorical, and less intent on mimetic illusionism, than Kracauer would have us believe. In response one could say, as Eisenstein in fact did in his 1926 essay "Béla Forgets about the Scissors," that the pro-*Stimmung* attitude of Balázs neglects the uses of alienation effects in film, especially montage editing.[43] More crucially, Balázs's work sees nothing problematic in the neoexpressionist shift away from the painterly, stylized sets à la *Caligari* toward the macrocosmic construction of entire screen worlds.[44] This is precisely what annoyed Kracauer the most: the fact that the film industry offered architects an all-too-tempting substitute for the building shortfalls of the crisis-ridden Weimar reality, a will to power facilitated by the very speed of on-set temporary construction and by the instant mass distribution of their works on screen—the will, that is, to create visual architectural effect for its own sake.[45]

But were Weimar filmgoers so wrong, then, to obsess and fantasize about their self-renewing and ever self-rebuilding "film-cities"? Perhaps Neubabelsberg represents, after all, the most truly modern or proto-postmodern aspect of Weimar film. As the Swiss reporter Walter Muschg more forgivingly remarked for the *Neue Zürcher Zeitung* in 1922, the forces at work in the Ufa film-city are still impressive by the very strength of their "conscious joy at the impossible."[46] There is within the multiworlded fake city a wholly *new* "fullness of life," as Muschg sees it, which imparts its dynamism in production and reproduction to the audiences at the receiving end of the film-item: it generates, in short, a highly credible "popular-aesthetic behavior" (B 140). As Muschg puts the contradiction of Neubabelsberg, it is literally fake, cheap, dirty, and loud, and yet simultaneously wholly true to its own art form, namely a pragmatics of production, tempo, and immediacy:

> Never before have I seen walls so covered with obscenities as in the film-city; never before have I received so strong an impression of how a culture must

> look where production springs from a real, fiercely driven need, where there are masters and succession, and where that which is accomplished is dragged out of the workshop right into the discussion. Here indeed the haste of production stands in reverse relation to the value and duration of the product. (B 140)

Nonetheless, Muschg reports that the medium of Babelsberg does not live up to its potential, insofar as the *Nibelungs*-type of pathos and the remedies for the postwar German spirit are full of "lazy magic" and "eternal yesterdays" (B 142).

Kracauer's polemical writings on Neubabelsberg and the Berlin movie palaces reveal the tension in the dual pull of his emotional attraction to, and political repulsion from, its effect-laden surfaces. We can, in particular, ask ourselves about Kracauer's evident fear of cinematic desire or scopophilia (*Schaulust*).[47] He does not allow himself to partake (at least textually) of any of Benjamin's self-indulgent *flânerie* in the noisy silent film-city, even though this site closely resembles his own excitedly allegorical and brilliantly cinematic city pictures of Weimar Berlin-by-night, collected decades later for the volume *Straßen in Berlin und anderswo.* However, it is interesting to note that where the Weimar Kracauer *does* praise the three-dimensionality of a film, it is in favor of an architectonically progressive, relatively dadaesque, anti-illusionist or Eisensteinian production: one such film for Kracauer is *The Street* (*Die Straße,* dir. Karl Grune, 1923), precisely because it keeps the wound or "gap" open between actors and their filmic setting, and hence between filmic effect and audience. As Kracauer states in his 1925 review article "Filmbild und Prophetenrede": "Instead of [the actors] living connected to the things [of the street], they sink down to the deathly objects themselves."[48] He insists on the urban dissonance of Grune's film, wherein the "middle" ground between film-picture and prophecy remains necessarily empty and "unbuilt." In an earlier review of *The Street,* Kracauer praises the "technique of associations" in the film as one in which "an object takes a shape that only film can form, and in which possibilities are realized that are only ever possibilities in film."[49] The space of the city street in Grune's film is not a site in which identities are constructed; on the contrary, it is where "only figures come together, events happen and situations pile up blindly one upon another: all of this without continuity and consequence, an uncannily unreal togetherness of unreal people."[50]

In the light of the preceding, then, it is all the more ironic that Kracauer does not acknowledge the extent to which the same kind of alienation effect was likewise part of a visitor's experience of Neubabelsberg itself (even if one concurs that it was mostly excluded from the Weimar moviegoing experience).[51] The dynamic red chaos that bespeaks George Grosz's *Metropolis,* a Dada painting of 1917,[52] for example, came to be most accurately re-represented, so to speak, on the terrain of Berlin's film production. Even the lewd graffiti scrawled on or behind the scenery was something the Berlin Dadaists consciously had to re-create, but Neubabelsberg came by its falsities naturally. All the mass ornaments that Dadaism embraced, Neubabelsberg, during the silent film years, already was: a total, shameless self-immersion in the culture industry. Its juxtaposed, lean-to sets formed a burlesque collage or incongruous series of overproduced images—a shrine of the new temporary art where several scenes could and would be built, filmed, or destroyed at any given moment. Again, it must be stressed that this posthumanist, creative condition does not refer to the bulk of the actual Weimar film-products, which strove toward ever more bombastic monumentalism (whether in architecture or in sentimentality), but rather to the Babelesque body of the film-city that quite inadvertently gave it birth. It is an immense, intriguing, and labyrinthine corpus, the artifices of which linger in the mind long after the hyperbole of Kracauer's defensive, corrective stance toward the stagings and building strategies of the Weimar film industry.

NOTES

1. Cf. Anton Kaes's reference to Weimar film as the "motor of modernity" in his chapter, "Film in der Weimarer Republik," in *Geschichte des deutschen Films,* ed. Wolfgang Jacobsen, Anton Kaes, and Hans Helmut Prinzler (Stuttgart: Metzler, 1993), 39–47. See also Siegfried Kracauer's discussion of film's role as generator of societal values in "The Little Shop Girls Go to the Movies," in *The Mass Ornament: Weimar Essays,* ed. and trans. Thomas Y. Levin (Cambridge: Harvard University Press, 1995), 291–304.
2. Kracauer states that Neubabelsberg covers 350,000 square meters; see his "Calico-World: The Ufa City in Neubabelsberg," in *The Mass Ornament: Weimar Essays,* ed. and trans. Thomas Y. Levin (Cambridge: Harvard University Press, 1995), 281. (Kracauer's essays in this volume are abbreviated in the main text as MO.) In a March 6, 1928, article for the *Berliner Tageblatt,* Alfred Polgar refers to it as a wonderful "children's playground." Polgar, "Im romantischen Gelände," reprinted in Wolfgang Jacobsen, ed., *Babelsberg 1912–1992: Ein Filmstudio* (Berlin: Argon Verlag, 1992), 144 (abbreviated in the main text as B). See also Hans-Michael Bock's account of the materials needed to build this new "film-city": "Die Filmstadt: Ateliergelände Neubabelsberg," in *Das Ufa-Buch,* ed. Hans-Michael Bock and Michael Töteberg (Frankfurt a.M.: Zweitausendeins, 1992), 86–89.
3. See Werner Sudendorf's summary, in "Kunstwelten und Lichtkünste," of the advantages Neubabelsberg enjoyed over the other Berlin film studios. In Wolfgang Jacobsen, ed., *Babelsberg 1912–1992: Ein Fimlstudio,* (Berlin: Argon Verlag, 1992), 45.

4. *Reichsfilmblatt,* December 22, 1926. Cited by Jürgen Schebera, *Damals in Neubabelsberg . . . : Studios, Stars und Kinopaläste der zwanziger Jahre* (Leipzig: Edition Leipzig, 1990), 51.

5. Fred Gehler and Ullrich Kasten, *Fritz Lang: Die Stimme von Metropolis* (Berlin: Henschel Verlag GmbH, 1990), 10. All translations are mine unless otherwise noted.

6. As Karl Prümm remarks in his essay "Empfindsame Reisen in die Filmstadt," reporters soon noted that the film-city produced a "second materiality of the [filmic] medium" (in Wolfgang Jacobsen, ed., *Babelsberg 1912–1992: Ein Filmstudio* [Berlin: Argon Verlag, 1992], 118).

7. *Ufa-Programm* (1925–26), 6–7; cited by Karl Prümm in his essay, "Empfindsame Reisen in die Filmstadt," 117. See also *Film-Kurier,* ed., *Das große Bilderbuch des Films* (Berlin: Film-Kurier, 1925).

8. Bruno Taut, "A Program for Architecture," in Anton Kaes, Martin Jay, Edward Dimendberg, eds., *The Weimar Republic Sourcebook* (Berkeley: California University Press, 1994), 432.

9. Kracauer's semi-autobiographical novel, *Ginster* (1928), sardonically recalls his years as an architect. Cf. Gerwin Zohlen's essay, "Schmugglerpfad: Siegfried Kracauer, Architekt und Schriftsteller," in *Siegfried Kracauer: Neue Interpretationen,* ed. Thomas Y. Levin (Tübingen: Stauffenburg Verlag, 1990), 325–44.

10. Wolfgang Pehnt, *Expressionist Architecture* (London: Thames & Hudson, 193), 65.

11. Cf. Friedrich Nietzsche's 1873 essay "Über Wahrheit und Lüge im aussermoralischen Sinne": "[T]ruths are illusions about which one has forgotten that they are illusions; worn-out metaphors that have become materially weak; coins that have lost their image and that now function only as metal and not as coins." (Nietzsche, *Sämtliche Werke: Kritische Studienausgabe in 15 Bänden,* ed. Giorgio Colli and Mazzino Montinari [Munich: Deutscher Taschenbuch Verlag / de Gruyter, 1980], 1: 880–81.

12. See the epigraph to Robert Musil's *Die Verwirrungen des Zöglings Törleß.* (Hamburg: Rewohlt, 1985), 7.

13. Siegfried Kracauer, *Das Ornament der Masse: Essays* (Frankfurt a.M.: Suhrkamp, 1963), 274. Abbreviated in the main text as OM.

14. For Kracauer's negative reception of *The Nibelungs* (his first film review), see "Der Mythos im Großfilm," *Frankfurter Zeitung,* May 7, 1924; reprinted in *Schriften 2,* ed. Karsten Witte (Frankfurt a.M.: Suhrkamp, 1979), 397–98.

15. Cf. Prümm's comments on Kracauer's narratorial tactics in "Calico-World": "The theoretical discourse is erected like a barrier between the spectator and the spectated event. Coldness and indifference govern this iron text that

immediately turns everything seen into elementary reductionism or into philosophical detour" ("Empfindsame Reisen in die Filmstadt," 123).

16. Kracauer describes the Schüfftan technique thus: "An impressive skyscraper does not tower nearly as dizzyingly as it does in its screen appearance: only the bottom half is actually constructed, while the upper section is generated from a small model using a mirror technique. In this way, such structures refute the colossi: while their feet are made of clay, their upper parts are an insubstantial illusion of an illusion [*Schein des Scheines*], which is tacked on" (*Mass Ornament*, 284; *Das Ornament der Masse*, 274). Cf. also Lotte H. Eisner, *The Haunted Screen: Expressionism in the German Cinema and the Influence of Max Reinhardt*, trans. Roger Greaves (London: Thames & Hudson, 1969), 233. On Schüfftan's suspicions of sabotage by screen architects, see Werner Sudendorf, "Kunstwelten und Lichtkünste," in Wolfgang Jacobsen, ed., *Babelsberg 1912–1992: Ein Filmstudio* (Berlin: Argon Verlag, 1992), 62.

17. See Michael Esser's definition of "flowing architecture" in the sets of Herlth and Röhrig: "Poeten der Filmarchitektur," in *Das Ufa-Buch*, ed. Hans-Michael Bock and Michael Töteberg (Frankfurt a.M.: Zweitausandeins, 1992), 118–23.

18. For an account of Ufa's production costs and takeovers, see Bruce A. Murray, "An Introduction to the Commercial Film Industry in Germany from 1895 to 1933," in *Film and Politics in the Weimar Republic*, ed. Thomas G. Plummer, Bruce A. Murray, et al. (Minneapolis: Minnesota University Press, 1982), 29; and also Julian Petley, *Capital and Culture: German Cinema 1933–45* (London: British Film Institute, 1979), 29–46.

19. Theodor W. Adorno and Max Horkheimer, *Dialectic of Enlightenment*, trans. John Cumming (New York: Continuum, 1944), 120.

20. Jean Baudry, "The Apparatus: Metapsychological Approaches to the Impression of Reality in Cinema", in *Film Theory and Criticism*, ed. Gerald Mast, Marshall Cohen, and Leo Braudy, 4th ed. (New York: Oxford University Press, 1992), 690–707.

21. Kracauer does not have kind words for montage films, either, particularly if they concentrate on a pure formalism at the expense of socially progressive content; see his attack on Walther Ruttmann in "Film 1928" (*Mass Ornament*, 318).

22. Cf. also Kracauer, "Berliner Lichtspielhäuser," *Das illustrierte Blatt* 14, no. 8 (February 21, 1926): 162. Deutsches Literaturarchiv, Marbach-am-Neckar (henceforth abbreviated as DL).

23. Dieter Bartetzko cites this emotive phrase of Kracauer's as part of his insightful but overargued thesis of the complicity of Weimar cinema's protofascistic "cultic-suggestive effectiveness" and "atmospheric architecture that stimulated feelings," as if these theatrical factors alone *caused* Nazism, rather

than being further used by the same. See Bartetzko, *Illusionen im Stein: Stimmungsarchitektur im deutschen Faschismus. Ihre Vorgeschichte in Theater- und Film-Bauten* (Hamburg: Rowohlt, 1985), 157.

24. Cf. Sabine Hake, who articulates how late Weimar cinema's "sensory overstimulation" gave rise to an "almost fetishistic attention to theater architecture and design." *The Cinema's Third Machine: Writing on Film in Germany 1907–1933* (Lincoln: Nebraska University Press, 1993), 266.

25. The *Marmorhaus* was built by Hugo Pál (1912–13), *Universum-Filmpalast* by Erich Mendelsohn (1928), the *Titania-Palast* by Ernst Schöffler, Carlo Schoenbach, and Carl Jacobi (1928), the *Mercedes-Palast* by Fritz Wilms (1927), the *Gloria-Palast* by Max Bremer and Ernst Lessing (1926), and the *Capitol* and *Babylon* by Hans Poelzig (1926 and 1929, respectively). See Peter Boeger's exhaustive historical guide to the movie palaces in Weimar Berlin, *Architektur der Lichtspieltheater in Berlin: Bauten und Projekte 1919–1930* (Berlin: Arenhövel, 1993); and Michael Töteberg, "Warenhaus des Films: Filmpaläste in Berlin," in *Das Ufa-Buch,* ed. Hans-Michael Bock and Michael Töteberg (Frankfurt a.M.: Zweitausendeins, 1992), 106–7.

26. Cf. Michael Töteberg's "Europas größtes Kino. Filmtheater und Varieté: Der Ufa-Palast in Hamburg," in *Das Ufa-Buch,* ed. Hans-Michael Bock and Michael Töteberg (Frankfurt a.M.: Zweitausendeins, 1992), 290–93.

27. Cf. Heide Schlüpmann, "Kinosucht," *Frauen und Film* 30 (1982): 44–51, on the feminizing architectural politics involved in the mass experience of Weimar cinema architecture.

28. Cf. Nietzsche's attack on Wagner's music for wanting "effect, . . . nothing but effect," for creating a "rhetorics of theater, a medium of expression, of a strengthening of gesture, of suggestion, of the psychological picturesque" (Nietzsche, "Der Fall Wagner," *Sämtliche Werke: Kritische Studienausgabe in 15 Bänden,* ed. Giorgio Colli and Mazzino Montinari [Munich: Deutscher Taschenbuch Verlag / de Gruyter, 1980], 6: 31, 30).

29. Indeed, Kracauer's fears regarding the dumbing-down of cinema audiences would appear to be justified in an unrealized project by Bruno Taut for a cinema amphitheater for patients brought in from nearby hospitals ("Bildvorführungen für liegende Zuschauer," *Bauwelt* 15, no. 32 [1924]: 743). This strange design enabled prostrate spectators to see movies by looking up at the screen, rather than down at it, positioned on horizontal, worshipful couches that descended in rows from the screen. See Janet Lungstrum, "Expressionist Towers of Babel in Weimar Film and Architecture," in *Visibility and Expressivity,* ed. Wilhelm S. Wurzer (Evanston, Ill.: Northwestern University Press, 1998).

30. Siegfried Kracauer, "Organisiertes Glück: Zur Wiedereröffnung des Lunaparks," *Frankfurter Zeitung* 74, no. 338 (May 8, 1930). DL.

31. In Frankfurt am Main in 1923, for example, Kracauer reports that only eight

to ten of the fifty-four registered architects in the *Bund Deutscher Architekten* were gainfully employed. Kracauer, "Die Notlage des Architektenstandes," *Frankfurter Zeitung* 67 (February 6, 1923). DL.

32. "Rabitz" is a term for the narrowly woven wire mesh (or expanding metal) that is stretched out over a wall and onto which the plaster is spread (named after its inventor, Karl Rabitz, a master builder, in 1880).

33. Siegfried Kracauer, "Über Turmhäuser," *Frankfurter Zeitung* 160 (March 2, 1921). DL. Quoted by Zohlen, "Schmugglerpfad," 332.

34. Siegfried Kracauer, *From Caligari to Hitler: A Psychological History of the German Film* (Princeton, N.J.: Princeton University Press, 1947).

35. Siegfried Kracauer, "*Frühlicht* in Magdeburg," *Frankfurter Zeitung* 66, no. 30 (January 12, 1922). DL.

36. In this sense Kracauer is, by implication, a proponent of the same impulse that fuelled the socialist modernist architecture of such figures as Hannes Meyer and Ludwig Hilberseimer. See K. Michael Hays, *Modernism and the Posthumanist Subject: The Architecture of Hannes Meyer and Ludwig Hilberseimer* (Cambridge: MIT Press, 1992).

37. Cf. Irmgard Keun's *Das kunstseidene Mädchen* (1932: reprint, Munich: Deutscher Taschenbuch Verlag, 1997), and Kracauer's use of the term *Glanz* as a signifier for Berlin in his essay, "Aus dem Fenster gesehen," in *Straßen in Berlin und anderswo* (Berlin: Das Arsenal, 1987), 41.

38. A postwar Kracauer condemned Lang's silent architectonic films as the proto-fascistic "triumph of the ornamental over the human" (*From Caligari to Hitler,* 95). Cf. Silberman in Stephen Eric Bronner and Douglas Kellner, eds., *Passion and Rebellion: The Expressionist Heritage* (New York: J.F. Bergin, 1983), 382.

39. Béla Balázs, "Der sichtbare Mensch, oder die Kultur des Films," in *Schriften zum Film I* (Munich: Carl Hanser Verlag, 1982), 90–92. Abbreviated in the main text as SM. See Frank Kessler's discussion of the debate concerning architectural and painterly *Stimmung* in "Les architects-peintres du cinéma allemand muet," *Iris* 12 (1990): 51–54. Cf. also Joseph Zsuffa's *Béla Balázs: The Man and the Artist* (Berkeley: California University Press, 1987) 114–21.

40. Balázs' subsequent book on sound film, *Der Geist des Films* (1930), was criticized by Kracauer for unquestioningly accepting Soviet film theory's valorization of the collective and the masses, and ignoring films where *das Massenhafte* did not feature. Kracauer, "Ein neues Filmbuch," *Frankfurter Zeitung* 75, no. 819 (November 2, 1930). DL.

41. See Hake's discussion of Balázs' limitations in *The Cinema's Third Machine*.

42. Miriam Hansen, "Decentric Perspectives: Kracauer's Early Writings on Film and Mass Culture," *New German Critique* 54 (1991): 68.

43. Cf. Sergei M. Eisenstein, *Schriften* (Munich: Carl Hanser Verlag, 1973).

Balázs was to compensate for this in *Der Geist des Films,* with its overt emphasis on montage. In point of fact, nothing tainted Balázs' reputation more for contemporary film studies than his script and scenography help for Riefenstahl's mountain film, *The Blue Light* (*Das blaue Licht,* 1932).

44. Leo Witlin notes this architectural divide in Weimar cinema in an article entitled "Filmarchitekt oder Filmmaler?" in *Filmtechnik* 3 (1926): 46; cited by Kessler, "Les architects-peintres," 52–53. The introduction of sound at the end of the 1920s signaled a swift formalization away from architectural monumentalism and a return to indoor shooting in newly equipped studios.

45. "The so-called picture has given way to the pictorial," remarked the film architect Herlth in "Die Aufgaben des Malers beim Film," *Gebrauchsgraphik* 6 (1924–25); cited by Kessler, "Les architects-peintres," 53.

46. Walter Muschg, "Filmzauber," *Neue Zürcher Zeitung* 997 (July 30, 1922); reprinted in Wolfgang Jacobsen, ed., *Babelsberg 1912–1992: Ein Filmstudio* (Berlin: Argon Verlag, 1992), 140.

47. Cf. Walter Serner's 1913 essay, "Kino und Schaulust," which first coins the term on the voyeuristic urge inherent to watching a film; reprinted in Anton Kaes, ed., *Kino-Debatte: Texte zum Verhältnis von Literatur und Film 1909–1929* (Tübingen: Max Niemeyer Verlag, 1978), 53–58.

48. Siegfried Kracauer, "Filmbild und Prophetenrede," *Frankfurter Zeitung* 330 (May 5, 1925) (n.p.). DL. See also Miriam Hansen's discussion of the role played by Grune's film in Kracauer's metaphysics of film in her "Decentric Perspectives," 47–49.

49. Siegfried Kracauer, "Ein Film," *Frankfurter Zeitung* 68, no. 93 (February 4, 1924) (n.p.). DL.

50. Ibid.

51. Prümm notes affinities in Kracauer's description of Neubabelsberg with his notion of the "spatial desert" of modernity in the latter's *Der Detektiv-Roman,* written from 1922 to 1925 but not published until 1971 (Wolfgang Jacobsen, ed., *Babelsberg 1912–1992: Ein Filmstudio* [Berlin: Argon Verlag, 1992], 125), but Prümm does not consider the architectural presence of the film-city Neubabelsberg itself in relation to the modern metropolis that provided Kracauer with so much material during his Weimar years.

52. See Hanne Bergius, "Berlin, the Dada-Metropolis," in *The 1920's: Age of the Metropolis,* ed. Jean Clair (Montreal: Montreal Museum of Fine Arts, 1991), 253–69.

2

COURTNEY FEDERLE

Picture Postcard: Kracauer Writes from Berlin

For over a century the figure of the *stranger* has represented a position in urban space that includes both the freedom and the suffering of a transitory, homeless, transgressive condition marginal to local social formations. Standing neither wholly inside nor wholly outside modern public culture, the stranger occupies a place that is simultaneously alien and participatory. In this essay, I will examine how Siegfried Kracauer, always a stranger in Berlin, wanders and reimagines the public spaces of Germany's capital city in the later years of the Weimar Republic. I want to assess how he experiences and represents the monumental sites of a city that was built up over the course of the late nineteenth and early twentieth centuries. I will attempt to convey how Kracauer occupies (and exploits) a position that enables him to invent a mode of critical urban analysis that reconfigures cityscapes precisely where nation, state, capital, and imperial desire most emphatically monumentalize themselves as static space. Given that Berlin is once again a dramatically contested site which is being reinvented and reconfigured for another uncertain future as the capital of Germany, it is important that we pore over Kracauer's reports from streets of the metropolis and his countermonumental discourse on the representative spaces of nationalism, statism, imperialism, and capitalism.

Wandering the modern capital city, Kracauer remains always a stranger in the sense suggested by Georg Simmel when he wrote of the stranger not

> in the sense that has already been dealt with often enough, as a wanderer who comes today and goes tomorrow, but rather as one who comes today and stays tomorrow—the potential wanderer, so to speak, who, even though he has not moved on, has not completely gotten over the freedom (*Gelöstheit*) of coming and going. He is fixed within a certain spatial sphere—or within a sphere the delimitations of which are analogous to spatial boundaries—but his position within this sphere is essentially defined by the fact that he does not belong in it from the very beginning, and that he brings qualities into this sphere that do not and could not stem from it."[1]

Simmel wants not only to identify a specific urban type and practice but also to locate the historical origins of that type and practice in the simultaneously alien and participatory position of the Jew. Furthermore, and perhaps most importantly for my consideration of Kracauer's estranged experience and representation of late-Weimar Berlin, Simmel argues that the stranger's position, which is neither fixed nor completely unbound, exemplifies the spatial aspect of social relations. I will demonstrate how for Kracauer, as for Simmel before him, the human formations of space provide both the conditions for and the symbols of social relations.

Kracauer comes to Berlin and stays for three years. He remains always a stranger in this metropolis, from which, in 1933, he flees precisely because the new regime has begun to transform the real and the symbolic spaces of the city in a totalitarian effort to completely efface the fixed and unbound position of the stranger (the Jew) that Kracauer occupies. We have to recall that Kracauer comes to Berlin as a sort of exile. In effect, the *Frankfurter Zeitung* banishes him to the capital rather than offer him a promotion in Frankfurt.[2] In 1929, I. G. Farben acquires a 49.5 percent share of the paper and begins to pressure the editorial staff to assume a more conservative stance. As an effect of the new politics at the paper, Kracauer receives the assignment in Berlin rather than the expected promotion to chief editor of the feuilleton, which would have kept him in Frankfurt. In 1931, it is made clear that the paper no longer needs him on its full-time staff. His articles are rejected with increasing frequency. Yet, despite offers from leftist democratic papers, he struggles to stay with the *Frankfurter Zeitung* because he feels it imperative, given the political situation in the capital, that he continue to address the paper's liberal bourgeois audience. On the night that the Reichstag is set aflame, Kracauer receives a telegram from the sympathetic publisher and chief editor of the paper, Heinrich Simon,[3] telling him that he has been assigned to the Paris bureau. On February 28, 1933 Kracauer leaves Berlin for Paris. Three weeks later he is unofficially laid off. In August he is officially dismissed from the paper.

Throughout his years in Berlin, Kracauer reports on the increasingly violent and threatening Nazi actions in the streets and squares of the capital. He recognizes and documents how the seizure of public space precedes and enables the seizure of political power. That Kracauer decides to flee Berlin the night of the Reichstag fire makes clear how acutely he understands that the representational sites in the city symbolically function to assert and project the order of political regimes. On the night of February 26, 1933, Kracauer experiences unequivocally that the reconfiguration of the capital's spaces under the new regime radically reduces the sphere within which he may participate.

As this brief account of his Berlin experience makes clear, Kracauer's urban practice is not, cannot be, that of the flaneur. During his wanderings he observes a city that is no longer available to the flaneur, a city that no longer affords a space for the flaneur. Kracauer documents how the flaneur's space continues to contract as a result of the ongoing transformations of the modern cityscape. For example, writing about the effect of advertising lights on the experience of the streets at night, Kracauer notes that the old urban practice of the flaneur is no longer possible beneath the fireworks of the modern city's night sky.[4] Kracauer himself is not as at home in the metropolis as was the flaneur who sauntered along the boulevards or walked his tortoise on a leash through the arcades of the nineteenth century's capital city. Kracauer differently experiences the city, from a position of estranged difference that in no way corresponds to that of the flaneur's aloof detachment. One may see in Kracauer, to paraphrase Benjamin, what has become of the flaneur when the context in which he belonged has been taken away.[5]

While working as the Berlin correspondent for the *Frankfurter Zeitung*, Kracauer files a number of reports from the streets of the continent's largest city. Kracauer walks a metropolis that has, to a great extent, taken form under the influences of, on the one hand, the emphatic evocation and assertion of nationalist/monarchist claims to the new nation's capital and, on the other, an unprecedented expansion in the key economic sectors of banking, communications, entertainment, transportation, and the electric, chemical, and heavy industries. Read together, Kracauer's Weimar era feuilleton pieces on the capital present a critical reading of the city as a modern urban space that continues to metamorphose under the powerful and often conflicting and asynchronic forces of nationalist and capitalist crisis and consolidation. In representing imaginary and material configurations of the metropolis that are forged in crisis, Kracauer offers something other than a vulgar Marxist critique of modern urbanism. Instead, while wandering the streets and recording his impressions, he discovers that Berlin's representational formations are complex symbolic constructs that can be deciphered through a practice of attentive looking which reveals the transformed city as the site of multiple and multivalent repressed, accidental, and asynchronic spaces. Kracauer claims to have accessed an urban unconscious, first by closely examining those spaces that accidentally reveal the unplanned and unnarrated forms of the modern city, and then by critically analyzing the fetishized places that service the grand narrative of the nation and its capital.[6]

With his investigations into the construction and fluctuation of meaning in urban formations, Kracauer discovers forms that stand as protean ciphers for the multiple and simultaneous crises of modernity, for the social, political, economic, and cultural transformations of the postwar years in Berlin. He documents exact moments and sites where the planned, representative architectural spaces break down and lose their intended significatory functions as public communicative forms. If we can agree that the grand urban structures of nineteenth-century Europe performed as a medium that narrated, staged, and sustained national myths, then we can better understand how Kracauer, in his essays on various urban formations, bears witness to the crisis of the grand narrative that represents the state as the telos of history.[7]

In recent years, a discussion has begun about the fact that Kracauer, in his Weimar era writings on cinema, evinces a subtle and differentiated reading of the emergent medium and its power to undermine the seemingly stable and literal referential space of the city through dispersal, distraction, dislocation, and disorientation.[8] In his early essays on cinema Kracauer anticipates not only Benjamin's argument on the new media in the artwork essay but also the postmodernist emphasis on the heterological and dislocative quality of mass media.[9] However, unlike Benjamin and even some postmodern authors, in the 1920's Kracauer does not envision a redemptive moment in the filmic medium. Similarly, in his Weimar era essays on city spaces Kracauer recognizes that the seemingly stable monumentality of the nation and its history, as evoked in its urban formations, is also susceptible to dispersal, distraction, dislocation, and disorientation. Again anticipating later critical theory, Kracauer understands that, as a result of the ambiguities of urban formations and their significatory functions, the masses are positioned more precariously now between the rock of the state and the hard place of capitalism. He discovers the paradox that these very formations and their functions become more effective as systems when their meaning becomes more dispersed. Kracauer recognizes and reveals both the effectivity and the potential slippage of an ideology that manifests itself in a system of protean and multivalent symbols.[10]

In what follows, I will demonstrate that Kracauer reads the metropolis as a dishomogeneous space not only filled by the mythologizing sites of representational and institutional architecture but also formed by a spatial practice that recognizes spontaneous and accidental formations.[11] I want to emphasize the historical significance of Kracauer's contribution to the formulation of a critical, modernist, urban epistemology—it must be remembered and emphasized how much Benjamin, Adorno, Bloch, and others learned (and failed to learn) from Kracauer about reading urban culture. I also want to point to the critical force that Kracauer's model might bring to the contemporary deciphering of the complex heterogeneity of late-twentieth-century urban space. In deciphering the city, he is interested not simply (and reductively) in revealing the false consciousness of a dominant ideological formation, in demythologizing the myths of nineteenth-century nationalist, capitalist, and imperialist culture.[12] Rather, he attempts to move beyond the critical negation and toward a "demythologizing of demythologizing"[13] that would allow for an analysis of the mythological formations of Berlin modernism that simultaneously exposes ideological formations and, in discovering the slippage in those symbolic systems, denies critical weight to the idea of totality. In situating Kracauer in this manner, I am, in effect, locating him simultaneously within and after modernism.

As I have already stated, Kracauer critically witnesses the multiple and contradictory formations of the urban space through which he moves when wandering the city. As an example of this critical practice I want to consider an essay entitled *Berlin Landscape* (1931). In this feuilleton piece Kracauer differentiates between planned and unplanned urban formations:

> One can distinguish between two types of urban formations (*Stadtbildern*): those that are consciously formed and those that result unintentionally. The first sort emerge from the artistic will realized in plazas, panoramic views, grouped buildings and perspectival effects, which *Baedeker* generally highlights with a little star. The second sort emerge without any prior planning. These are not compositions . . . rather they are creations of accident that cannot be accounted for. Wherever massive buildings and streetways meet whose elements are produced by interests that are oriented in completely different ways, a sort of urban formation (*Stadtbild*) emerges that was itself never the object of any particular interest. It is consciously formed just as little as nature and is similar to a landscape in that it unconsciously asserts itself. . . . This landscape is unaffected Berlin. Without intention, Berlin's contrasts, its severity, its openness, its juxtaposition, its glamor express themselves in this landscape that has grown of its own accord. Knowledge (*Erkenntnis*) of cities is connected to the deciphering of urban formations that are articulated in a dream-like manner.[14]

The two types of urban space identified here correspond to conscious and unconscious constructs, to what Deleuze and Guattarri call state and nomad space. The intended city is broken up and complicated by the accidental city, which, in its chance character, permits the experience of a cityscape not *authored* by any particular interest. In this passage, Kracauer analyzes one such urban formation—the street scene before his apartment window—that exemplifies how these unaffected cityscapes escape the authority of urban planners and architects and reveal the heterogeneity that their designs deny.[15] Even though Kracauer does not problematize landscape as social-cultural configuration, in employing the term he draws an ironic and critical parallel between the moral-aesthetic construct of scenes in nature and the political-economic construct of scenes in the metropolis. The anti-aesthetic quality of these creations of accident suggests not natural growth and harmony but instead urban growth and crisis: urban configurations of monopoly capitalism, nationalist consolidation, and imperialist ambition in the late nineteenth and early twentieth centuries assume forms that escape all intention and design. Kracauer would replace the old aesthetics of landscape with a new *aisthetikos,* that is, with a new way of perceiving that would be adequate to the experience of urban formations.

Several months before writing *Berlin Landscape,* Kracauer observes and deciphers the other type of urban formation that he identifies as planned: state space. In a piece entitled *On the Employment Office: The Construction of a Space* (1930), Kracauer claims that the enciphered meaning of the specific space of an (un)employment office becomes apparent only by the inadvertent eruption through its surface of a hidden discourse:

> Every typical space is produced by typical social conditions, which express themselves in that space without the disturbing interference of consciousness. Everything that is denied by consciousness, everything that is otherwise intentionally overlooked, participates in the construction of that space. Spatial formations (*Raumbilder*) are society's dreams. Wherever the hieroglyph of any spatial formation is deciphered, there the ground of social reality presents itself.[16]

Kracauer's reflection on the social production of space leads to the insight that the intentional, conscious construction of any discrete space will always be haunted by the unintentional, unconscious expression of the social conditions that produced that space. The architecturally repressed, which of course means the socially, culturally, politically repressed, returns in the very process of the space's construction.[17] Kracauer does not attempt a psychoanalytic interpretation of society's dreams— there is no indication of a topological series of displacement and distortion.[18] Rather, as this passage makes clear, his *analytic* practice deals with the deciphering of hieroglyphic spatial formations that, like any hieroglyphic language, could make sense only when read in juxtaposition with other formations.[19] Most importantly for the present discussion, Kracauer softens the distinctions that he makes in *Berlin Landscape* when, here in his analysis of an (un)employment office, he discovers that even planned spaces are transformed by accidental, unconscious forces that escape planning design. Kracauer has complicated his distinction between conscious (intended) and unconscious (unintended) urban formations by discovering that the consciously repressed returns and participates in the very production of precisely the most consciously constructed state spaces.[20]

During his Berlin years, Kracauer frequently describes this very sort of slippage in the architectural language of consciously constructed urban spaces in essays on train stations, hotel lobbies, arcades, amusement parks, movie palaces, sports arenas, and city streets. I will turn now to one such essay, entitled *Ansichtspostkarte* (Picture postcard), where he demonstrates his method of deciphering urban formations as the complex constructs of intention, displacement, experience, accident, and memory. The title deserves some attention. The picture postcard is simultaneously an image for remembering and for forgetting, for representing and for promoting, for selling and for collecting, is always a representation of an idea as space. Postcards are always souvenirs and, as such, always belated in their indexing of sites that have become tourist destinations precisely because they are not only *representative* but also *represented* sites. More specifically, early-twentieth-century postcard images of urban spaces contribute to the construction of an urban picturesque characterized by nostalgic representation of monumental, representative nineteenth-century spaces. With his picture postcard, Kracauer sends the message that there exists simultaneously an urban space available only to the critical *tourism* of a new *aisthetikos*.

In this short feuilleton piece from 1930, Kracauer describes how, when approaching the Kaiser Wilhelm Memorial Church at night, he discovers that the luminescence of the advertising lights from the cinema palaces across the street transforms the static, monumental, and representational memorial structure into a transient, unnoticed, and improbable urban formation:

> The Kaiser Wilhelm Memorial Church at night: anyone coming from the zoological gardens train station who catches a view of it—and the urbanite only sees it at all at night, since during the day it is nothing more to him than a gigantic hindrance to traffic—gets a view of a remarkable, almost divine (*überirdisches*) drama. Out of the sacral structure there radiates a soft light that is as becalming as it is unexplainable, a brightness which has nothing in common with the profane red shimmer of the spotlights, but which strangely detaches (*abhebt*) itself from its environment and seems to have its source in the Kaiser Wilhelm Memorial Walls themselves. Does the pale glow force its way out of the church's interior? But this cathedral, which joins sword with altar, obviously has only one ambition: to represent outward into the world (*nach außen hin zu repräsentieren*). . . . The mysterious glow is in reality only a reflection. Reflection of the facades of light, which, from the Ufa-Palace down to the Capitol theater and beyond, turn the night into day so as to drive the horror of the night out of the theatergoers' workday. . . . The mild radiance that surrounds the Kaiser Wilhelm Memorial Church is the unintentional reflection of this dark glow. That which remains from this spectacle of light and which is thrown out from the [pleasure] industry—the desolate walls collect. The exterior of the church, which is no church, becomes the refuge of the wasted and forgotten and radiates as beautifully as if it were the most holy itself. Secret tears find their memorial place in this manner. Not in the hidden interior— right in the middle of the street the unnoticed, the improbable is gathered and transformed, until it begins to shine, for everyone a consolation.[21]

Kracauer locates the church in the city as a protean form that has escaped its original, intended, representational function. During the day the memorial church, built to represent the order of the monarchy—already emphatically imaginary, asynchronic, nostalgic, and reactionary when constructed—performs the negative function of hindering traffic and the circulation of goods, labor, services, and consumers. The anachronistic monumentality of the structure literally stands in the way of the development of the city center as the hub of a general circulation. Its reactionary assertion defies, and simultaneously and inadvertently manifests, the reality that late-nineteenth- and early-twentieth-century capitalism has outstripped and made obsolete the order of the *imperial age*.[22] At night the memorial church, built of stone as a massive and insistent monumental structure, is transformed into an ethereal luminescence which, to all appearances, strangely transcends and detaches itself from the surrounding city. Yet, upon closer inspection, Kracauer notes that the church does not radiate but rather reflects light, that the sublime, celestial radiance reveals itself as merely the accidental, unintended reflection of the pleasure industry's (*Vergnügungsbetrieb*) own dark glow. In the moment that Kracauer records, the memorial church has become the mere surface that captures and weakly reflects the excess of the spectacle of advertising lights, the mere surface that collects the discarded and the forgotten and returns them as the pale glow of a symbolic system in crisis.[23]

This is not the only moment in his Weimar-period essays where Kracauer speaks of the paradoxical quality of advertising lights that escape the limits of their intended function and reveal a world-historical formation as illusion. In *Advertising Lights* (1927) he observes how the monumentality of advertising lighting design, which, as we have seen in *Picture Postcard*, threatens to supersede the monumentality of the nation, is itself threatened by the very medium through which it constructs itself as monumental:

> Advertising lights rise towards a heaven in which there are no longer any angels, but also one in which all is not just business. The advertising lights shoot out beyond the economy, and what is intended to be advertising becomes illumination. This results when business people get involved in lighting effects. Light remains light and, if it radiates in all its colorfulness, then it truly exceeds the limits that have been prescribed for it by its employers. Colorful letters which are supposed to advertise white laundry veer somewhat from their task even when they are five stories tall. The accountability of the marketing director is limited in the empire of lightbulbs, and the signals that he gives slip from his control and take on new meaning. Thus the juxtaposition of shops produces a teeming of light whose gleaming disorder is not purely terrestrial. One can still recognize signs and texts in this teeming of light, yet signs and texts here have transcended their practical purpose, their dissolution into colorfulness has shattered them into glitter fragments that come together according to laws that differ from the usual ones. The drizzle of advertisements that the business world showers down forms constellations in a strange heaven.[24]

Advertising lights transcend their function, leave behind their persuasive-communicative purpose, and become pure and meaningless to the further circulation of commodities—become *illumination*. Yet the dialectical transcendence of the message and medium does not lead to redemptive synthesis. Rather, the illumination only makes plain how profoundly estranged the experience of the modern cityscape has become. There is little hope offered by this vision in the urban heavens, only the dire revelation that in the *empire of lightbulbs* no meaning adheres to the signs.

In looking at Kracauer's essay on the Kaiser Wilhelm Memorial Church, we see that, in the light of day, the memorial is blockage. As such, the representational form reveals itself for what it is when, in its presence as hindrance, it disappears as memorial only to reappear as antimodern structure. On the other hand, in the light of the night, the memorial is reflection. As such, monumentality is dialectically transformed through a negation of the negation: the "progress" of the capitalist city, the very progress that has negatively transformed the memorial during the day, reveals itself as the force that has hollowed out all monumentality and left only the surface as the site of any possible countermonumental significance. Kracauer makes clear that only in the excess material accidentally collected, reversed, and diffused in the reflections on the memorial's desolate walls can the discarded and the improbable be transformed and deciphered, can the memorial still be read as a meaningful, contemporary urban formation, as a chance and fleeting monument to the new world historical formation of the double injunction to work and enjoy, to produce and consume. We have seen how lights at night transform the cityscape and create lightscapes, how, every night, lights transform the monumentality of the city. Kracauer understands the new urban formations not only as symptoms of the crisis of the state and its self-representation but also as part of capitalism's injunction to enjoy, precisely in a time of crisis. In the specific instance of the Kaiser Wilhelm Memorial Church, the monumental (and in-the-way-of-things) representation returns each morning to remind everyone that the state is still, always, there. But the monumental injunction to pleasure also returns each night, evoking and provoking a return of everything repressed during the workday. Here time is granted for discharge. This is not the haunted night of romanticism and individuals. This is the luminous night of modernism and the masses.

As his "Picture Postcard" suggests, Kracauer devises an urban geography sensitive to how the urban space is practiced and to the fact, in practice, that space is never static. Baldly stated, Kracauer observes slippage in ideologies of space.[25] He sees the Kaiser Wilhelm Memorial Church as a structure located in the heterogeneous urban environment of Berlin in the late 1920s where the static space imagined and constructed by the state over the course of the preceding half century is transformed by the practice or use that is made of that space every day and every night. By day, a past age's mythological state formation clogs the present age's rational, economic space. By night, that same rational, economic space in turn creates an accidental, mythological formation. Kracauer registers the transformative potential of the accidental experience and being of city spaces. The stable forms intended to represent memory, wholeness, and ideal identity now dialectically represent forgetting, dispersal, and material estrangement. Given the contemporary discussion on and actual rebuilding of historically representational spaces in the German capital, Kracauer's analysis of the social production and transformation of Berlin as urban space deserves renewed attention.

NOTES

1. Georg Simmel, originally as "Exkurs über den Fremden," in *Soziologie* (München: Duncker & Humblot, 1908), 509: "Es ist hier also der Fremde nicht in

dem bisher vielfach berührten Sinn gemeint, als der Wandernde, der heute kommt und morgen geht, sondern als der, der heute kommt und morgen bleibt—sozusagen der potenziell Wandernde, der, obgleich er nicht weitergezogen ist, die Gelöstheit des Kommens und Gehens nicht ganz überwunden hat. Er ist innerhalb eines bestimmten räumlichen Umkreises—oder eines, dessen Grenzbestimmtheit der räumlichen analog ist—fixiert, aber seine Position in diesem ist dadurch wesentlich bestimmt, daß er nicht von vornherein in ihn gehört, daß er Qualitäten, die aus ihm nicht stammen und stammen können, in ihn hineinträgt." Donald Levine has translated the excursus as "The Stranger," in *On Individuality and Social Forms* (Chicago: University of Chicago Press, 1971).

2. My account of Kracauer's assignment to and departure from Berlin derives from Inka Mülder's *Siegfried Kracauer: Grenzgänger zwischen Theorie und Literatur* (Stuttgart: Metzler, 1985), 8–10, where she discusses Kracauer's career with the *Frankfurter Zeitung* from 1920–1933. She documents Kracauer's growing unease with both the political situation in Berlin and the changes at the paper in the early 1930s.

3. In early 1934 Simon is driven from the paper, losing not only his position but a great deal of his fortune. Mülder, *Kracauer*, 149.

4. "Hier kann man nicht wie auf den Boulevards flanieren. . . ." *Schriften*, vol. 5, pt. 2 (Frankfurt: Suhrkamp, 1990), 20.

5. I paraphrase Benjamin's description of the man in the crowd in his discussion of Poe's story: "The man of the crowd is not a flaneur. . . . One may rather see in him what would become of the flaneur when the context in which he belonged would be taken away" (Walter Benjamin, *Gesammelte Schriften* 1 [Frankfurt: Suhrkamp, 1974], 627). Benjamin's argument posits not only the historicity of the flaneur's experience but also that of the flaneur's way of seeing. Benjamin does not merely identify an urban type; rather, he fashions an ideal position which would best mediate the experience of modernity.

6. There are a number of key texts from the contemporary theoretical discourse of urban space that I have turned to in my reading of Kracauer. Those that bear most directly on the language and theoretical basis of my argument are: Henri Lefebvre, *The Production of Space* (London: Blackwell, 1991), which presents the most elaborate, critical, and imaginative theory of space and "spatial practice" yet written. He begins with a critique of semiological reductions of social space to the status of a message and asks "to what extent a space may be read or decoded?" He insists that, in questioning what occupies space and how it does so, his method can analyze the historically contingent processes of spatial signification. In arguing that space is a social product produced differently in each society, he elaborates a method for analyzing the ideological content of *spatial practices*, particularly those that partake in the fetishization of space in service of the state. Michel de Certeau, *The Practice*

of Everyday Life (Berkeley: University of California Press, 1984) develops a complex, though sometimes whimsical, theory of how urban space is read. He bases his theory on a semiological model that accesses "ways of operating, ways of using urban space" (xi), or what he calls "practices of space" (91) that transform urban space and disrupt the "constructed order" or "proper geometrical space" (100) of urban planners and architects. Paul Virilio's essay, "The Overexposed City," (in *Zone ½* [New York: Zone Books, 1986]) reflects on postmodern urban space in terms of a crisis of the whole, of the grand narrative, of the homogeneous in urban and architectural space. In *The Architectural Uncanny* (Cambridge: MIT Press, 1992), Anthony Vidler provides a number of provocative, though often unresolved, points for consideration. Most pertinent to the present discussion is his essay entitled "Vagabond Architecture," in which he considers John Hejduk's "critique of conventional monumentality and fixed urban architecture in favor of the mobile and nomadic . . . countermonumentality" (207). Vidler locates Hejduk's architectural imagination in the modernist tradition of "vagabond imagination" (209) exemplified by the urban imaginary of such authors as Baudelaire, Rimbaud, Aragon, Benjamin, and Dubord. (I would add Kracauer's name to this list of modernist vagabond authors.) In elaborating his definition of the "vagabond imagination," Vidler discusses Deleuze and Guattari's distinction between *state* space and *nomad* space in *Nomadology: The War Machine* (Gilles Deleuze and Félix Guattari, trans. Brian Massumi [New York: Semiotext(e), 1986]). Vidler paraphrases their account: "A sedentary space that is consciously parceled out, closed, and divided by the institutions of power would then be contrasted to the smooth, flowing unbounded space of nomadism; in western contexts, the former has always attempted to bring the latter under control" (214).

7. Paul Virilio relates the postmodern discourse on the crisis of the grand narrative to the crisis of the modern/postmodern city, to "the crisis of the whole . . . as the crisis of a substantial, homogeneous space, inherited from archaic Greek geometry, to the benefit of an accidental, heterogeneous space where parts and fragments become essential once again" ("The Overexposed City," 29).

8. Miriam Hansen, "Decentric Perspectives: Kracauer's Early Writings on Film and Mass Culture," *New German Critique* 54 (Fall 1991): 47–76.

9. Here I refer generally to the postmodern reception of Benjamin in literature and film theory, epistemology and philosophy of history, sociology and political theory, and most recently, urban geography and architectural theory. I refer specifically to Gianni Vattimo's discussion of Heidegger and Benjamin's artwork essays: "Perhaps we have now reached the stage where we can recognize that the superficiality and fragility of aesthetic experience in late-modern society do not necessarily have to be signs and symptoms

of alienation linked to the dehumanizing aspects of standardization. . . . The advent of the media enhances the inconstancy and superficiality of experience. In so doing, it runs counter to the generalization of domination, insofar as it allows a kind of 'weakening' of the very notion of reality, and thus a weakening of its persuasive force. The society of the spectacle spoken of by the situationists is not simply a society of appearance manipulated by power: it is also the society in which reality presents itself as softer and more fluid, and in which experience can again acquire the characteristic of oscillation, disorientation and play." *(The Transparent Society* [Baltimore: Johns Hopkins University Press, 1992], 59)

10. "Contrary to what critical sociology has long believed (with good reason, unfortunately), standardization, uniformity, the manipulation of consensus and the errors of totalitarianism *are not* the only possible outcome of the advent of generalized communication, the mass media and reproduction. Alongside these possibilities—which are objects of political choice—there opens an alternative possible outcome" *(The Transparent Society,* 59).

11. Michel de Certeau tries to account for an "ordinary practice of the city" that remains "foreign to the 'geometrical' or 'geographical' space of visual, panoptic, or theoretical constructions. These practices refer to a specific form of *operations* . . . 'another spatiality' (an 'anthropological,' poetic and mythic experience of space), and to an *opaque and blind* mobility characteristic of the bustling city. A *migrational,* or metaphorical, city thus slips into the clear text of the planned and readable city" (*The Practice of Everyday Life,* 93).

12. Inka Mülder-Bach discusses Kracauer's reading of the early Marx from the 1840s through the *German Ideology* and his usage of the term *Entmythologisierung* in her essay "Der Umschlag der Negativität: Zur Verschränkung von Phaenomenologie, Geschichtsphilosophie und Filmaesthetik in Siegfried Kracauers Metaphorik der Oberfläche," *Deutsche Vierteljahresschrift* 61, no. 2 (1987): 359–73.

13. Gianni Vattimo provides the term in *The Transparent Society:* "To demythologize the demythologization does not mean to restore the rights of myth, if only because amongst the myths we recognize as legitimate is that of reason and its progression. Demythologization, or the idea of history as the emancipation of reason, is not at all easy to exorcise. . . . If we wish to be faithful to our historical experience, we have to recognize that once demythologization has been exposed as a myth, our relation to myth does not return as naive as before, but remains marked by this experience. A theory of the presence of myth in today's culture must start afresh from this point" (40).

14. "Mann kann zwischen zwei Arten von Stadtbildern unterscheiden: den einen, die bewußt geformt sind, und den anderen, die sich absichtslos ergeben.

Jene entspringen dem künstlerischen Willen, der sich in Plätzen, Durchblicken, Gebäudegruppen und perspektivischen Effekten verwirklicht, die der Baedeker gemeinhin mit einem Sternchen beleuchtet. Diese dagegen entstehen, ohne vorher geplant worden zu sein. Sie sind keine Kompositionen . . . sondern *Geschöpfe des Zufalls,* die sich nicht zur Rechenschaft ziehen lassen. Wo immer sich Steinmassen und Straßenzüge zusammenfinden deren Elemente aus ganz verschieden gerichteten Interessen hervorgehen, kommt ein solches Stadtbild zustande, das selber niemals der Gegendstand irgendeines Interesses gewesen ist. Es ist so wenig gestaltet wie die Natur und gleicht einer Landschaft darin, daß es sich *bewußtlos* behauptet. . . . Diese Landschaft ist ungestelltes Berlin. Ohne Absicht sprechen sich in ihr, die von selber gewachsen ist, seine Gegensätze aus, seine Härte, seine Offenheit, sein Nebeneinander, sein Glanz. Die Erkenntnis der Städte ist an die Entzifferung ihrer traumhaft hingesagten Bilder geknüpft" ("Berliner Landscaft," *Schriften,* vol. 5, pt. 2 [Frankfurt: Suhrkamp, 1990]), 399–401, emphasis added). All translations are by me. I use the original title as it appeared in the *Frankfurter Zeitung.* The title as given in the collected works, "Aus dem Fenster gesehen," corresponds to the title of the essay as it appeared in the collection *Straßen in Berlin und Anderswo.* I prefer the original title because it emphasizes the paradoxical space and structure represented in Kracauer's essay.

15. Kracauer develops his critical analysis of planned urban space during a period when high modernist urban design has laid claim to a postaesthetic position from which it intends to perform the social-transformative, utopian activity of which bourgeois art was no longer capable. Kracauer's postmodern critique of the grand narrative of modernist urban/architectural discourse (Le Corbusier, Hilbeseimer, Bauhaus, etc.), not the topic of this essay, derives from his more general critique of Weimar-era Berlin as cityscape. Manfredo Tafuri discusses and documents the impact that the utopianism of early Soviet design aesthetics had on Central European avant-gardes in the early 1920s, a utopianism that envisioned *"Art as the organization of one's entire existence,* in the same manner as science and technology. . . ." See his essay "U.S.S.R.-Berlin, 1922: From Populism to 'Constructivist International,'" in Manfredo Tafuri, *The Sphere and the Labyrinth: Avant-Gardes and Architecture from Piranesi to the 1970s* (Cambridge: MIT Press, 1987), 119–48. In his essay "From Utopia to Heterotopia," Gianni Vattimo speaks of the avant-garde's "ideology of design" as "the dream of an aesthetic rehabilitation of everydayness by an elevation of the forms of objects and the appearance of our surroundings." In Vattimo, *The Transparent Society,* 64.

16. "Jeder typische Raum wird durch typische gesellschaftliche Verhältnisse zustande gebracht, die sich ohne die störende Dazwischenkunft des Bewußtseins in ihm ausdrücken. Alles vom Bewußtsein Verleugnete, alles, was sonst

geflissentlich übersehen wird, ist an seinem Aufbau beteiligt. Die Raumbilder sind die Träume der Gesellschaft. Wo immer die Hieroglyphe irgendeines Raumbildes entziffert ist, dort bietet sich der Grund der sozialen Wirklichkeit dar" ("Über Arbeitsnachweise," *Schriften*, vol. 5, pt. 2 [Frankfurt: Suhrkamp, 1990], 185–91).

17. Kracauer discusses elsewhere in his writing the other structures that serve as the uncanny storage spaces for society's refuse and repressed. For example, in his essay "Farewell to the Linden Arcade," he tells us how the anachronistic space of the arcade became the "nesting place" of everything that was banished from bourgeois life because it could not serve to represent that life or indeed because clashed with the official worldview (*der offiziellen Weltanschauung*). The arcades "housed that which had been thrown out and crammed in, the sum of all those things that could not be used as facade ornament." (Sie beherbergten das Ausgestoßene und das Hineingestoßene, die Summe jener Dinge, die nicht zum Fassadenschmuck taugten.") ("Abschied von der Lindenpassage," *Schriften*, vol. 5, pt. 2 [Frankfurt: Suhrkamp, 1990], 260–65.)

18. Inka Mülder speaks in terms of " *Träumen ohne Traumarbeit*" in her discussion of this passage. See *Kracauer*, 87f.

19. Kracauer has already begun to work out this interpretive model in his discussion of the sequential juxtaposition of images in film. His 1924 essay on Karl Grune's film *Die Straße*, for example: "The film *The Street* . . . is one of the few works of modern film direction in which an object is given the form that only film can give it and in which possibilities are realized that are only possible in film. . . . This film places one shot after another and mechanically creates the world out of them as they flip by. . . . (Der Film *Die Straße* . . . ist eines der wenigen Werke moderner Filmregie, in denen ein Gegenstand Gestaltung erfährt, den nur der Film so gestalten kann, und Möglichkeiten verwirklicht werden, die nur für ihn überhaupt Möglichkeiten sind. . . . Aufnahme stückt er an Aufnahme und setzt aus ihnen, die hintereinander abwirbeln, mechanisch die Welt zusammen. . . .) *(Abendblatt, Feuilleton* [Frankfurt], February 4, 1924). I thank Miriam Hansen for drawing my attention to and making available this unreprinted essay.

20. Paul Virilio writes: "Constructed space is thus not simply the result of the concrete and the material effect of its structures, its permanence and its architectonic or urban references, but also the result of a sudden proliferation, an incessant multiplying of special effects, which, with consciousness of time and distance, affects perception of the environment" ("The Overexposed City," in *Zone* ½ [New York: Zone Books, 1986], 29).

21. Die Kaiser-Wilhelm-Gedächtniskirche am Abend: Wer sie, vom Bahnhof Zoo her kommend, erblickt—und der Großstädter erblickt sie überhaupt nur abends, da sie ihm tags über nichts als ein riesenhaftes Verkehrshindernis

ist—, dem wird ein merkwürdiges, ein beinahe überirdisches Schauspiel zuteil. Von der religiösen Baumasse strahlt ein sanftes Leuchten aus, das so beruhigend wie unerklärlich ist, eine Helle, die mit dem profanen rötlichen Schimmer der Bogenlampen nichts gemein hat, sondern sich fremd von der Umwelt abhebt und ihren Ursprung in den Kaiser-Wilhelm-Gedächtniswänden selber zu haben scheint. Dringt der fahle Glanz aus dem Kircheninnern hervor? Aber dieser Kuppelbau, der Schwert und Altar miteinander verkuppelt, hat ersichtlich nur den einen Ehrgeiz: nach außen hin zu repräsentieren . . . Der geheimnisvolle Glanz ist in Wirklichkeit ein Reflex. Reflex der Lichtfassaden, die vom Ufapalast an bis über das Capitol hinaus die Nacht zum Tage machen, um aus dem Arbeitstag ihrer Besucher das Grauen der Nacht zu verscheuchen. . . . Der milde Glanz, der die Kaiser-Wilhelm-Gedächtniskirche umfließt, ist der unabsichtige Widerschein dieser finsteren Glut. Was vom Lichtspektakel abfällt und vom [Vergnügungs-]Betrieb ausgestoßen wird—öde Mauern bewahren es auf. Das Äußere der Kirche, die keine Kirche ist, wird zum Hort des Vergossenen und Vergessenen und strahlt so schön, als sei es das Allerheiligste selber. Heimliche Tränen finden so ihren Gedächtnisort. Nicht im verborgenen Innern-mitten auf der Straße wird das Unbeachtete, Unscheinbare gesammelt und verwandelt, bis es zu scheinen beginnt, für jeden ein Trost ("Ansichtspostkarte," *Schriften,* vol. 5, pt. 2 [Frankfurt: Suhrkamp, 1990], 184–85).

22. Writing in 1843 on the state of political affairs in Germany, Marx notes the anachronistic, nostalgic, reactionary, and comic character of the "German régime [which] . . . only imagines that it believes in itself and asks the world to share its illusion. If it believed in its own nature would it attempt to hide it beneath the semblance of an alien nature and look for its salvation in hypocrisy and sophistry? The modern *ancien régime* is the comedian of the world order whose real heroes are dead. History is thorough, and it goes through many stages when it conducts an ancient formation to its grave. *The last stage of a world-historical formation is comedy.* . . . The old, rotten order against which these nations revolt in their theories, and which they bear only as chains are borne, is hailed in Germany as the dawn of a glorious future. . . ." ("Contribution to the Critique of Hegel's 'Philosophy of Right' Introduction," in *The Marx-Engels Reader,* ed. Robert C. Tucker [New York: Norton, 1978], 16–25). Adorno, in his afterword to Walter Benjamin's *Berliner Kindheit* (Frankfurt: Suhrkamp, 1992), speaks of Benjamin's sensitivity to the new German capital's lack of tradition being compensated for by the evocation of tradition as such in an ideological displacement that has the recent past stand in for the most distant past.

23. Inka Mülder reads this essay as part of her effort to distinguish between Kracauer's and Benjamin's *Städtebilder.* She characterizes Kracauer's texts as

being concerned with the present and the transformations of the structures of everyday experience. *Kracauer,* 114–16.

24. "Die *Lichtreklame* geht an einem Himmel auf, in dem es keine Engel mehr gibt, aber auch nicht nur Geschäft. Sie schießt über die Wirtschaft hinaus, und was als Reklame gemeint ist, wird zur Illumination. Das kommt davon, wenn die Kaufleute sich mit Lichteffekten einlassen. Licht bleibt Licht, und strahlt es gar in allen Farben, so bricht es erst recht aus den Bahnen, die ihm von seinen Auftraggebern vorgezeichnet worden sind. Bunte Lettern, die weiße Wäsche ankündigen sollen, sind nicht ganz bei der Sache, selbst wenn sie fünf Stockwerke bedecken. Die Zuständigkeit des Propagandachefs ist im Reich der Glühbirnen begrenzt, und die Signale, die er erteilt, wandeln unter der Hand ihren Sinn. So erzeugt das Nebeneinander der Läden ein Lichtgewimmel, dessen gleißende Unordnung nicht rein die terrestrische ist. Man kann in diesem Gewimmel noch Zeichen und Schriften erkennen, doch Zeichen und Schriften sind hier ihren praktischen Zwecken enthoben, das Eingehen in die Buntheit hat sie zu Glanzfragmenten zerstückelt, die sich nach anderen Gesetzen als den gewohnten zusammenfügen. Der Reklame-sprühregen, den das Wirtschaftsleben ausschüttet, wird zu Sternbildern an einem fremden Himmel ("Lichtreklame," *Schriften,* vol. 5, pt. 2 [Frankfurt: Suhrkamp, 1990], 19).

25. Henri Lefebvre makes clear the connection between ideology and space through a series of questions: "What is an ideology without a space to which it refers, a space which it describes, whose vocabulary and links it makes use of, and whose code it embodies? . . . More generally speaking, what we call ideology only achieves consistency by intervening in social space and in its production, and by thus taking on body therein. Ideology *per se* might well be said to consist primarily in a discourse upon social space" (*The Production of Space* [London: Blackwell, 1991], 44).

3

SABINE HAKE

Provocations of the Disembodied Voice: Song and the Transition to Sound in Berger's *Day and Night*

The years of the early sound film remain, together with the cinema of the 1950s, one of the least researched periods in the history of German cinema. Such persistent neglect follows an unquestioned preference for historiographical models based on aesthetic or political categories, as well as an emphasis on formal, thematic, and ideological cohesion rather than on moments of adjustment and compromise. Technological advances and their impact on narrative strategies, visual styles, and generic traditions have for the most part been ignored. The following investigation draws attention to the productivity of such transitional moments and analyzes the thematization of sound in an unjustly neglected early sound film, Ludwig Berger's *Ich bei Tag und du bei Nacht* (1932; literally: I by Day and You by Night), subsequently referred to here as *Day and Night*.[1] Produced during years of great economic uncertainty, fundamental changes in the film industry, and heated debates over the future of German film, Berger's musical fantasy offers a playful reflection on the new sound technology prior to its full integration into the classical realist text. This it does by means of the self-referential gestures and hybrid styles typical of all transitional moments. By thematizing the new technology, *Day and Night* bears witness to the hopes and fears that accompanied the most important paradigm shift in the history of cinema.[2] Through its combination of experimental and commercial perspectives, Berger's musical comedy also challenges the typical rise-and-decline models of historical explanation and draws attention to the textual strategies through which mainstream cinema responds to technological innovation.

Until very recently, German film histories have preferred periods of emergence over those of decline. Whereas the former celebrate new filmic styles in relation to larger artistic movements and cultural traditions, the latter are often associated with scenarios of corruption and deterioration. The heroic narratives of formal and technical innovation validate film as an art form, whereas the processes of appropriation foreground the pressures brought to bear on cinema because of its precarious position between art and entertainment, culture and industry. Of course, the conceptualization of a period according to the rise-decline model depends very much on the point of reference, the choice of constituent elements, and the forms of internal relationships. The consequences are especially pronounced in the case of Weimar cinema. While Kracauer's sociopsychological history of Weimar cinema establishes a teleology of pre-fascist tendencies, Lotte Eisner's formalist approach privileges an art cinema committed to the traditions of German romanticism. However, both critics dismiss the cinema of the Wilhelmine period as primitive, and both attack the early sound film as a betrayal of the medium's inherent potential.

Recent studies on an early "cinema of attractions" and its affinities with popular and working-class culture have challenged such views. In particular, the trend toward historical contextualization at the intersection of film studies and German studies has shifted attention from the properties of the work to the larger cultural formation, including the regimes of visuality and the cinema as a public sphere. In these contexts, the so-called cinema of narrative integration has been theorized as an ongoing negotiation of visual styles, narrative strategies, and ideological positions that invariably comes into conflict with both the self-reflexive qualities of modernist cinema and the promise of an emancipatory mass culture. Missing in all of these scenarios is an adequate assessment of the paradigmatic rupture brought about by the introduction of sound film. An indication of the insufficient attention thus far given to technological innovation as an agent of historical change, the early sound film continues to be described in terms laid out by its contemporaries; that is, it is either denounced as the premature abandonment of an aesthetic practice with many yet unexplored possibilities, or it is characterized as just another stage in the inevitable move toward what Rudolf Arnheim once called the "total film" (*Komplettfilm*).

In the German case, any reassessment of the transition from silent to sound film is complicated by the overlaps with another paradigmatic break, the rise of national socialism. Film historians have followed Weimar critics in denouncing the early sound film for its submission to economic and, by extension, political pressures. Film operettas and musical comedies continue to provide the most convenient target for an opposition to technological change that, behind its legitimate aesthetic concerns, betrays a conservative approach to modern mass media and new technologies of perception. Notwithstanding the fact that the project of leftist filmmaking culminated in two sound films, *Mutter Krausens Fahrt ins Glück* (Mother Krause's Journey to Happiness, 1929) and *Kuhle Wampe oder Wem gehört die Welt?* (Whither Germany? 1932), the years between 1929 and 1933 are often associated with escapism and commercialism. While the canon of Weimar cinema includes a surprising number of sound films, most notably *Der blaue Engel* (The Blue Angel, 1930) and *M* (1931), its greatest contributions continue to be equated with silent film. *Day and Night* suggests that these transitional years provided a rare occasion for combining generic convention and formal experimentation and for infusing quality entertainment, to use producer Erich Pommer's term, with self-critical moments. Moreover, this exemplary early sound film allows me to outline a model for integrating technological change into economic, social, cultural, political, and aesthetic histories of Weimar cinema: not as an addition, but as a critical device that articulates relationships between the economics and politics of representation in new and surprising ways. Instead of conflating the introduction of sound technology, the process of economic concentration, and the rise of national socialism in a historical moment of unchallenged hegemony, I want to present sound as a destabilizing element that, within the confines of genre cinema, draws attention to the means and processes of filmic representation.

The transition to sound took place in two stages, an early period of controversy and experimentation and a later one of institutionalization and standardization. The first screening of a sound film, in 1929, caused great excitement and curiosity among audiences. It became apparent that the most basic elements of filmmaking had to be redefined. These included the approach to mise-en-scène, framing and editing, and the conventions of screen writing and acting; but they also extended to the conditions of film production and exhibition and the place of cinema in definitions of national culture. Not surprisingly, many film critics responded with hesitation and concern: about the future of the silent film and its highly codified visual language; about the utopian promise of a democratic mass medium unhindered by language barriers; about the abandonment of uniquely filmic techniques in favor of filmed theater; and about the ascendancy of dialogue-based plots and conventional narratives that might more easily be appropriated by nationalistic and reactionary ideologies. Much has been written about the technical, economic, and legal implications of the transition to sound film, including changes in the studio system, the competing sound systems, the patent wars, and the impact on German film import and export. The translation of these changes into narrative and visual strategies remains a much more complicated matter, especially if one wants to take seriously the productive role of technology as an agent of film history.

For analyses that move beyond the customary complaints about the inadequacy of the first sound films, the second phase of consolidation from 1932 to 1935 is particularly interesting. By 1933 silent films were no longer produced, and by 1935 all theaters were equipped for sound projection. An ingenious but ultimately unprofitable solution to the new language barriers was provided by multi-language versions—that is, the practice of shooting several versions simultaneously with different actors. For instance, the musical comedy *Die drei von der Tankstelle* (The Three from the Filling Station, 1930) and the adventure drama *F.P.1 antwortet nicht* (F.P.1 Doesn't Answer, 1932) had French and English versions. As long as the new sound technology still required advertising and self-promotion, the cinema experienced a period of creativity and originality. Yet, in the end, the idea of a sound cinema that would combine national and international characteristics proved illusory. The multilingual versions often reduced national culture to stereo-typical physiognomies, and the representation of difference remained limited to idiosyncratic acting styles and speech patterns. Despite efforts to preserve the dream of film as a universal language and to accommodate national peculiarities on the level of idiom and voice, the new sound technology ultimately paved the way for the instrumentalization of filmic narratives by the project of German nationalism. Profiting from the historical connection between music and language in the national imagination, sound helped to stabilize the image and its precarious vacillation between mimetic representation, iconographic signification, and poetic symbolism; the voice and its hidden claims about body and identity played a crucial part in this process.

Day and Night opens by restaging its aesthetic dilemmas in the form of a sound check in the projection room of a small neighborhood movie theater. Even before the first image appears, we hear impatient calls from offscreen to "Start!" A slow traveling shot reveals the outlines of a sound projector and stops on the hand of a projectionist adjusting the volume and responding to the demand with a calm "Don't panic!" From a blaring loudspeaker the camera makes the transition from booth to auditorium and, in a swift pan, follows the conical beam of light from the projector to the screen. However, instead of moving pictures, the frame shows the silhouette of a man repairing the sound system behind the screen. After a quick return to the booth, where the annoyed projectionist is seen eating a sandwich, the camera moves out onto the street and inspects the announcements of new releases posted around the entrance of the theater. The tune that constitutes these three locations as part of an extended narrative space is picked up by a young man in evening attire who inquires about the new film and the whereabouts of the projectionist. Whistling, he follows the music back to the source and enters the theater through the back door—of course with the noticeable change in volume that in the early days of sound always accompanied the opening and closing of doors. Responding to his friend's inquiries about the new release, the projectionist brandishes an enthusiastic review. The reviewer's claim that "This real-life fairy tale shows clearly that the golden moment will come for all of us some day" elicits an angry response: "Nonsense, it's all a pack of lies!" The scornful remark seems confirmed by the credit sequence for the film in question, a production by the Bombastik Film AG, entitled *All of This Is Yours!* However, the film's hit song, "When I go to my movie theater on Sundays!" systematically disproves such skepticism once it establishes an interpretative framework for Berger's playful reflection on music and fantasy in contemporary urban life. "The flickers (*Kientopp*) as a social narcotic made an entrance through characters"[3]—this is how contemporary reviewer Willy Haas described Berger's mixture of self-promotion and self-mockery.

Responding to the larger controversy over sound, the opening sequence serves two distinct purposes: to compare two musical genres and, through music as a social and cultural marker, to present two very different approaches to popular cinema. In so doing, Berger's film problematizes sound in relation to the promises of realism and the dangers of illusionism. With its obligatory counts and countesses, spectacular sets, exquisite costumes, numerous extras, and sentimental melodies, the film operetta from the neighborhood movie theater stands for escapism in its most trivial and contrived form. This caricature of the dream factory provides the backdrop against which the working-class characters from the film formulate their own relationships to the movies, whether in the form of simple pleasures and diversions or through expressions of suspicion and disbelief ("a pack of lies!"); it also serves as a ubiquitous reference point in their conception of love and romance. To be sure, the introduction of themes like mass unemployment, social iniquities, women's emancipation, and sexual harassment is not necessarily tantamount to social criticism. As catalysts in the juxtaposition of traditional arias and contemporary tunes, these themes merely link the change in musical tastes to the living conditions in the big city. On the level of narrative, the protagonists are forced to revise their naive views on wealth, romance, and happiness. Yet, on the level of individual desire and its musical articulation, the illusion is rescued across any superficial differences in musical styles and realigned with what for Berger represents a legitimate need for make-believe. The critique of fantasy in relation to music serves only to strengthen the truthfulness of desire against the pervasiveness of social injustice and economic hardship. Turning songs into a critical commentary makes possible such an improbable, but not necessarily unproductive solution.

The story line contributes to such doubling effects as it tests the implications of fantasizing "too much" and "too little" in the contemporary setting of Berlin. Where other city films from the period convey a sense of disillusionment, this modern fairy tale strives for a reenchantment of the world. Already the names of the main protagonists, the nightclub waiter Hans (Willy Fritsch) and the manicurist Grete (Käthe von Nagy), recall the proverbial Jack and Jill characters from countless popular stories.[4] They unknowingly share the same bed in a furnished room that he rents by day and she by night—a common practice during the depression. In trying to escape the problems of everyday life, the young man and woman repeatedly fall victim to their fantasies of social ascent. When Grete meets Hans during the morning rush hour, she mistakes his sartorial splendor for a sign of wealth. When Hans sees Grete being picked up by a chauffeur-driven limousine, he mistakes her for the daughter of one of her wealthy customers. Their ensuing romance illustrates to what degree movie images interfere with everyday life and how perceptions can activate, complicate, and inhibit desire. Eventually all problems are resolved, once they realize that they have been sleeping in the same bed all along. The ending finds Hans and Grete happily reunited in the movie theater—proof that even in real life love conquers all.

Day and Night was not the first sound film to reflect on the social and psychological effects of cinema through an investigation of its means of production.

The new technology provided the appropriate setting in an earlier murder mystery, *Der Schuß im Tonfilmatelier* (The Shot on the Sound Stage, 1930). It also inspired silent film parodies like *Das Kabinett des Dr. Larifari* (The Cabinet of Dr. Larifari, 1930), and, beginning with *Zigeuner der Nacht* (Gypsies of the Night, 1932), introduced the projectionist as the main protagonist. Widespread speculation about what some critics described as a cinema of hyperrealism found expression in stories about the deceptiveness of the image and the pitfalls of perception; that these stories were often set in the world of image production only underscored the perceived need for control. Berger's film was one of the first to thematize the new technology from the perspective of reception and to assess the impact of mechanical reproduction in the context of cultural consumption. Only one year later, Fritz Lang's *Das Testament des Dr. Mabuse* (The testament of Dr. Mabuse, 1933) would mobilize the scenarios of listening for purposes of urban terrorism and mass control. Whereas Lang would concentrate on the speaking voice, Berger remained committed to the singing voice as a perfect compromise between the regimes of language and music. Throughout his career, he found inspiration in the immensely popular genre of the film operetta. Like their precursors from the stage, these film operettas habitually use mistaken-identity plots to deal with social and sexual differences in a mildly critical, but ultimately affirmative manner. Vacillating between the conventionality of social roles and the rhetoric of true selfhood, the plots almost demand the addition of musical numbers which, like false identities, offer both a heightened view of reality and an affirmation of the primacy of emotions. From a historical spectacle like *Der Kongreß tanzt* (The Congress Dances, 1931) to the contemporary settings of *Ein blonder Traum* (A Blonde Dream, 1932), all tensions between the sexes and the classes are magically overcome through the smooth transitions between dialogue and song and their evocation of a reality unburdened by the demands of probability.

Day and Night's parody of conventional film operettas and its commitment to more contemporary approaches reveal two decisive influences—the program of good entertainment introduced by star producer Erich Pommer and the belief in film as a modern fairy tale realized in the work of director Ludwig Berger. Both men had spent time in Hollywood, from 1924 to 1929 and from 1926 to 1932, respectively, studying American methods of filmmaking. Produced by the Erich Pommer unit at Ufa, *Day and Night* profited immensely from the insights Pommer had gained from a series of highly successful productions. Beginning with *The Blue Angel*, he had explored the creative possibilities of sound in *The Three From the Filling Station, The Congress Dances,* and *A Blonde Dream,* sometimes utilizing elements from the traditional operetta, sometimes moving toward the revue film, and sometimes emulating the American musical. In creating such a new hybrid genre, Pommer reached a workable compromise between the demands of a changing marketplace and the new economy of filmic means.[5] He combined the self-conscious approach to filmic representation, so often described as the distinguishing mark of German silent cinema, with the unmistakable American influence in the staging of performances and the choice of musical styles.

If Pommer stands for the reconciliation of artistic ambitions and economic exigencies, then Berger personifies the affinities between cinema and fairy tale.[6] His lifelong fascination with this traditional narrative form is evident already in his artistic endeavors of the 1920s. Berger published several books of fairy tales, and even his theater productions of the classics were praised for their dreamlike quality. For Berger, music brought out the fantastic elements of cinema and afforded pleasures traditionally identified with regression and dream. This belief in the liberating powers of music connects his first big success, *Ein Walzertraum* (A Waltz Dream, 1925), to his last German film, the lighthearted musical comedy *Walzerkrieg* (Waltz Wars, 1933). In connection with the release of *Der verlorene Schuh* (The Lost Shoe, 1922), based on motifs from the Cinderella story, Berger wrote: "The fairy tale gives to the film what the film greatly needs: the simple song themes with all the possibilities of colorful variation, the primitive structure, and the multitude of visions poured over it. The film gives to the fairy tale what the fairy tale needs: reality and credibility, tempo and drive, and an entire colorful dream world full of light and shadow."[7] That is why Dahlke's characterization of *Day and Night* as "a pretty realistic painting of everyday life during those years" is as misleading as his praise for the director's ability to avoid "an operetta-like down-playing and trivializing of conflicts."[8] Berger always preferred the world of ordinary wonders and everyday miracles to realistic or illusionist styles. Against the polemical opposition of realism and escapism, he introduced a third possibility: a cinema based on the reality of desire. That reality for him arose from the affinities between cinema and dream and the transformation of spectatorship into a means of deliberate regression.

Using a film-within-the-film to reflect on the social and cultural aspects of filmmaking has been a common practice since the earliest years of cinema. Especially during transitional periods, the emphasis on film as a production rather than a product has allowed filmmakers to refute claims about the medium's status as a mere reflection of reality. It has also infused elements of aesthetic distancing and critical reflection into a popular art form often accused of mass deception. *Day and Night* approaches the problem of sound within this tradition. By setting up two paradigms of spectatorship, the film distinguishes between its naive and sophisticated forms. Identification with the critical consumers of escapist fare in the diegesis places the spectators where they can suspend disbelief without succumbing to the illusion. This double articulation foregrounds the active aspects of looking and cultivates fantasy without the usual negative connotations. Whether such strategies only hide a more devious process of appropriation, as some reviewers of the film have claimed, needs to be clarified through a closer look at the narrative and discursive function of music.

The differences between the film's contemporary setting and the fantasy world of *All of This is Yours!* are articulated on three levels: narrative, set design, and music style. In accordance with the worst gender stereotyping, the young woman serves as the demonstration object for the dangers of movie addiction; perhaps that is why Arnheim advised his readers: "Watch this film in the company of young girls."[9] It is significant within the larger debates on the sound film that the new technology is associated not with the masculine aesthetics of modernist montage but with the allegedly feminine realm of popular culture and its formal and social conventions. Given the strong aesthetic and political divisions at the end of the Weimar Republic, Berger's balancing act between musical fantasy and cinematic metaphor was not well received, and inspired more general complaints about the escapist nature of then-contemporary film production. Kracauer's review of an earlier Berger film is very revealing here: "While inflation grew all-devouring and political passion was at its height, these films provided the illusion of a never-never land in which the poor salesgirl triumphs over the conniving queen, and the kind fairy godmother helps Cinderella win Prince Charming. . . . However, this never-never land was not beyond the range of politics."[10] In making women audiences responsible for the enduring appeal of escapist entertainment, Kracauer's analysis establishes an opposition that allows for only two alternatives, either a critique of the social conditions and their representation in mainstream cinema or complete identification with the laws of the market and the affirmative function of mass culture in modern society.

Resisting such deceptively simple models, Berger insists on a constant slippage between convention and subversion, compliance and resistance, that, in his view, distinguishes the cinema as the mass medium most responsive to the needs of contemporary audiences. The convergence of urban mentality, modern consciousness, and cinema culture finds expression in the female lead, one of Kracauer's proverbial little shop girls at the movies—but in a way that collapses the usual oppositions.[11] Trapped in a menial job without a satisfying social life, Grete seems all too eager to escape her daily routine to the "small shimmer of light" provided, both figuratively and literally, by the motion-picture theater. Her enthusiastic declaration, "Just like the movies!," delivered in moments of happiness, functions as the hinge between the two stories, but it also introduces a new model of experience based on her close knowledge of the cinema and its narrative conventions. By measuring life against its cinematic double, Grete demonstrates her familiarity with modern mass media and the aesthetics of simulation. During a visit with Hans to Sanssouci, a more than appropriate location given its meaning ("without worry"), she feels compelled to compare their first kiss with its standard portrayal on the screen. Miraculously, her insistence on musical accompaniment is granted by the museum warden playing a flute concerto; he, of course, is only imitating Frederick the Great—or, rather, Otto Gebühr from the popular *Fridericus Rex* series and its most recent sequel, *Das Flötenkonzert von Sanssouci* (The Flute Concerto of Sanssouci, 1930). The cinematic citations do not stop here. Back in her working-class neighborhood, Grete walks past a movie poster that repeats the framing of her face in the presentation of the famous star. For a moment her wildest dreams seem to come true when a wealthy admirer sends her expensive gifts and her landlady declares, "Now it is really like the movies here." Even the return to reality in the ending only confirms for her that life is just as fantastic as the most unbelievable film story; hence her conclusion: "We were sleeping in the same bed all this time? You know what this is like? The movies."

The use of locations and set designs in a film shot almost entirely on the Ufa lot in Babelsberg further complicates the comparisons between old-fashioned and contemporary tunes. On the level of surface effects, the differences between *Day and Night* and *All of This Is Yours!* seem all too evident. Against the cheap extravagance of the fantasy castle, Sanssouci presents its historical splendor in a lengthy quasi-documentary sequence. Through these superficial similarities, the reality effect becomes implicated in the filmic portrayal of modern city life. Here realistic settings predominate (e.g., the small furnished room, the nail salon, the nightclub, the modern villa) and close attention is paid to the social hierarchies established by urban spaces. In the presentation of shabby tenements and working-class neighborhoods, the film follows the conventions of the street film from the expressionist period. The exterior scenes on crowded boulevards and in modern suburbs imitate the functionalist look of city films in the tradition of New Objectivity. Yet precisely in its function as a marker of the real, the big city betrays its status as a construction. The montage of product names, posters, and shop windows remains a calculated effect, and the choreography of passers-by, buses, and cars a controlled chaos. In the contemporary world of the diegesis, the deceptions of cinema appear the least transparent.

For Berger, the conventions of realism are not only less attractive; they also provide for a more treacherous simulation of the real. These layers of illusionism and their respective regimes of pleasure are repeated in the juxtaposition of two musical genres, classical operetta and modern song. The high standards of 1920s musical culture are evident in the contribution of well-known film composer Werner Richard Heymann, the cheerful tunes performed by the new Ufa-Jazz-Orchestra,and the participation of the decade's most famous a cappella group, the Comedian Harmonists. There are even mildly critical overtones in the way Eisler's "Solidarity Song" from *Whither Germany?* resonates in the assertive mood of "We Fear Nobody." For the most part, however, Berger introduces the sentimental tunes from *All of This Is Yours!* into the "real world" of the diegesis in order to make fun of their old-fashioned musical and lyrical formulas. Accordingly, the countess in the film makes a spectacular exit in the typical style of the Ufa costume dramas, complete with liveried servants announcing in recitative, "Madame is going out"—then the scene cuts to Grete catching a crowded bus on her way to work. Standing in a sea of roses, the admirer of the countess sings, "If you don't come, the roses have bloomed in vain"—then we see Hans waiting impatiently for Grete, holding three tiny roses. The chorus announces "She's coming!" and both women arrive, with the modern protagonist delayed because of work obligations.

Not surprisingly, the romantic yearnings expressed by this old-fashioned song find less and less resonance in the contemporary setting of Weimar Berlin. Overlaid by themes from the song, the first test of romantic expectations occurs when the two lovers miss each other during a rainstorm. The tune's sentimental melody accompanies Grete's short-lived transformation from a jobless manicurist into a woman of the world. When she admires herself in an elegant evening gown, her landlady remarks solemnly: "It's the fault of this music." This statement may hold true for the kitschy arias from the operetta, but as the film sets out to demonstrate, it does not apply to the lively songs that offer the protagonists guidelines for modern living. They accompany the budding romance between Hans and Grete from its promising beginnings through various complications to the double happy ending in the operetta and film. Performed by the Comedian Harmonists with their usual unbridled optimism, "Wenn ich sonntags in mein Kino geh'" functions both as a programmatic and narrative device and thus deserves to be quoted in full:

Wenn ich sonntags in mein
   Kino geh'
Und im Film die feinen Leute seh'
Denk ich immer wieder
Könnt ich mal, ach könnt ich mal
Genauso glücklich sein.
	When I go to the movies
	   on Sundays
	And see the people in their finery
	I think to myself
	Could I, oh, could I but
	Be as happy as them.

Alle Tage Sekt und Kaviar Und ein Auto und ein Schloß sogar So was schleicht schon lang' In meine süßen Träume rein.	Everyday champagne and caviar And a car and a castle too Such are the thoughts that for so long Have sweetened my fondest dreams.

Auf dem fünfundsiebzig
   Pfennigplatz
Sehn' ich mich nach einem süßen
   Schatz
Der genauso wie im Film
Am Schluß mich glücklich macht.
	On the seat for fifty-seven
	   pfennigs
	I yearn for a sweet darling
	
	who like in the movies
	makes me happy in the end.

Wenn ich sonntags in mein
   Kino geh'
Und den Himmel voller Geigen seh'
Träum' ich noch am Montag früh
Einmal leben so wie sie
Doch zu sowas kommt man nie.
	When I go to the movies on
	   Sundays
	And see the sky full of violins
	I still dream on Monday morning
	About once living like them
	But such things never become true.

First heard in the opening sequence described above, this song travels from the projection booth to the room across the street, where Grete picks up the lyrics and repeats the melody while gargling during her morning rituals. When the song appears for the second time, Hans rejects its insipid message and demands his "Quiet!" By contrast, Grete literally takes the music to bed when she listens to a radio performance of Monosson appearing at the Casanova Club. When her landlady complains that "These hits spread like the plague," Grete responds, "These hits! In real life, things always turn out differently anyway." That she needs to distinguish more clearly between the dreamworld of the movies and the problems in her life becomes glaringly obvious during the last performance of the song, when a rendezvous with her rich admirer ends in complete disaster. However, the closing scene indicates that she continues to believe in the promise of a better life. At the movies, Berger suggests, fiction and reality become identical through the sheer power of song.

The innovative sound editing and staging of the songs is largely responsible for the remarkable expansion of the auditory realm in *Day and Night*. In its flowing, seemingly weightless quality, Berger's musical editing style resembles most closely René Clair's *Sous les toits de Paris* (Under the Roofs of Paris, 1930) and Ernst Lubitsch's *Monte Carlo* (1930). Berger's disregard for the exaggerated acting styles and static mise-en-scène of the theater is evident in the overly theatrical demeanor of the landlady, formerly an actress at the court theater of Lippe-Detmold. Against such theatrical conventions, Berger allows the songs to determine the pace and direction of all camera movements and to open up narrative space beyond its physical boundaries. The emotional charge of the melodies occasions numerous pans and tilts and finds expression in extensive traveling shots. Music at once anchors and delimits the image and redefines the relationship between frame and offscreen space in ways not possible in the tight mise-en-scène of Expressionism and the didactic montage sequences of Russian film.

The self-referential function of the songs draws attention to the openness and versatility of music-based genres during the transitional period. Obviously, *Day and Night* defies easy classification as a film operetta, but it also has little in common with the self-contained cabaret performances in *The Blue Angel* or the distancing achieved through the street ballads from *Die Dreigroschenoper* (The Threepenny Opera, 1931). Unlike in the film operetta, there are no characters in the diegesis who, in an abrupt departure from the conventions of filmic realism, suddenly break into song and dance. Berger always cast actors (not singers) in the leading roles and thus avoided the typical problems of film operettas, with their barely developed characters and story lines. Whereas the performative aspect of music tends to disrupt the flow of the narrative, its association with new technologies of reproduction (radio, gramophone, film) in this strange hybrid of romantic and musical comedy has the opposite effect: it allows the songs to take an active part in the construction of narrative space. No longer limited to the conditions of live performance, the songs combine the stabilizing functions of "mood music" (e.g., expressing emotions, facilitating transitions) with the defamiliarizing effects of song as critical commentary.

Because the conventions of classical narrative cinema are maintained throughout, the contribution of the songs to an expanded auditory mise-en-scène and metatextual structure is all the more remarkable, and this for several reasons. For one, the film's conventional story is predicated on the pervasiveness of mass media in the modern world; this is evidenced by the characters' awareness of popular culture as a multimedia production and their close familiarity with new modes of perception modeled on the cinema. Berger has little interest in the expressive potential of the human voice and the underlying tension between repressed desire and enunciatory excess. Instead, he explores the technologies of sound reproduction and measures the impact of a dramatically expanded auditory field on the social and psychological functions of popular music. Once the new hit song by the Comedian Harmonists appears simultaneously on the screen, the radio, and the stage, the qualitative distinction between embodied and disembodied voice, so crucial for traditional approaches to musical performance, can no longer be maintained. Music becomes an extension of the everyday; its lyrics and melodies give the characters an opportunity to find a workable compromise between the pleasures and pitfalls of cinematic illusion.

Facilitating transitions, making connections, and heightening dramatic situations—such functions endow the songs with attributes typically associated with film music. In the same way that mood music anchors the meanings conjured up by the images, the songs mediate between actions and perceptions and integrate both into a narrative continuity. From the cue sheets of the silent film to the original scores of the later sound film, this kind of semiotic anchorage through nondiegetic music has hinged on its imperceptible presence. By contrast, the musical numbers in the film operetta arrest the flow of the story and draw attention to their performative aspects. *Day and Night* combines both possibilities, narrative integration and cinematic excess. The film moves back and forth between the theatricality of music and the visuality of the image. While the characters and their everyday lives bear the burden of realistic representation, the songs continue to celebrate the power of the imagination against all concessions to the laws of contingency.

In distinguishing image and sound along these lines, Berger draws attention to the dramatic changes in the field of vision brought about by the introduction of sound. The symbolic use of objects and spaces in the classical German cinema of the early 1920s became more and more inappropriate in the new linguistic order. Continuity editing triumphed over the various forms of associative and conceptual montage, and performance styles relinquished their more stylized elements before the new regimes of naturalism. Through the strategic positioning of its songs between critical commentary and narrative integration, *Day and Night* preserves some of the discursive functions abandoned by the image in pursuit of greater verisimilitude; in particular, the theme song cited above orchestrates the kinds of real and imaginary moves achieved previously through framing and editing. As the placeholders of desire, the songs relieve the human voice of the pressures of self-expression and become floating signifiers in the sound film's new scenarios of sensory deception and critical illumination. By using the disembodied voice to show the emotional appeal of a thus redefined cinematic consciousness, Berger moves beyond the simplistic opposition of realism and fantasy and draws attention to the need to integrate both tendencies in a formally innovative and profoundly self-critical popular cinema.

Berger's thematization of the dramatic changes in representational practices and modes of reception can be understood only in the context of the extensive debates on the early sound film. Summarizing the main positions and identifying the major concerns will help in assessing the film's contribution to the controversy over sound as a signifier both of the cinema's inevitable decline and of its ongoing self-transformation. In a kind of repetition-compulsion, the arguments against the sound film emulated the rhetorical strategies from the cinema debate of the late 1910s. Both moments, the transition from the "primitive" to the "classical" silent cinema and the transition from the silent to the sound film, conjured up images of impurity and contamination. However, where the critics of the early film drama expressed concern about the film's muteness, which they regarded as proof of its incompatibility with dramatic traditions, the opponents of the early sound film saw the addition of a sound track as a threat to inherently filmic means. They feared a return to the theatricality of the early film drama and a depletion of the visual field under the demands for dramatic unity and narrative continuity. In their view, the sound film reversed the liberation from technology that, after tedious beginnings, had elevated film to an art form and freed the image from the pressures of verisimilitude. Thus aesthetic opposition to the sound film formed around the following points: the much-praised internalization of the silent cinema; the pictorial, metaphoric, and rhetorical functions of the image in the silent film; and the affinities between silent cinema, visual pleasure, and the cult of diversion. A few critics resisted such essentialist positions. Willy Haas refused to separate art and technology and argued in a way not dissimilar to Benjamin's later Art Work Essay: "An art form that is as closely linked to technology as the film participates in the concept of 'technological process' not only externally, but also internally."[12] Kracauer pointed to the social and cultural developments that had given rise to a progressive mass culture, and he asserted that "the internationalism of the silent film did not arise automatically from the universal accessibility of the images, but was the result of a methodologically-executed distribution of images. . . . The silent film, in a way, did not originate in the internationalism of visual impressions; it moved toward it."[13]

Responding to the coming of sound meant either relegating sound to the category of a supplement without intrinsic value or making it the unifying force in an entirely new art form defined precisely through its radical otherness from the aesthetic project of silent cinema. The conceptualization of sound as a supplement confirmed claims about the inevitable trend toward cinema as a *Gesamtkunstwerk,* (total work of art) whereas the assumption of an essential difference between silent and sound film allowed film critics to hold on to the dream of cinema as a new visual language. An effective method for dealing with technological change and its impact on aesthetic practices was to separate the innovative sound film (*Tonfilm*) from the mere talking picture (*Sprechfilm*). Critic Herbert Ihering wrote that "the talking picture (*sprechende Film*) is nothing more than a reproduction of reality. The moving picture (*Bewegungsfilm*), through its own laws, stands apart from reality as something new."[14] Composer Kurt Weill argued in a similar vein "that the sound film must find its own autonomous forms of expression."[15]

Accordingly, the leading film critics of the Weimar period used the provocation of sound to revise their theories of film with a view toward new creative possibilities. Rudolf Arnheim maintained that "the sound film is more than an addition, that it is an artistic activity *sui generis*";[16] he used gestalt psychological categories to examine sound montage, shot sizes, framing, and other filmic devices under this aspect. Béla Balázs continued his investigation into the liberating qualities of visual culture and concluded that "the acoustic film will open up for us the language of things, just as the optical film revealed the face of things. It will teach us to hear the world, just as the optical film taught us to see."[17] Last but not least, Kracauer declared that just as sound was more than an addition to the image, the sound film was anything but a continuation of the silent film: "Sound has its own time, its own space. Only after the successful fusion of the distinct aesthetic worlds of sound and image will the word in film take on form."[18]

These statements not only identify the place attributed to technological innovation in the critical imagination, they also shed light on Berger's own filmic and musical staging of the controversy. A number of highly charged terms informed the critical responses to sound film: realism, verisimilitude, simulation. As I have argued, the relationship between *Day and Night* and *All of This Is Yours!* and their constituent systems of difference (e.g., music, acting, set design) hinges on a similar engagement with conflicting definitions of the real. In the context of film criticism, the introduction of sound revived older fears about a blurring of boundaries between representation and reality and the anticipated return to modes of spectatorship that provided no distance from the cinema's perceptual and emotional effects. The supplement of sound, it was feared, would complete the transition from representation to simulation and turn the cinema into an even more effective instrument of mass manipulation. This pessimistic view of sound as yet another move toward a delusional media technology was shared by all those who, like Arnheim, believed in the limitation of formal means as a prerequisite of true art. However, it also appealed to more politically oriented critics, like Balász, who held the new sound technology responsible for the growing political pressures on filmmakers and who saw a direct connection between the changes in the film industry, the promotion of new genres, and the suppression of artistic innovation and political activism.

Just as *Day and Night* set out to disprove those critics who dismissed sound as a mere supplement, it put into question all simplistic equations between sound film, popular entertainment, and female audiences, but—and herein lies its real provocation—it did so from the perspective of a real appreciation for fantasy and imagination. Again, we can discern clear connections between the film's use of woman as a heuristic device and the discursive positioning of the feminine in debates on the early sound film. For obvious reasons, the introduction of sound threatened the binary opposition that, up to this point, had organized the public perception of mass-cultural practices in Weimar Germany. The relationship between the cinema and the traditional arts was from the beginning articulated in gendered terms, with high culture endowed with "masculine" traits like active engagement, total immersion, and critical detachment, and with the cinematic experience defined as passive, emotional, uncritical—in a word, feminine. Confronted with the first sound films, critics began to claim the image for a masculine trajectory, by pointing to its formal unity and coherence, for instance, and by emphasizing its affinity for symbolism and abstraction. Film sound, especially in its evocation of the absent body, came to be identified with the undifferentiated and uncontrollable qualities of the feminine. According to the new defenders of the moving image, song and music created an emotional excess that represented the opposite of art. The old high-low divide returned in the opposition between the silent and the sound film, with the former now claimed for an avant-garde aesthetic and the latter associated with escapist entertainment. Even the seemingly progressive alignment of the silent film with internationalism, and of the sound film with nationalism, contains elements of this problematic mapping of new divisions along gender lines.

To conclude: the close attention to music in *Day and Night* must be read as both an acknowledgement of these larger concerns and an attempt to demonstrate the creative potential of sound in the new constellations of film, art, and mass culture. By emphasizing the active qualities of listening, Berger offers a tempting solution to the perceived crisis of the filmic image prior to its full integration into the classical realist text. Just as the film refuses to subordinate auditory to visual relations, it insists on combining good entertainment with formal experimentation. As I have argued, the generic conventions occasion a playful reflection on the status of cinema. *Day and Night* responds to the widespread claims about the decline of the cinema by exploring the liberating qualities found in music, artifice, and, above all, fantasy. Berger's modern fairy tale offers an alternative to the mutually

exclusive paradigms of realism and illusionism and embraces fully the reality effect
of the imagination in the cinema and in everyday life. At the same time, the film
responds to a feared confusion of fiction and reality by telling its story at two
levels and by examining their terms of engagement through the perspective of a
typical and an ideal spectator. With these qualities, this delightful musical comedy
from the early 1930s not only responds to the main paradigm shift in the history
of cinema but also makes its self-referential strategies an integral part of popular
entertainment.

NOTES

1. Following established practices at the time, Pommer shot *Day and Night* in
several versions, a French version, *A moi le jour, à toi la nuit,* coproduced with
Alliance Cinématographique Européenne (ACE) and featuring Käthe von
Nagy and Fernand Gravey, and an English version, *Early to Bed,* coproduced
with Gaumont British and starring Fernand Gravey and Heather Angel.
2. On the invention of sound, see Harald Jossé, *Die Entstehung des Tonfilms:
Beitrag zu einer faktenorientierten Mediengeschichte* (Freiburg and Munich:
Alber, 1984). More filmographical references can be found in Ulrich J. Klaus,
*Deutsche Tonfilme: Filmlexikon der abendfüllenden und deutschsprachigen
Tonfilme nach ihren deutschen Uraufführungen. 1929/30. 1931. 1932* (Berlin
and Berchtesgarden: Klaus, 1988–92). On the historical reception of the
early sound film, see Helmut Korte, *Der Spielfilm und das Ende der Weimarer
Republik* (Göttingen: Vanderhoeck & Ruprecht, 1998). On the transition to
sound in its economic and political implications, compare Wolfgang Mühl-
Benninghaus, *Das Ringen um den Tonfilm: Strategien der Elektro-und der
Filmindustrie in den 20er und 30er Jahren* (Düsseldorf: Droste, 1999). For
recent contributions to the historiography of this period, see Karl Prümm,
"Historiographie einer Epochenschwelle: Der Übergang vom Stummfilm
zum Tonfilm in Deutschland (1928–1932)," in *Filmgeschichte schreiben:
Ansätze, Entwürfe und Methoden; Dokumentation der Tagung der GFF 1988,*
ed. Knut Hickethier (Berlin: edition sigma, 1989), 93–103 and Wolfgang
Jacobsen, "Wortdämmerung: Auf dem Weg zum Tonfilm," in *Der deutsche
Film: Aspekte seiner Geschichte von den Anfängen bis zur Gegenwart,* ed.
Uli Jung (Trier: WVT Wissenschaftlicher Verlag, 1993), 79–80. On some
theoretical implications, see Tom Levin, "The Acoustic Dimension," *Screen*
25, no. 3 (1984): 55–68 and Kaja Silverman, *The Acoustic Mirror: The Female
Voice in Psychoanalysis and Cinema* (Bloomington: Indiana University Press,
1988).

3. Willy Haas, *Film-Kurier,* 29 November 1932. Also see the enthusiastic comments from the advertisement in *Lichtbildbühne,* 3 December 1932. For a review that takes issue with the film-inside-the-film-construction, see *Lichtbildbühne,* 29 November 1932.

4. Fritsch and Nagy had already tested the romantic possibilities of role-playing in *Ihre Hoheit befiehlt* (Her Highness Commands, 1931), where they fall in love as a hairdresser and a greengrocer—even though they really are a princess and a lieutenant.

5. On Pommer's formative influence on the film operetta, see Wolfgang Jacobsen, *Erich Pommer: Ein Produzent macht Filmgeschichte* (Berlin: Argon, 1989), 105. For two recent publications about musical genres in the early sound period, see *Musik Spektakel Film: Musiktheater und Tanzkultur im deutschen Film 1922–1939,* ed. Katja Uhlebrok (Munich: text + kritik, 1998) and *Als die Filme singen lernten: Innovation und Tradition im Musikfilm 1928–1938,* eds. Malte Hagener and Jan Hans (Munich: text + kritik, 1999).

6. For further information about this unjustly neglected director, see Hans-Michael Bock and Wolfgang Jacobsen, eds., *Ludwig Berger* (Munich: edition text + kritik, 1992); Ulrich Gregor, "Märchenträumer mit Intellekt," in *Ludwig Berger 1892–1969* (Berlin: Akademie der Künste, 1969), 6–8.

7. Hans-Michael Bock, "Ludwig Berger," in *Cinegraph: Lexikon zum deutschsprachigen Film* (Munich: text + kritik, 1984–), B3.

8. Günther Dahlke and Günter Karl, eds., *Deutsche Spielfilme von den Anfängen bis 1933* (Berlin: Henschel, 1988), 308.

9. Rudolf Arnheim, "Filmnotizen," *Die Weltbühne* 49 (1932): 848.

10. Siegfried Kracauer, *From Caligari to Hitler: A Psychological History of the German Film* (Princeton, N.J.: Princeton University Press, 1974), 108. The reference is to *The Lost Shoe.*

11. The reference is to Kracauer's "Little Shopgirls Go to the Movies," in *Mass Ornament: Weimar Essays,* translated and edited with an introduction by Thomas Y. Levin (Cambridge, Mass: Harvard University Press, 1995), 291–304. See my article on "Girls and Crisis—The Other Side of Diversion," *New German Critique* 40 (1987): 147–66.

12. Willy Haas, "Wortdichtung im Film?" *Die literarische Welt* 3, no. 30 (1928): 1–2. The reference is to Walter Benjamin's "The Work of Art in the Age of Mechanical Reproduction," in *Illuminations,* intro. Hannah Arendt, trans. Harry Zohn (New York: Schocken, 1969), 217–51.

13. Siegfried Kracauer, "Internationaler Tonfilm?" in *Von Caligari bis Hitler,* trans. Ruth Baumgarten and Karsten Witte (Frankfurt am Main: Suhrkamp, 1979), 469.

14. Herbert Ihering, *"Von Reinhardt bis Brecht: Eine Auswahl der Theaterkritiken* (Berlin: Aufbau-Verlag, 1961), 1:429.

15. Kurt Weill, "Tonfilm," in *Theorie des Films,* ed. Karsten Witte (Frankfurt am Main: Suhrkamp, 1982), 188.

16. Rudolf Arnheim, "Die traurige Zukunft des Films," in *Kritiken und Aufsätze zum Film,* ed. Helmut H. Diederichs (Munich: Hanser, 1977), 18.

17. Béla Balázs, "Neue Mittel—neue Zwecke," in *Schriften zum Film,* ed. Helmut H. Diederichs, Wolfgang Gersch, and Magda Nagy (Berlin, Budapest: Hanser, 1982), 2:235. On a more cautionary note, Balázs also wrote: "If the sound film should become a new art form that can well hold its own next to the other arts and the silent film, then it must treat sound not only as a supplement, an addition for dramatic scenes, but as the central and decisive dramatic event and the main motif of the narrative" (*Der Geist des Films* [Halle/Saale: Wilhelm Knapp, 1930], 177).

18. Siegfried Kracauer, "Der erste deutsche Tonfilm," in *Von Caligari bis Hitler,* trans. Ruth Baumgarten and Karsten Witte (Frankfurt am Main: Suhrkamp, 1979), 417.

MARY BRODNAX

4 Man a Machine: The Shift from Soul to Identity in Lang's *Metropolis* and Ruttmann's *Berlin*

Is more needed . . . to prove that man is but an animal, or a collection of springs which wind each other up without our being able to tell at what point in this human circle nature has begun? If these springs differ among themselves, these differences consist only in their position and in their degrees of strength, and never in their nature; wherefore the soul is but a principle of motion or a material and sensible part of the brain, which can be regarded, without fear of error, as the mainspring of the whole machine, having a visible influence on all the parts. The soul seems even to have been made for the brain, so that all the other parts of the system are but a kind of emanation from the brain.

JULIEN OFFRAY DE LA METTRIE, *Man a Machine*

Metropolis (1925/26): Freder steps in to replace a worker struggling to shift the arms on a huge dial as lights flash. Although the pointing arms appear to control some industrial process, the task seems both pointless and endless. Sympathy for the worker presumably motivates Freder's action, along with the assumption that, should the worker collapse, a disaster would befall his fellows. The task performed, the very image of alienating labor, facilitates the transfer of undefined information. By replacing the worker, Freder becomes "a principle of motion" and "the mainspring of the whole machine."

Berlin, Symphony of a City (1927): In a montage sequence edited to create the impression of speed and repetition, employees dial telephones, strike the keys of "Torpedo" typewriters, and send messages through vacuum tubes. Even more so than Freder, who retains individuality, they have become "a principle of motion" devoted to the exchange of information. As the "mainspring of the whole machine," the people in this film function as part of a larger organism for which they provide the animal vitality. The city comprehends the activity she encompasses; her inhabitants appear to have only energy, not comprehension.

Metropolis (1925/26), directed by Fritz Lang.

Lang's *Metropolis:* From Spiritual to Economic Identity

Metropolis lends itself to an economic interpretation. The metallic Maria circulates with disastrous effect among the workers and, capitalizing on their inability to recognize a counterfeit, stimulates a run on the market that bankrupts their community by destroying both their homes and the factories that provide their livelihood in the underground city. Delivered into the hands of Fredersen, the workers accept his terms in order to regain the small degree of market participation they once enjoyed. Fredersen, although shaken by the near collapse of the entire metropolitan system his economic deviousness has elicited, stabilizes fluctuations by bringing in new management—his son Freder—under the guise of cooperation with labor. *Metropolis* imitates the inflationary process that nearly destroyed the businessmen, salaried employees, wage earners, and pensioners of the Weimar Republic before the advent of the 1924 Dawes Plan.

In this scenario, the original Maria complicates the otherwise straightforward economic mimesis performed by the film. Her name a reference to the Virgin

74

Berlin, Symphony of a City (1927), directed by Walter Ruttmann.

Mary, she first appears in the film as a mother figure ushering innocent children through the gates of paradise (her appearance cites Goethe's Charlotte as well, who, slicing bread for a group of children, makes a lasting impression on Werther). The paradise, a pleasure garden where Freder chases his playmates around glittering fountains, is a pallid imitation of the ideal garden Maria promises the children they will someday enter. Her second appearance pointedly marks her association with the mother of God for those who may have overlooked the introduction of Christianity into the film. Appearing before an altar and a background of crosses in a catacomb, Maria bears witness to the good news that a savior will come to alleviate the workers' suffering. When contrasted with the scene in which the subterranean machines transmogrify into a fire-spewing sacrificial god, the catacomb setting suggests that the workers, like the Israelites tempted to celebrate a golden calf or to imitate the Ammonites' obeisance to Moloch, have the alternative of worshiping at a different altar. The setting also suggests that their choice, like that of the early Christians, will bring them into conflict with established powers and require that they suffer until redemption occurs. Maria introduces a jumble of Christian overtones into *Metropolis;* her presence not only encourages discussion of the mesalliance of Thea von Harbou's religiosity and Lang's cinematic inventiveness,[1] but also of the fear of technology and sexuality, particularly feminine sexuality, accessible to a psychoanalytic reading of the film, and of the transition from Expressionism to New Objectivity in Weimar culture provided by earlier studies, such as those by Andreas Huyssen and Paul Coates. Such perspectives, however, address neither the juxtaposition of the two models of history displayed by the film (i.e., salvation history and economic history) nor what such a juxtaposition reveals about the nature of a developing national identity that would be compatible with totalitarianism under National Socialism (and with other political models as well).

The difficulty of reconciling the idealism Maria represents, teleological in that it promises a solution outside of history, with the material situation of the workers lends the oft-noted naivete to the concluding message of the film that "between the hands and the brain . . . the heart acts as mediator." Lang called the denouement a "Märchen" (fairy tale) decades later in an interview with director Peter Bogdanovich and ascribed its superficiality to his lack of political awareness at the time. He further defended himself and his five-million-mark blockbuster by suggesting that machines motivated his interest.[2] The film admittedly does not address the complexity of Weimar culture in the epic manner of a work like *Berlin Alexanderplatz,* but Lang's disavowal of political sophistication late in his life— perhaps his answer to *From Caligari to Hitler*—rings false. Siegfried Kracauer's analysis of *Metropolis* suggests this when he remarks that Lang "could not possibly overlook the antagonism between the breakthrough of intrinsic human emotions and his ornamental patterns." The film's display of "these patterns up to the very end," Kracauer argues, advances Nazi political objectives.[3] On the other hand, elements of the concluding scene that gloss the European investigation of the relationship of body, soul, and history challenge the argument that Lang's film allied him with Nazi political positions.[4]

The teleological nature of Maria's presence—the way in which she points to a salvation history outside of economic history—may limit the aesthetic dimension of the film, but precisely this feature shows that Lang's fascination with machines includes the human-as-machine. Huyssen argues that the film reflects a fear of technology merged with a fear of the feminine, but it is also preoccupied with arguments that elide radical distinctions between soul and body and deflate salvation models of history.[5] *Metropolis* introduces a scale by which a spectator can evaluate definitions of "soul" against a background of political and industrial interests. If Freder represents "man a machine"—that is, the human with a mechanical or material soul—then Maria represents the human with an ideal soul, and the robot Maria represents the creaturely soul of beings animated by a vital force but lacking in comprehension. The film offers these representations as competing models for a German identity during the Weimar period.

The robot Maria and her creator, Rotwang, whose prosthetic hand links him to his mechanical offspring, join a family of artificial humans and their creators that includes the literary figures of Jean Paul's mechanical man, von Arnim's clay puppet, Tieck's scarecrow, and Hoffmann's Olimpia, as well as the historical figures of Vaucanson and his flute player or the Jaquet-Droz family and their three automatons—a piano player, a draughtsman, and a scribe (to exclude von Kempelen's famous hoax of the chess-playing automaton). As Peter Sprengel points out, many of these literary creations enabled their authors to satirize German aristocratic and bourgeois culture, while others, notably Jean Paul's and Hoffmann's, addressed the anxiety that no essence distinguished man from machine.[6] Rotwang's counterpart in German film history is the rabbi in Paul Wegener's *Golem* films, the first of which appeared in 1914. Unlike Rabbi Loew, who uses his skills as an alchemist and wise man to animate his clay assistant (in *The Golem, How He Entered the World,* 1920), Lang's magician-scientist uses his talents to endow an already animated robot with a flesh-and-blood appearance. A double for a human, a mechanical "Doppelgänger," so it seems, would enable the men to achieve their end by agitating the workers. They realize, however, that a mere double for a human, despite its sex appeal or rhetorical proficiency, would accomplish little for them. In acquiring Maria's face, the robot gains access to a specific human history. Fredersen and Rotwang need not only an agent, but Maria's record as a representative of the promise of salvation at the end of time if they are to manipulate the workers in Metropolis. At stake in *Metropolis,* then, is not only a notion of history shaped by the uncanny (characterized by attempts to cope with the return of the repressed—whether motivated by a sexophobia, a technophobia, or a sophistophobia—which *The Student of Prague* vividly introduced to filmgoers a decade earlier), but a concept of history that would replace the hope offered by teleological promises with the calculability of economics.

Kracauer reads the reconciliation concluding *Metropolis,* in which the "industrialist acknowledges the heart for the purpose of manipulating it,"[7] as corroborating evidence for his thesis that Weimar cinema reflects a national psychology susceptible to totalitarian rule, the mechanisms of which a psychoanalytic vocabulary enables him to reveal. The film leaves room, however, for an analysis that situates it within the tradition of a European discussion of two conflicting models of history and a concept of human identity neither ethnic nor psychoanalytical, but economic in character. *Metropolis* suggests that by privileging economic history over salvation history (whether Marxist or Christian), German men and women could enter a national marketplace that would guarantee their physical and "spiritual" well-being.

Lang's vision of souls in the balance became a commonplace. The Olympian sons of Metropolis, their gargantuan buildings, and their mythic machines were adopted humorlessly as reference points by Hitler protégé Albert Speer, the sculptor Arnold Brecker, and Fritz Todt, who directed construction on the Autobahn. More than half a century later, American popular culture recycled Lang's alienated workers and heroic capitalists by updating his film with a Giorgio Moroder soundtrack

(1984) and citing it in film and in advertising: Ridley Scott's *Bladerunner* (1982), Apple MacIntosh campaigns of the 1980s, and Tim Burton's *Batman* series (1989, 1992) stand out among the works influenced by *Metropolis*.

Heide Schönemann's *Fritz Lang: Filmbilder, Vorbilder*, a compilation of Lang's references to the graphic arts, enables us to see that the director preceded his imitators in the technique of citation; by pairing images from his films with artworks primarily from the first two decades of the twentieth century, Schönemann illustrates Lang's proclivity for this practice.[8] She also documents Lang's influence on his contemporaries Eisenstein, Chaplin, Buñuel, and Brecht.[9] Citations of Kurt Schmidt's *Der Mann am Schaltbrett* (Man at the Control Panel, 1924) and Oskar Schlemmer's *Drahtkostüm* (Wire Suit, 1922) best illustrate Lang's interest in "man a machine." The first work depicts a figure reminiscent of a robot, with its arms raised before a stylized control board. The figure looks over its shoulder toward two humanoid figures composed of more radically geometrical shapes. The lifted arms and legs of all three figures, which suggest a dancing motion, convey that, in La Mettrie's words, humans are "a collection of springs which wind each other up." Schmidt's design, for a ballet celebrating the fifth anniversary of the Bauhaus, seems to have inspired the portrayal of Freder standing in for the collapsing worker.[10] The second work, a wire outline of a human figure clothed by a skirt and hat of vertical wire rings, suggests a body enveloped by energy fields; it apparently motivated Lang to depict shimmering rings of energy moving up and down the robot's metallic body as it becomes the false Maria.[11]

Schönemann's collection of references omits one that is central to the thesis of the present essay. *Metropolis* concludes with a tableau depicting Frederson, Freder, and the foreman Gyorgy as they shake hands. This picture of harmony accompanies Maria's sentimental instruction regarding the mediation of the heart between the head and the hands. The scene suggests that Freder's mediation will enable brutish laborers and enlightened capitalists to reconcile and cooperate in a conflict-free marketplace. Maria's marginal presence—she encourages Freder to intervene but does not appear in the frame as the men embrace—intimates that the eradication of conflict in the secular sphere of profit depends on the continued influence of the sacred sphere; thus, the reconciliation takes place neither on the market square where the assembled workers stand nor in the cathedral proper. Rotwang, whose cooperation with Frederson has subordinated both alchemical and empirical science to market forces, clears the way for the merger not only of capital and labor but also of salvation history and economic history by crashing to his death in a rooftop struggle with Freder.[12] The latter's heartfelt reconciliation of brain and hands occurs on the cathedral steps, linking the spheres of religion and commerce, as if the film were celebrating a world order in which business would mock Lord Thurlow's trenchant observation that the corporation lacks precisely the corporeal element that would subject it to moral or ethical restrictions enforced by physical punishment.[13] Is the reconciliation illusory? Lang's claim that he was politically naive when he directed *Metropolis* coexists uneasily with the irony that Kracauer attributed to Lang's alignment with a fascist ideology and condemned in the otherwise saccharine staging of this central scene.

Lang's citations make deciphering his position vis-à-vis the political implications of *Metropolis* more complex. The background of assembled workers and the deployment of the central male figures refer visually to Jacques Louis David's 1791 *The Tennis Court Oath*. The drawing depicts three clergymen embracing before a crowd of impassioned French nationalists swearing "never to be separated and to meet wherever circumstances so require, until the Constitution of the Kingdom is established firmly on solid foundations."[14] Prepared for a painting commissioned by the Club des Jacobins in 1790, *The Tennis Court Oath* is an emblem both of French nationalism and of a revolutionary free market individualism. Jean Starobinski acknowledges the position (frequently labeled Western) that collective action, particularly in a national context, comprises expressions of individual will. *The Tennis Court Oath* and the 1784–85 *Oath of the Horatii,* its visually related predecessor emphasizing the masculine self-sacrifice necessary to achieve republican goals, reveal the roots of such concepts in a European cultural vocabulary.[15]

Lang's citation of *The Tennis Court Oath* is teasingly ambiguous. The reference could suggest that through the mediation of the sacred both capital and labor can profit, or it could highlight ironically the cynical cooperation of Fredersen and his foreman (who warns Frederson about the workers' revolt and shields him from their frenzied attack) as they restore the market status quo against the backdrop of a crumbling cathedral. The depiction of the laborers, which by inverting the position of the worker spectators vis-à-vis the three focal figures turns *The Tennis Court Oath* on its head, suggests that the second reading of the scene is more appropriate: dehumanized as a mass, with their backs to the film spectator, the workers' march toward the cathedral parallels their earlier march into the subterranean industrial tunnels. The workers have gained nothing, the master of Metropolis retains his power, and his son has joined him. Lang's visual citation of *The Tennis Court Oath* introduces a complexity into the staging of the scene which Kracauer, censuring Lang for employing an "all-devouring decorative scheme," does not address. The implication that Lang's continued use of ornamental patterns reinforces the deployment of totalitarian power in Weimar culture overlooks the relationship to David's drawing. The embrace depicted does not advance totalitarian politics, nor does it bless a union of "liberation theology" and commercial idealism; it ridicules revolution as a force for social change and as a historical concept rooted in the utopian thought of salvation history. Lang's reference to David's *Tennis Court Oath* can thus be understood as a commentary on the relationship between salvation history and the ideal soul versus economic history and the material soul. The two models of history are irreconcilable, but the cleverness of economic history is to obfuscate their opposition. *Metropolis* reveals this mechanism with an ironic allusion—whether intended or unintended, whether

Jacques-Louis David, *The Tennis Court Oath,* pen on paper, 1791. 66 x 101.2 cm. Chateaux de Versailles et de Trianon. @Photo RMN-Gérard Blot.

critical or accepting must remain unclear—by its "politically naive" director. While doing so, the film suggests not a preference among the competing models for a national identity provided by Freder, Maria, and the robot Maria, but an awareness of an emerging dominant model for such an identity.

As one of the earliest philosophical works to characterize the human being as a machine with a material soul, Julien Offray de La Mettrie's *Man a Machine* (1748) marks a moment in the vivisection of human moral nature to which the mad scientist genre refers. Huyssen, in his discussion of *Metropolis,* quite rightly introduces La Mettrie as an author whose ideas shape the materialist philosophy that influences the reception of technology in nineteenth- and twentieth-century arts and letters. The physician's description of movement in decapitated chickens, kittens, and puppies, in the chopped-off paws of moles, and in caterpillars, worms, and eels thrown into hot water, along with his speculations about the continued beating of the heart in the still-warm, dissected corpses of executed criminals, could have served as a model for the activities of Mary Shelley's Dr. Frankenstein.[16] Like Frankenstein's experiments, however, La Mettrie's dispassionate investigations into the workings of nature coincided with a passionate love for Enlightenment humanism and its subjects. Contrary to what Huyssen maintains in his brief characterization of *Man a Machine,* La Mettrie does not conclude that "the body is nothing but a clock," nor does his view strictly represent an "extreme materialist view with its denial of emotion and subjectivity."[17]

La Mettrie defines the soul as the material consequence of sensation and rejects the conceptualist notion that it is an immaterial addition to the physical body that radically distinguishes the human from the animal. Although he admires Descartes's innovative analysis of the ideal nature of the human soul, La Mettrie posits that, limited by a lack of scientifically grounded observations of the human being, his forerunner lacked the necessary information to draw valid conclusions about human nature (142).

In *Man a Machine,* La Mettrie prophylactically concedes (an effort which failed) that the origin of consciousness in the sum of sensations does not exclude the possibility of a divine entity at work to endow sentient life with self-awareness, but he argues that to ignore empirical science "is to regard nature and revelation as two contraries which destroy each the other, and consequently to dare uphold the absurd doctrine that God contradicts Himself in His various works and deceives us" (86). In all beings, the capacities of memory, judgment, and feeling support an ability to distinguish between good and evil that varies according to intelligence level, not soul. La Mettrie's philosophical treatise, therefore, was intended to support ethical behavior; nonetheless, it blatantly challenged a Christian moral imperative and the view of human history defended by his eighteenth-century Christian detractors. For them, human history was transparently teleological and man's soul "spiritual"; both progressed on a linear path toward the dissolution of the physical body, the release of an immaterial essence, and the suspension or *Aufhebung* of history. La Mettrie countered that, given the inability of humans to draw conclusions based on observations regarding the goal of history or the relationship to an ideal sphere, "pure naturalism" provides the best means of organizing social relations in a history that is not linear, but, for beings endowed with material souls, a "human circle" (135). He understood human events as revolutions independent of the teleological end implicit in Christianity and would no doubt have rejected other forms of utopian thought, such as Marxism, that posit a moment at which history empties into stasis. The materialist definition of human life that La Mettrie recognized privileges a differently defined "revolution," typified by free-market commerce, which understands human history as the circulation of capital (intellectual or mercantile) invested, accumulated, and bequeathed in perpetuity, and which finds in commerce (likewise intellectual or mercantile) the good works to ensure salvation in the event the promises of teleological history enter fulfillment. Commerce thus replaces political revolution in the rational social order as the means of creating both equitable social conditions and a stable identity in a Europe defined by the national marketplace. Within the parameters provided by empiricism, La Mettrie understood the soul as an "enlightened machine," not only dependent on "the proper organization of the brain and of the whole body," but a result of "this organization itself":

> For finally, even if man alone had received a share of natural law, would he be any less a machine for that? A few more wheels, a few more springs than in the most perfect animals, the brain proportionally nearer the heart and for this very reason receiving more blood—any one of a number of unknown causes might always produce this delicate conscience so easily wounded, this remorse which is no more foreign to matter than to thought, and in a word all the differences that are supposed to exist here. Could the organism then suffice for everything? Once more, yes; since thought visibly develops with our organs, why should not the matter of which they are composed be susceptible of remorse also, when once it has acquired, with time, the faculty of feeling? (128)

For La Mettrie, the human body indeed resembles a large watch, but a vulnerability to moral feeling and a potential for remorse characterize its intelligence. It shares with animals the property of a soul, the force that moves organic matter (141–43). What distinguishes the human from the animal is the degree of sophistication of its brain, which allows the human soul a greater sophistication also. Essential for this development is time, or rather history.

In contrast to La Mettrie's conception of the soul generated by sensation, the ancient idealist conception of the anima bound to the body by invisible threads informs Maria's nature. She acts not to rescue the workers from inhumane conditions, but to introduce them into an inhuman order. Freder, ruled by physical sensation, awakens to a moral sphere because his pursuit of Maria enables him to experience history self-consciously—not because of a transforming encounter with the ideal she represents. The robot Maria remains devoid of moral direction; seeking neither evil nor good, it incites rebellion among the workers, dances erotically before a crowd of aroused onlookers, and shrieks with laughter at its own immolation. In each instance, it watches change for its own sake, without interest in moral or temporal consequences and without reflecting on the feeling change engenders; that is, it leads an immediate existence in which it is completely consumed by the present and has no concept of history. Like some perverse version of Kleist's marionette, it exists in a peculiar state of grace.[18]

Metropolis introduces Christian teleology, personified in Maria, as an antidote to the economic anxiety experienced by the workers in the underground city, but the film also represents the argument over the nature of the human soul that contributes to the dismantling of teleological reassurances in commercial culture. It depicts the victory of the commercial while pressing the teleological into the background, yet retains an unresolved tension between the two systems. Maria, Freder, and the robot provide the bodies through which the film distinguishes among competing relationships to history. *Metropolis* concludes with the half-hearted election of Freder as the model for a German national identity in an era when, across the sea, to cite Lang discussing the negative American reception of *The Song of the Nibelungen*, "the people in Pasadena" knew nothing of "Siegfried's fight with the dragon."[19]

Ruttmann's *Berlin, Symphony of a City:* From Economic to Cybernetic Identity

Let mans Soule be a Spheare, and then, in this,
The intelligence that moves, devotion is,
And as the other Spheares, by being growne
Subject to forraigne motions, lose their owne,
And being by others hurried every day,
Scarce in a year their naturall forme obey:
Pleasure or businesse, so, our Soules admit
For their first mover, and are whirld by it.
Hence is't, that I am carryed towards the West
This day, when my Soules forme bends toward the East.[20]

With these words, written early in the seventeenth century, the English divine John Donne remarked upon the shift in thought characteristic of the modern era. For an earlier time, a prime mover had guided those who properly performed their devotions, just as it guided the heavenly spheres in their movements. The human soul, in celestial imitation, attained through religious piety a roundness that granted an otherwise vegetative self the locomotion of intelligence. Donne recognized that the discoveries of modern science would alter not only these laws of nature but also the sacred and secular laws that regulated private devotions and public functions. Motions of secular entertainment and business, once considered alien to the soul's contemplation of life and death, would by virtue of a greater speed cancel the grave force of contemplation and whirl the soul, fraught with anxiety, toward expansive modernity.

Three centuries later, similar concerns couched in similar metaphors preoccupied the secular preachers of the declining modern age, an age populated by persons, not souls, termed "postmodern" in 1917 by Rudolf Pannwitz (*The Crisis of European Culture*).[21] Thus Kracauer, in a 1924 essay titled "Langeweile" (Boredom), also wrote of the sphere that moves persons regardless of their will:

> Es ist, als träumte man einen jener Träume, die der leere Magen gebiert. Eine winzige Kugel rollte ganz aus der Ferne auf dich zu, sie wächst sich zur

Großaufnahme aus und braust zuletzt über dich her; du kannst sie nicht hemmen, noch ihr entrinnen, gefesselt liegst du da, ein ohnmächtiges Püppchen, das von dem Riesenkoloß mitgerissen wird und in seinem Umkreis vergeht. Flucht ist unmöglich.[22]

It is as if one dreamed one of those dreams produced by an empty stomach. A tiny ball rolls out of the distance towards you, it grows to a close-up and finally roars over you; you can neither check it, nor escape it. You lie there chained, a powerless little doll, that is torn along by the huge colossus and wastes away in its orbit. Flight is impossible.

Kracauer saw in the entropy discovered by natural science, in the helplessness of bodies in the pull of decaying gravitational forces, a metaphor to describe the fate of modern beings for whom the self is "missing" ("verschollen") because technology has focused attention elsewhere: the close-up is no longer on the player, but rather on the giant pinball. The souls Donne described, whirled loose from an anchored individuality, were for Kracauer flattened into the external layer of a juggernaut, whose projectile speed rolled members, not persons, in an increasing mass toward what Kracauer also termed an "antenna fate." Humans shared—in an age Siegfried Gideon would describe as "anonymous history"[23]—in one of two fates: rolled under by a colossal ball, they became the groping arms of that urbane globe; or they became swarming soldiers, all antennae, in a mechanized formicary. Both images suggest that the human body was to become or had already become a genderless receiver, a relayer of information, and a component of a larger organism.

Berlin, Symphony of a City captures these modern bodies, performs vivisection on them (the film belongs to the genre of the "Querschnitt" or "cross-section" film), and represents an improved human being, an integrated information circuit. Walter Ruttmann announced his intentions of redesigning humans in a newspaper article titled "How I Filmed my Berlin Film," published in the *Lichtbildbühne* of October 8, 1927. His first step would be to capture them as they milled through the city: "Nun konnten wir auch hier die Menschen überlisten, nachts durch die Straßen fahrend Verkehr und Leben einfangen" ("Now here also we could outwit the people, capture traffic and life, driving through the streets by night"). Ruttmann professed to be possessed by a desire to build "from living material . . . from the million-fold energies of motion actually present in the city organism" ("aus lebendigem Material . . . aus den millionenfachen, tatsächlich vorhandenen Bewegungsenergien des Großstadtorganismus").[24]

Constructing his "Berlin film," Ruttmann visualized modernity as a relay of information that gave what Georg Simmel, in *The Philosophy of Money*, called "an otherwise unobtainable transparency and calculability" ("eine sonst unerreichbare Durchsichtigkeit und Berechenbarkeit") in the "content of life" ("Inhalte des

Lebens") to the state, commerce, and entertainment. Time and the money analogy, as Simmel discussed them, organize a day in the life of the city that Ruttmann depicts. Acts of weighing, calculating, and evaluating link shots depicting business, transportation, advertising, street vendors, window shopping, and sports events. Sequences from the film equate persons with dolls in mechanical perpetual motion or with mannequins whose function is to display goods. That this movement of information, a product of "the superstructure of money relations over qualitative reality" ("der Überbau der Geldrelationen über der qualitativen Wirklichkeit"), determined "in a much more invasive manner the inner image of the same" ("in noch viel eingreifenderer Weise das innere Bild derselben"),[25] is the essential principle of the film, but it is a principle not comprehended by those participating in it, whether "it" be the film or the life the filmmaker claimed to have captured and transformed when he wrote that he believed that most persons "who experience the intoxication of movement in my Berlin film, do not know where their intoxication comes from" ("die an meinem 'Berlin-Film' den Rausch der Bewegung erleben, nicht wissen woher ihr Rausch kommt").

Ruttmann depicted a merger of human and machine into an information processor whose presence would support the movements of commerce and entertainment in the early twentieth-century metropolis. The secretary's body became the launching tube for missives from the Torpedo typewriter, the human hand became a secondary handset of the telephone as well as a digital dialing system, waiters became the arms and legs of a mechanized, conveyor-belt restaurant kitchen. Spectators watching *Berlin, Symphony of a City* were to undergo a similar process: interacting with the cinematic machine, they would become a part of the apparatus. This transformation would endow them with the ability to experience life; that is, the cinema would supply self-consciousness and an entry into history to beings otherwise incapable of comprehending the world around them. The film theory term "suture" would seem to describe a similar operation. Ruttmann's intentions, however, were more global than this term suggests.

In Huyssen's and Coates's readings of *Metropolis,* Lang's and von Harbou's vision defines the conflict between labor and capital, as well as between woman and man, in terms of technologies capable of replacing human workers and religious sentiment. Burning the female robot restores the status quo of class, of gender, and, to a lesser extent, of salvation history by reassuring the frightened masses that a common biology allies them with the masters of *Metropolis* against machines. Kracauer, Huyssen, and Coates examine the fears beneath the overlay of the film's conciliatory conclusion. This essay attempts to take their work a step further by considering the interest *Metropolis* and *Berlin, Symphony of a City,* two otherwise quite different "city" films, share in addressing the investigation of a German identity that one can trace at least as far back as Frederick the Great's 1748 eulogy for La Mettrie.

85

Ruttmann, in a state of "aroused hunting fever," went into the streets of Berlin with the intention of creating life by using cinema technology to seduce the city. "With infinite perfidy and prudery" ("Tücke und Sprödigkeit"), he wrote, the city attempted "to withdraw itself from the inexorability of my lens" ("sich der Unerbittlichkeit meines Objektivs zu entziehen"). A mechanically enhanced Casanova thrilled by the ability to achieve an otherwise impossible intercourse, Ruttmann pursued an unending "series of adventures" in which the least "false tone" would interrupt "in the last moment a situation already nearly grasped." Ruttmann's description of his activities postulates an ability to constitute subjects first by penetrating both the abstract metropolitan body (with the camera) and the undeveloped mental faculties of its organic members (with the projection apparatus). His rejection of a preexisting subjectivity resembles that expressed by La Mettrie nearly two centuries earlier.

Ruttmann argued that as a potent, mechanically enhanced father, he could impregnate the city of Berlin. The Berliners, the offspring of his cinematic liaison, would awaken to true life after experiencing a rebirth as intelligent beings, as organic cyborgs. The proof of their vivacity was to be a symphonic movement quite different from that which they experienced as hapless bodies torn along by the spheres of business and pleasure. A second proof was to be their recognition of Berlin, their mother (and, presumably, recognition of the self-proclaimed father as well): "And when I have managed to make the people resonate [zum Schwingen zu bringen], to enable them to experience the city of Berlin, then I will have reached my goal." The resonance that for Ruttmann marked the entry into historical consciousness recalls La Mettrie's analysis of mental processes in the brain capable of advanced thought. Comparing the "cerebral fibres . . . stimulated to render or repeat the words that strike them" to a "violin string or harpsichord key," which "vibrates and gives forth sound," La Mettrie locates the origin of intelligence—or soul—in the external world. Penetrating the brain with information, as Ruttmann wished to do with the cinematic apparatus, would stimulate a birth that likewise compares to La Mettrie's description of the acquisition of soul: "And as the structure of the brain is such that when eyes well formed for seeing, have once perceived the image of objects, the brain can not help seeing their images and differences, so when the signs of these differences have been traced or imprinted in the brain, the soul necessarily examines their relations—an examination that would have been impossible without the discovery of signs or the invention of language." (105)

In this inversion of the notion that the eyes are the window of the soul that allow a unicum to reveal itself, La Mettrie posits that the organic matter of the brain rests quiescent until images of external stimuli already organized in terms of their differences impress themselves on receptive tissue. Without such intervention, the soul remains utterly silent. Ruttmann compares the birth out of such a silence to a symphony, but that symphony originates in the movements of a complicated machine, "which can resonate if each smallest part grasps the other with the most exact precision" ("die nur in Schwung geraten kann, wenn jedes kleinste Teilchen mit genauester Präzision in das andere greift"). Like La Mettrie, for whom the soul is a repository of the signs of countless sensory impressions, Ruttmann understands the origin of consciousness to depend on an accumulation of impressions ("smallest parts") which function like the teeth on cogs; however, whereas La Mettrie suggests that exposure to the semiotic technical apparatus of language arouses the analysis of material relationships, Ruttmann's comments in the journal *Lichtbildbühne* and his film suggest that a contemplative experience of life remains beyond the reach of the human unshaped by a more mechanical technical apparatus, because that human otherwise remains cowed by the sign nature of the world. It is useful to turn once again to La Mettrie to understand the nature of the relationship to external stimuli that characterizes the cybernetic identity Ruttmann's work posits as desirable.

> All this knowledge, with which vanity fills the balloon-like brains of our proud pedants, is therefore but a huge mass of words and figures, which form in the brain all the marks by which we distinguish and recall objects. . . . These words and the objects designated by them are so connected in the brain that it is comparatively rare to imagine a thing without the name or sign that is attached to it.
>
> I always use the word "imagine," because I think that everything is the work of imagination, and that all the faculties of the soul can be correctly reduced to pure imagination in which they all consist. Thus judgment, reason, memory are not absolute parts of the soul, but merely modifications of this kind of medullary screen upon which images of the objects painted in the eye are projected as by a magic lantern. (106–7)

Ruttmann's intentions vis-à-vis a cinema audience differed radically from La Mettrie's analysis of the human condition, despite a similarity in the conceptualization of the human brain as a screen across which projected images play. For La Mettrie, a play of images adequately mediated by the organic technical apparatus of the eye and by language generated the characteristics celebrated as human: judgment, reason, and memory. For Ruttmann, only with the assistance of the filmmaker's tools could a human become more than a sum of assembled members and function in the flow of information characterizing urban existence. Even after this transformation, it would be a rare individual—Spengler's predator, Jünger's warrior in a storm of steel, Ruttmann himself—who could wield the technical apparatus to generate "life" in an age flooded with information.

For Ruttmann, it was the cinematic apparatus in his hands, the hands of a "pinball wizard," that first gave the mass members life. Just as some machines sustain life in the physical body, and others in the social bodies of the state, commerce, and entertainment, so the movie machines were to sustain the newly encoded life of the affective body—the body as information switchboard. The camera, like the lightning-harnessing machinery of Dr. Frankenstein, enabled Ruttmann and his crew to take members from the maternal body of Berlin, stitch them together, and then, with the projector, effect the merger of human and machine, thus creating what soon could be called a cybernetic system.

Ruttmann used the montage principle not to analyze, criticize, or interpret life, but to create rhythms of what Kracauer called "ambiguous neutrality." Carl Mayer, the author of the idea for the film, parted ways with Ruttmann rather than participate in making a film on this basis, and Kracauer dismissed Ruttmann's film for failing to move from the aesthetic to the political.[26] Why was Ruttmann's neutrality, noted disparagingly, so distressing? It was not merely that it partook of both conservative and modernist sentiment—although not in the manner described by Jeffrey Herf as incorporating "modern technology into the cultural system of modern German nationalism, without diminishing the latter's romantic and antirational aspects"[27]—but that its rhythms lay claim to creating life, as if the spectators in the audience were awaiting the input that would make them sentient beings and provide them with an identity. This method implied that the circulation of information, rather than the contemplation of the sign nature of the world, was to become the ultimate goal of the cinematic system. The interest in national identity broached by Ruttmann's film does not resemble that expressed by German nationalists or Nazi ideologues, whose desire to "recover" authentic experience saw in technology the means of cultivating a German soul; as in Lang's *Metropolis*, Ruttmann's *Berlin* locates in economic structures based on the circulation of information or goods the material relations that define identity.

Conclusion: Bodies Transcribed, Movement Transfixed

Any information system, Ruttmann's film suggests, functions best when mechanized. Likewise, the human body will perform at its best when integrated into the cybernetic system, the purpose of which is to stimulate, regulate, and perpetuate the circulation of information. *Berlin, Symphony of a City* suggests that there is to be no mere human use for information any longer, no intention of using information to inspire and supplement contemplation, no intention of using information to manipulate sign systems. Instead, Ruttmann's cybernetic being beyond the interests of gender and race will ensure the perpetual circulation of information in an effort to transcend Nature. Information will become the thriving, "natural" organism maintained by human regulators, like new Adams in a new Eden.[28]

This shift in ideas from human as intellect to human as information switchboard, not foreign to Ruttmann in view of his comments about his adversarial role in filming the citizens of Berlin, was part of the contemporary public discussion of the significance of technological instruments. In the 1920s, some thinkers and artists understood information as an otherwise empty container for the expression and revelation of the human soul, while others understood it as the means of giving the human a credible form. Rudolf Arnheim and Adolf Behne, for example, argued in the *Weltbühne* in 1925 over the relationship between body and machine. Speculating about the effect on the body of using the typewriter, Arnheim wrote in an article titled "Die Seele in der Silberschicht" (The soul in the film of silver): "We save time thereby and remain in close touch with the tempo of the present—but do we not also lose important values of an aesthetic and human type? Do we not lose the rich magic which resides in the written? Do we not lose graphology?" Behne answered in an article referring to a typewriter (in German literally a writing machine), "Schreibmaschine, Frans Hals, Lilian Gish und Andres":

> Die Handschrift mit ihren Formenschnörkeln ist "fixierte Ausdrucksbewegung"—die Maschinenschrift ist, eben weil die manuelle Ausdrucksbewegung, das Zufällige der Stimmung, der Hemmungen durch Papier, Feder, Tinte, fortfällt, eine (relative) viel prägnantere Fixierung des Geistes und des Willens. . . . Die Prägung des Menschlichen verliert sich nicht durch die Benutzung einer Maschine: sie wird deutlicher, sicherer und klarer; sie wird einfach und meßbar.

> Handwriting with its ornamental forms is "fixed movement of expression"—the machine script is a (comparatively) much more precise fixation of spirit and will, exactly because the manual expressive movement, the incidental of mood, of restraints by paper, quill, ink cease. . . . The shaping of the human does not subside through the use of a machine: it becomes more decipherable, more certain and clearer; it becomes simple and measurable.[29]

Although Arnheim and Behne shared a notion of the human shaped by a belief in essence, for Arnheim the magical status of that essence was threatened by technological apparatuses that displaced tools, such as pen and paper, which because of their relative simplicity he paradoxically considered subordinate to the human spirit. Behne, on the other hand, saw mechanical devices providing not only the means of controlling the signs proliferating in the world, but also the means of eliminating the arbitrary interference of the physical body and its transitory emotions that distort the expression of essence.

Ruttmann proposed to create an improved human with the cinematic apparatus and *Berlin, Symphony of a Great City,* one that would move the definition of "human" beyond that articulated by Behne's position. The transcription of the body in the simple and measurable terms effected by Ruttmann's technology was to transform "fixed movement"—the traces of human presence in history—into a "fixity of spirit and will" pregnant with a new human identity. In contrast to Lang, Ruttmann did not offer competing representations as models for a German national identity; with an identity in hand, he offered to install it in spectators in the cinemas.

Ruttmann, as Kracauer and Mayer pointed out, did not interpret or criticize the world in a traditional sense in *Berlin, Symphony of a City.* According to Ruttmann's ideas, however, this was not the failure his critics called it; rather, it was the expression of his thesis: the humans on the streets of Berlin were not ready for works of criticism and interpretation. They had to acquire an identity through technology before they could participate in the circulation of information. Thus, Ruttmann proposed to merge the body with the cinematic apparatus in order to induce the birth of an adequate, cybernetic person.

The revolution or "human circle" that for La Mettrie characterized history became, as questions of ethnicity and nationality dominated the European sphere over the next two centuries, a figure for an economic identity that offered an alternative to identities sentimentally nationalistic, "reactionary modernist" in nature, Marxist, or pseudo-adamically pan-European, each of which takes its terms from a concept of ideal soul. Partaking as it does of a technological materialism with its roots in eighteenth-century modernity, the economic identity defined in the Weimar period by *Metropolis* and *Berlin, Symphony of a City* rejects the salvation history framework that allies the nationalist and internationalist models for identity mentioned above, despite their apparent differences. Lang's film treats economic identity as a means of replacing the promises of teleological systems with the calculable benefits of participation in a national intellectual or commercial market. *Metropolis,* however, particularly in the citation of David's *The Tennis Court Oath,* expresses an ironic awareness of the potential for abuse of an identity grounded in economic relations. Simmel best described this potential in *The Philosophy of Money* as "an exactitude and possibility of fixed determination which remains forbidden to the direct inclusive expression of the entire range of its qualities" ("eine Genauigkeit und Fixierungsmöglichkeit, die seinem direkten, den ganzen Umfang seiner Qualitäten einschließenden Ausdruck versagt bleibt").[30] Ruttmann's work posits the possibility of a more direct intervention in the development of identity in a political and cultural environment determined by market relations by challenging La Mettrie's attribution of intellect to the human with a mechanical soul. For Ruttmann, the mass members of modernity, of which the Germans of the Weimar period constitute but one example, would gain from the incisive encounter with the technological apparatus of the cinema a clarity and consistency of a completely different order than that they experienced in a "prenatal" consciousness. The identity Ruttmann offered was, like that represented by Freder in *Metropolis,* economic in its dependency on relations established by material conditions, but it sought to alter the fundamental biology of the subject. Such a transformation in the service of the circulation of information as the ultimate commodity—in that it combined the products of the intellectual marketplace with those of the commercial marketplace—resulted in a cybernetic identity for the human who would regulate the flow of information.

NOTES

1. One notes the references to Moloch, the Tower of Babel, the Virgin Mary, the seven deadly sins, and other features of the Judeo-Christian tradition. Luis Buñuel praised Lang for the film's dynamic portrayal of the machine world but blamed von Harbou for its religious trappings: "Although we must admit that Fritz Lang is an accomplice, we hereby accuse as the presumed author of this eclectic experiment and bold syncretism his wife, the film script author Thea von Harbou" (Michael Töteberg, *Fritz Lang* [Reinbeck: Rowohlt, 1985], 55–56). All translations from the German are my own, unless otherwise noted.

2. Ibid., 55.

3. Siegfried Kracauer, *From Caligari to Hitler* (Princeton, N.J.: Princeton University Press, 1947), 164.

4. Paul Coates agrees that the film does not reveal Nazi tendencies, "except in the sense that its effort to fuse opposites matches that of National Socialism" (*The Gorgon's Gaze* [Cambridge: Cambridge University Press, 1991], 46).

5. Andreas Huyssen, "The Vamp and the Machine: Technology and Sexuality in Fritz Lang's *Metropolis*," *New German Critique* 24–25 (1981–82): 221–37.

6. Peter Sprengel, "Maschinenmenschen: Ein zentrales Motiv in Jean Pauls Satire," *Jahrbuch der Jean-Paul Gesellschaft* 12 (1977): 101–3.

7. Kracauer, *From Caligari to Hitler,* 164.

8. Heide Schönemann, *Fritz Lang: Filmbilder, Vorbilder* (Berlin: Edition Hentrich, 1992). Schönemann's extremely useful study parallels examples from the graphic arts with images from Lang's films. She does not consider, however, whether Lang was engaging in the technique of allusion or that of citation. I would argue that Lang cites images in a manner similar to that termed "postmodern" in reference to later twentieth-century cultural products. Making this distinction in regard to Lang's filmic practice might also provide a way of defining the difference between the film *Metropolis* and von Harbou's novelization or traces of her influence in the film. Lang's citations would undercut a sentimental reconciliation of a subject and the world, whereas von Harbou's novel would seek to reinsert a whole subject into a public sphere that coexists harmoniously with an ideal sphere.

9. Ibid., 99–104.

10. Ibid., 52–53.

11. Ibid., 56.

12. Töteberg refers to this merger as the "fraternization of capital and labor through a Führer-figure" (*Fritz Lang,* 61).

13. Lord Thurlow, an eighteenth-century English jurist and statesman, said, "Did

you ever expect a corporation to have a conscience, when it has no soul to be damned and no body to be kicked?"

14. Luc de Nanteuil, *David* (New York: Abrams, 1990), 74.

15. Jean Starobinski, *1789: The Emblems of Reason*, trans. Barbara Bray (Cambridge, Mass.: MIT Press, 1988), 110–11.

16. Julien Offray de La Mettrie, *Man a Machine* (La Salle, Ill.: Open Court, 1912), 129–32. All subsequent references to this work appear parenthetically in the text.

17. Huyssen, "The Vamp and the Machine," 225.

18. Coates reads these characters in terms of gender relations, arguing that *Metropolis* "both unmasks the paternal order and consolidates it" (*Gorgon's Gaze*, 52). While such a reading illuminates a central feature of the film, one can also read the sexual frenzy aroused by Maria's, Freder's, and the robot's rather free-floating desire for one another as a symptom of a different relation, which, like the worker's frenzy in the film, marks the anxiety in Weimar culture and in other industrial cultures that the economic productivity of the working class, intended to support a well-defined social order, is threatened by the reproductive productivity of that same class, a contribution that threatens to overturn the social or national order that "invited it in." Reproduction in this context refers neither to a biological difference, nor to an ideological or psychological construct, but to the consequences of biological reproduction that are economic: the reduction of the significance of humans not to a biological gender, but to simple numbers.

19. Töteberg (*Fritz Lang*, 51) cites a 1975 interview with Lang, Gene D. Philips, "Fritz Lang Remembers," *Focus on Film* 20 (1975): 43–51.

20. John Donne, "Goodfriday, 1613. Riding Westward," in *The Poems of John Donne*, ed. Herbert Grierson (London: Oxford University Press, 1933), 306.

21. Cf. Wolfgang Welsch, *Unsere postmoderne Moderne* (Weinheim: VCH, Acta Humaniora, 1988), 12.

22. Siegfried Kracauer, *Das Ornament der Masse* (Frankfurt am Main: Suhrkamp, 1977), 323.

23. Siegfried Gideon, *Mechanization Takes Command* (New York: Norton, 1969).

24. Walter Ruttmann, "Wie ich meinen 'Berlin'-Film drehte," *Lichtibildbühne*, October 8, 1927, 24. All subsequent citations of Ruttmann are from this source, this page.

25. Georg Simmel, *Philosophie des Geldes*, 5th ed. (Munich and Leipzig: Verlag von Duncker & Humblot, 1930), 500.

26. Kracauer, *From Caligari to Hitler*, 184–88.

27. Jeffrey Herf, *Reactionary Modernism: Technology, Culture, and Politics in Weimar and the Third Reich* (Cambridge: Cambridge University Press, 1984), 2.

28. In some ways, the identity posited by Ruttmann's work recalls that discussed

by R. N. Coudenhove-Kalergi in *Revolution durch Technik* (Leipzig and Vienna: Paneuropa-Verlag, 1932; first published as *Apologie der Technik*, 1922). For Coudenhove-Kalergi, who envisioned a pan-European state, technology would transform the earth into "a single Garden of Eden." Although he describes this return "by unceasing progress" to a "state of nature" that will exist "on a higher level," the steps necessary to bring about and, presumably, to maintain the transformation of the earth—"through streets and canals, irrigation and drainage, hygiene and engineering, central heating and cooling"—very much suggest an identity for the denizens of this realm predicated upon a carefully controlled flow of regulatory information (100–101).

29. Ulrich Ott, ed., *Literatur im Industriezeitalter,* Marbacher Katalog 42, no.2 (Marbach am Neckar: Deutsche Schillergesellschaft, 1987), 1008–9.

30. Simmel, *Philosophie des Geldes,* 500.

5

ANNE LEBLANS

Inventing Male Wombs:
The Fairy-Tale Logic of *Metropolis*

Certain early critics of Fritz Lang's *Metropolis* took issue with fairy-tale patterns in what they otherwise considered a realistic movie. The American critic Welford Beaton expressed the opinion of many when he wrote:

> I refuse to believe that a century hence workingmen will be slaves who live underground. If Pommer wished to produce a story laid in a mythical country, and showed me bullfrogs driving rabbits tandem, I would not quarrel with him, for it is his own mythical country and I must accept all that his brain peoples it with; but when he says, "That is what your descendants will be doing one or two hundred years hence," I refuse to follow him. . . .[1]

Beaton's stance (a filmmaker should either create a fairy-tale world or represent the world realistically) is understandable in light of the autonomy that fairy tales such as those of the Brothers Grimm exhibit vis-à-vis the real world. In their tales, the formulaic "Once upon a time" functions as a kind of gate that shuts out everyday reality and signals the entrance into another realm whose separation from the real world is absolute.

Already in the nineteenth century, however, there also existed another type of fairy tale in which the mother-witch, so typical of the Brothers Grimm, is replaced by a father-magician—think of Pate Droßelmeier in E. T. A. Hoffmann's *Nußknacker und Mausekönig* (*The Nutcracker*)—and nature by technology. This second type of tale, which could be called a "fairy tale of modern life," is saturated with the particularities of everyday existence in an industrial capitalist society. They can be integrated easily into the structure of fairy tales because, under capitalism, life itself gained fairy-tale characteristics. These came to the fore on special occasions such as Christmas and the world exhibitions, festive occasions that responded to social tensions and attempted to neutralize or resolve them in an imaginary way. Together with fairy tales these festivities provide us with an important context for understanding Lang's film. Although the fairy-tale patterns in *Metropolis* preclude a literal interpretation of the movie, they do not make it

95

unrealistic. On the contrary, it is their adherence to a fairy-tale logic that helped sensitize Lang and von Harbou to particular (under)currents of contemporary life. *Metropolis,* I would suggest, is a seismograph that with great accuracy registers concerns, conflicts, and developments of the mid-1920s. Lang's and von Harbou's adherence to fairy-tale logic also had a more problematic side, however, for it allowed them to address the challenges of modernity in terms of seemingly obsolete nineteenth-century paradigms.

In the first part of this essay, I will present aspects of fairy tales and festive life that provided Lang and von Harbou with a blueprint for *Metropolis.*

I

In *All That Is Solid Melts into Air,* Marshall Berman, who characterizes modernity as "a struggle to make ourselves at home in a constantly changing world,"[2] distinguishes between three different stages in the history of modernity. During the second stage, which roughly coincides with the nineteenth century, "a great modern public abruptly and dramatically [came] to life."[3] Although this public shared the excitement and exhilaration of living in a fast-paced, modern age, it "[could] remember what it [was] like to live, materially and spiritually, in worlds that [were] not modern at all."[4] For many members of the bourgeoisie, the memory of earlier views and practices (such as those reflected in the rapidly disappearing tales and festivities of the lower classes) became the raw material out of which new homes were produced.

During the first stage of modernity, when capitalism had already begun its ascent but when many were still unaffected by the new climate, folktales and carnivalesque festivities were among the residual pockets of a premodern mentality.[5] In the late eighteenth and early nineteenth century, however, they were transformed into fairy tales and bourgeois Christmas celebrations. Although both the collectors of fairy tales and the creators of Christmas celebrations tried to preserve traditions that were in danger of being eroded by modernity, their efforts carry signatures of modern life. In the fairy tales of the Brothers Grimm, for example, the structures of older traditions survive but undergo a transformation that leads to an inversion of many of their characteristics—an inversion in line with a capitalist economy. By transforming the premodern in the image of the modern, nineteenth-century folklorists wittingly or unwittingly contributed to the third stage of modernity, when—still following Berman—the process of modernization expanded to incorporate the entire world.

Both carnival and folktales were expressions of a gift economy.[6] The quintessential gift in such an economy, Lewis Hyde has argued, is food that would perish if not consumed.[7] In the agrarian communities of early modern Europe, carnivals were a time of celebratory excess in which the social hierarchy was turned upside down and those at the bottom of the social order were allowed to act above their station. The whole community participated in rituals of gift exchange that were initiated by the poor, who forced the rich to keep "open house."[8]

Capitalism, by contrast, is an exchange of commodities. Commodities, Hyde argues, are like bread made with chemicals to keep it from perishing.[9] During the same period in which collectors tried to preserve fairy tales for future generations, Christmas presents, at least in bourgeois households, became collector's items. The quintessential Christmas present in the nineteenth century was the kind of gift that the Stahlbaums in Hoffmann's *Nutcracker* put on the top shelf of their home museum, far out of the reach of the children for whose benefit it was created.

Although mothers seem to be a more formidable presence than fathers in most of the *Kinder- und Hausmärchen* (Children's and Household Tales), the Brothers Grimm had already contributed to the development of a "fairy-tale of modern life," in which the mother-witch is replaced by a father-inventor. "Hänsel und Gretel," for example, features a powerful mother-witch, but ends with the extermination of the witch and a transition to a father-dominated household. The mother-witch, who first feeds the children milk and pancakes but then tries to enlist Gretel's help in fattening up and cooking Hänsel, remains a monstrous threat to the children until they destroy her and rob her of her jewels. With these jewels, they return to the house of their father to lead a life from which all hardship is removed.

What is important in this context is that the transition from a mother- to a father-dominated household is accompanied by a transition from one economy to another, from an economy of gift giving (represented by the milk, the pancakes, and the gingerbread house) to one of accumulation (represented by the jewels). Burning the witch in the oven is part of an alchemical process that turns bread and milk into precious stones. The stones are preferable because they are less transitory. Hänsel and Gretel discover that they are not dependent on (mother) nature's whims if they take possession of her jewels. The jewels allow them to possess the mother without having to be afraid that they will be possessed by her.

The link between Christmas and fairy tales is made explicit in *The Nutcracker,* which Hoffmann wrote in the fall of 1816 for a Christmas anthology of fairy tales. In this work Hoffmann goes one step further than the Brothers Grimm. His story begins on Christmas Eve, when nature is brought into the home in the form of a Christmas tree. Laden with gold and silver apples and with "buds" and "blossoms" in the form of sugar-coated almonds and colorful candy, the Christmas tree has much in common with the gingerbread house. The edibles used to decorate the Christmas tree are there to be seen rather than to be eaten, however. Whereas in "Hänsel und Gretel" the children learn to replace the gifts of the living (edibles) with those of the dead mother (jewels), edibles function as jewels in Hoffmann's narrative. There is another important difference between the two tales. In "Hänsel und Gretel," the children rob the mother of her jewels; in *The Nutcracker,* on the other hand, the "jewels" are purchased with the money earned by a father-educator who tries to wean his children of their dependence on a mother-witch by showering them with gifts that are substitutes for those they once received from the mother.

Both the gingerbread house and the Christmas tree belong to the common stock of German Christmas decorations. Under the Christmas tree, the gingerbread house is often flanked by another building in miniature: the Christmas crib. These two dwellings represent two different stages in the bourgeois domestication of women. Whereas the gingerbread house is the domain of the mother-witch who threatens to devour children that feast on her body, the Christmas crib is inhabited by a virgin mother who dotes on the son that God the Father has given to her. In the course of the nineteenth century, the hierarchy within the bourgeois family was such that every bourgeois child was to a certain extent a Christ-child, born to a virgin mother, her sexuality strictly confined to the master bedroom, and a Godlike father. The bourgeois Christmas celebration communicated two seemingly conflicting messages. On the one hand, it marked the birth of a child and thus the mother's capacity to bestow the gift of life. On the other hand, it emphasized the superiority of the Father/God over the mother, who was only human. The virgin/mother would not have given birth to this special child if she were not Jehovah's bride elect. It is not surprising that in Thomas Mann's first novel, Hanno Buddenbrook needs to recite the "Our Father" before receiving his Christmas gifts. It is equally unsurprising that the bearer of gifts—the symbol of abundant and gratuitous giving—became in much of middle and northern Germany the *Weihnachtsmann*, a decidedly male figure. Of greatest importance here is that the celebration of the father is grafted onto a celebration of the mother and that, as a consequence, things that are purchased with money are presented as if they belonged to the realm of the gifts offered by the mother: life itself, nurturance, care (things that remained more or less outside of the market). Christmas thus represented an attempt by the father to assert his power over the domestic sphere by suggesting that the domain of the mother—including her capacity to give birth—was really his.[10] This might explain why the figure of the male gift-giver often adopts features of the mother. Especially in America, Santa Claus is often depicted as a man with an enormous belly—a belly comparable in size to that of a woman in the advanced stages of pregnancy. Rather than being pregnant with child, however, he is pregnant with merchandise.

That children become the main recipients of Christmas presents might suggest that, like the carnival for Bakhtin, Christmas is a celebration of the young. Bourgeois children pay a high price for their elevated status, however. Insofar as the Stahlbaums satisfy their childrens' longing for nature and for mother nature with a Christmas tree—with a substitute, in other words—there is an element of deception in their generosity. One can argue that they seemingly give to their children what they actually deprive them of. Given the changed social climate of the nineteenth century, it is not surprising that the king in *The Nutcracker* refuses to share and that mice—parasites—occupy the position of the poor. Given that children take over the role of the poor as the prime recipients of Christmas gift-giving, it is equally unsurprising that they, too, are in danger of becoming associated with mice. Whereas Hänsel and Gretel acted like mice when they nibbled at the sweets from which the gingerbread house was made, Fritz and Marie have already learned to delay oral gratification. Marie, especially, has perfected the art of transforming oral into visual pleasure to such an extent that she does not even seem tempted as she travels through candyland. It is not by accident, however, that it is on Christmas Eve, the night of gift-giving, that the mice invade the Stahlbaums' residence. For as long as children receive the benefits of their parents' wealth without contributing to the family's economic survival, latent similarities between mice and children will continue to assert themselves.

The fact that bourgeois children are assigned the role of parasites by their elders might drive feelings of parental resentment underground but does not necessarily make them disappear. Although Marie helps the Nutcracker destroy the mice, she suffers a fate that resembles theirs. Not by accident, the Nutcracker's kingdom is an artificial world created by the same father-magician who fabricates mousetraps. *The Nutcracker* is a variation on the story of the Pied Piper of Hamelin. Droßelmeier's present—the music box in the form of a castle—functions as a mousetrap for children. Marie begins to enter it when the mechanic starts to play the music of his story. By the end of the tale, she is trapped in a golden cage—the land of eternal childhood. The pampered bourgeois child is a child who is not allowed to grow up. (S)he is simultaneously the family's redeemer and a sacrificial lamb.

The logic at the heart of the bourgeois Christmas celebrations also fueled the world exhibitions. Like Christmas, they were simultaneously an interruption and a festive intensification of normal life under capitalism. Like Christmas, they were a celebration of male birth. One of the hallmarks of the world fair of 1900 in Paris, for example, was an enormous globe that symbolized the universe. This globe, hollow on the inside, enveloped a second globe which represented the Milky Way. A third globe—minuscule in size compared with the two others—occupied the center of the second globe and represented the earth. To be sure, the earth was tiny. But what did this matter, as long as it was nestled securely at the inside of a gigantic man-made universe, a kind of technological womb, which could be viewed from the inside and the outside by visitors of the exhibition?

II

In "Weihnachtlicher Budenzauber" (The Magic of the Christmas Market, 1932), Siegfried Kracauer suggests that during the Christmas season little demons, whose exuberance has been suppressed all year long, are released to celebrate their saturnalia.[11] Although the nineteenth-century bourgeoisie transformed carnival, it did not eradicate it. The spirit of the older tradition survived below the surface of many Christmas rituals and contributed to ideological tensions at the heart of Christmas. On the one hand, Christmas, as a celebration of the Father, helped preserve the status quo. At the same time, however, it interrupted normal life and, by reminding people of the ideal of social justice, it could—under the pressure of historical circumstances—increase social tensions and evoke associations with revolution. In America, during the second half of the nineteenth century, the month between Thanksgiving and Christmas became a time for "ragamuffin parades":

> those parades had been popular from at least the midnineteenth century— especially in New York City, where they brought both children and adults dressed in homemade colorful costumes, blowing horns and carrying bells and banners, into the Streets. As the Novelist Dean Howells wrote in 1907 of the New York tradition, "the poor recognize [Thanksgiving] as a sort of carnival. They go about in masquerade on the eastern avenues, and the children of the foreign races who populate the quarter penetrate the better streets, blowing horns, and begging of the passers.[12]

In Germany, too, the children of the poor penetrated the quarters of the rich. In *Berliner Kindheit,* Walter Benjamin writes: "Along with these [toys, nuts, straw, and tree decorations] something else poured forth: poverty. Just as apples and nuts and a bit of glitter could appear on the Christmas plates next to the marzipan, so too the poor people with lametta and bright candles in the better quarters of the city."[13] Paradoxically, Christmas provided many protected bourgeois children with one of their first glimpses of social inequality. Although the Christmas markets, which shot up like mushrooms throughout Berlin during the Christmas season, were magic spaces—worlds set apart—they also mirrored the real world. "Christmas came, and all at once, before the eyes of the bourgeois child, it divided his city into those who shuffled [with their parents] past the booths on Potsdam Square and those, who alone, indoors, offered their dolls and farm animals for sale to children of their age."[14]

In *Berliner Chronik,* the victory in the conflict between the two forces at work during the Christmas season goes to the status quo. For the very fairy-tale atmosphere of Christmas prevents the child from interpreting what he sees in the cold light of class differences. Rather than a symptom of social inequality, the gap between rich and poor strikes him as an artifice of the same order as, for example, the paper figures that make up the Christmas cribs. The visit to the Christmas market works as a kind of inoculation that provides the Christ-child with a small dose of social reality—a dose small enough to preserve his ignorance—and protects him against more serious attacks on his immune system. During each Christmas season, a conflict is re-enacted which allows the Father to establish his power all the more effectively.[15]

Benjamin grew up around the turn of the century. One would expect the carnivalesque to have a much better chance of gaining the upper hand during a period of accelerated change and political frenzy such as the Weimar Republic. The Weimar years, after all, correspond with the period in Russian history that inspired Bakhtin's study on carnival. During these years, normal life and festive exuberance began to permeate each other in unprecedented ways, creating a climate in which many of the nineteenth-century strategies for warding off threats seemed obsolete. Why would one turn the family into a vessel of wealth when economic crises such as rampant inflation could empty the vessel in only a fraction of the time needed to fill it? Cultural capital, too, seemed an unstable currency during this golden age of mass culture and cultural leveling. And what about the ideals of interiorization and domestication during a time when growing numbers of bourgeois women joined the workforce, and gangs of children, destitute and fatherless in the aftermath of World War I, roamed the city and continued, in their own way, the war on the streets? In the aftermath of World War I, once carefully cultivated oppositions between private and public, inside and outside, collapsed and the whole world seemed to be turned topsy-turvy.

This crisis produced what I would like to call "a fear of reversed imperialism"—a fear of being swept away by things one had previously managed to contain. How this fear manifested itself can be gleaned from comparing the optimistic image of the gigantic globe proudly displayed at the Parisian world fair with an image conjured up by Siegfried Kracauer in an essay, "Langeweile" (Boredom), published in 1924 and devoted to the effects of radio, film, and advertising on the modern city dweller. The radio-listener, Kracauer argues, is pregnant with what he receives from the magic box. Rather than enclosing the embryo, however, he is taken into possession and consumed by it: "While one endures such an antenna-destiny, the five continents draw nearer and nearer. In reality, it is not we who embrace them. On the contrary; their cultures—in a kind of limitless imperialism—take possession of us. . . ."[16] His image takes the following twist: "A tiny globe, coming from very far away, rolls toward you; it grows into a close-up and, finally, roars over you; you cannot escape it, you are lying there, tied up, a little powerless doll that is swept away by a gigantic force and dissolves in its radius."[17]

There is another side to Weimar, however. Weimar's entertainment industry provides us with examples of the kind of defenses that a social immune system under attack can muster. In many ways, Weimar was a golden age for the creation of technological wombs. Among the many examples of attempts to construct male wombs in which to recreate and transform the world were the so-called pleasure palaces. One of these was the "Haus Gourmenia." A brochure celebrating its opening in 1929 heaps lavish praise on Gourmenia's most distinctive feature, its roof garden.[18] The roof garden is more than an urban nature substitute, it is also a contained area, a hermetically closed environment in which nature is transformed into a more perfect version of its former self. Even in one's own backyard, one runs the risk of being surprised by rain or a thunderstorm. On Gourmenia's roof, however, one has nothing to fear. Gourmenia has "outwitted nature."[19] With great pride, the author of the brochure exclaims: "One is capable of producing one's own weather."[20]

Also important for understanding *Metropolis* are those sites of entertainment, such as amusement parks, where people could learn how to confront the new threats of urban life. In Berlin, the *Lunapark,* situated at the western end of the Kurfürstendamm, became enormously popular during the 1920s. Both its orientally stylized main building and its displays of people, mostly Africans from the former colonies, were reminiscent of the world exhibitions. The Lunapark was also a gigantic laboratory, however, where new technological inventions, such as radio, were tested and introduced to an enthusiastic public. Much to the puzzlement of some observers, people would visit the Lunapark to be thrown around and get dizzy. "Various entertainment devices seem to be invented and created only to make one sick," Fedor von Zobelitz complained in 1910 after a visit to the Lunapark. "One suffers from artificially induced seasickness, dizziness, lack of blood in the brain, hallucinations, itching in arms and legs, and a presentiment of insanity . . . ."[21] During the 1920s, it might be suggested, one did not need to go to the Lunapark to get dizzy. Experiencing the real-life events of those years must have been enough to give people the impression that, at least in a figurative way, they were riding a roller coaster. Yet this might be precisely the reason why they flocked to the Lunapark. By voluntarily submitting themselves to the crazy pace of a topsy-turvy world, visitors could regain a sense of control.

One of the major attractions of the Lunapark, which was modeled after Coney Island, was a cable railway which moved past a painted cityscape of New York. Americanization and cultural leveling became synonymous for some critics. The Lunapark was, according to Hans Kafka in a feuilleton in 1928, a place where one could watch philosophy professors ride the merry-go-round; a place where the elaborate and rigid principles of German high culture were toppled and its representatives—much like Professor Rath in *The Blue Angel*—made fools of themselves by succumbing to the lures of American mass culture.[22] It is not without significance that Kafka casts himself in the role of onlooker rather than participant. He enjoys the pleasures of the merry-go-round vicariously through identification/disidentification with fictitious philosophy professors.

Kafka's ambivalence is characteristic of Weimar's ambivalence toward America. On the one hand, one is fascinated by American mass culture. At the same time, one fears being swept away by foreign influences, and tries to uphold superior German standards. The fear of Americanization is one of the most common manifestations of the fear of "reversed imperialism," which, as I have pointed out, is a fear of being overwhelmed by something previously contained. Applied to Americanization, this would turn American popular culture into a genie that had escaped from a German bottle. We might be too attuned nowadays to notions of American cultural imperialism to appreciate the grain of historical truth in this image. Yet, part of what reached Germany from America in the 1920s was a transformation of what had been exported from Germany to America only a few decades earlier. In his well-documented book, *Land of Desire,* William Leach argues convincingly that German immigrants contributed more to the creation of American mass culture than immigrants of any other nationality. A point in case is Tony Sarg, a famous German-born puppeteer who had grown up with "a passion for objects in miniature—toys, small dolls, and many boats."[23] In 1924, he fabricated grotesquely enlarged versions of these miniatures for Macy's Christmas parade. Thanks to the give-and-take between Germany and America in the realm of popular culture, it is not surprising that the Lunapark was perceived by some as a piece of Americana in the middle of Berlin and by others as so typical of Berlin that foreigners would not understand its appeal. During the 1920s, America functioned as a mirror in which many Germans saw an image of their own country—an image grotesquely distorted, but an image nevertheless. Kracauer, with his sixth sense for cultural ironies, called the painted cityscape of New York at the Lunapark "ein überberlinishes New York." Dialogues with America were often attempts at putting the genie back in the bottle—at regaining balance and control over something that had run out of hand.

In 1924 the Lunapark became the setting for a movie by Jaap Speyer.[24] This movie, *Die Puppe vom Lunapark,* deserves some attention here, because, like *Metropolis,* it centers on a father-son conflict, but it links this conflict to aspects of contemporary life (amusement parks, the dialogue between Germany and America) that appear only in a much more allegorized form in Lang's movie. The father in Speyer's film was an American millionaire, a first-generation immigrant from Germany, who had made his millions by selling pianos—by capitalizing on a symbol of German high culture, in other words. According to one reviewer, this father sent his late-adolescent son to Europe to wean him from his addiction to radio (by reducing music lovers to passive listeners, radio reduces the need for pianos). According to another reviewer, however—and this is interesting because it shows how easily the characteristics usually attributed to Germany and America can be reversed—the father wanted to distract his son, a too serious student of philosophy, from his intellectual pursuits, to awaken in him a flair for business and an interest in the more practical aspects of life. The journey itself provides the son with the opportunities for social mingling that reminded us of the carnivalesque origins of Christmas when we encountered them in descriptions of bourgeois Christmas celebrations. During his time on board the ship, he crosses class boundaries to explore the world of those at whose expense millionaires like his father make their fortune. Under a false name, he becomes a stoker and further subverts his father's wishes by using his travel money to become an anonymous benefactor to people in need. The female protagonist he meets upon his arrival in Germany also crosses class boundaries, but, predictably, in the opposite direction. She is a poor girl from Berlin-Ost who plays piano every night on the Vox recording station. After the protagonists fall in love, the girl is fired from the radio station and forced to accept a rather dubious position as barmaid at the Lunapark. (A surviving photograph of the female protagonist as barmaid shows striking similarities with shots of the "false" Maria in *Metropolis*). When her boyfriend discovers her at the Lunapark, he decides to drop her, though they reconcile later. Significantly, their reconciliation is inaugurated by another one, that between father and son. It turns out that the female protagonist is the daughter of a woman the father once loved. At the end of the movie, the balance between America and Germany, father and son, is firmly reestablished. The ride on the roller coaster is over, so to speak.

III

Although Bakhtin optimistically associates carnival with renewal and the possibility of historical change, even he emphasizes that carnival gives only temporary license to the underdog. It should not surprise us that in Weimar Germany, the very sites of carnivalesque reversal, such as the Lunapark, also provided revelers with the means to regain control. What makes the attempts at regaining one's balance problematic, however, is that they also involve submission or resubmission to the kind of authoritarian father figure whose fantasies are familiar from the Christmas rituals discussed earlier. Ultimately, the reconciliation between father and son in *Die Puppe vom Lunapark*—a reconciliation that foreshadows the reconciliatory ending of *Metropolis*—serves the interests of the father rather than those of the son. With only slight exaggeration, one can argue that the father and his old sweetheart marry each other by proxy of their children. The wedding, which turns a potentially "bad" Maria ("bad" through her dubious position as barmaid) back into a "good" Maria, restores the world according to the father's wishes. When the young woman remarks that she could go back to the radio, he responds: "To the competition? Then I would rather have you as a daughter-in-law."

If nineteenth-century narrative patterns keep reasserting themselves in some of the most modern products of Weimar's entertainment industry, this might have something to do with the way that memories of World War I cast dark shadows on postwar exuberance. During long months in the trenches, soldiers had experienced the body's vulnerability to fragmentation, mutilation, and dismemberment. These experiences reactivated the fear of women and nature to which the creation of male wombs had been a response in the first place. In *Lustmord: Sexual Murder in Weimar Germany*, Maria Tatar (who comes to this topic after two books on fairy tales) points out that many literary and artistic representations of the war are charged with an incredible erotic energy.[25] In a truly carnivalesque fashion, the earth is depicted as a maternal body—as a "site of regeneration but, more importantly, despite the womb-like protection it offers the soldiers, the locus of an explosive, violent death."[26] The earth becomes a cosmic, cannibalistic mother who slaughters and devours her children.

After the war, the dangers represented by "Mother Earth" were transferred to the city. Unlike the battlefield, however, the city was a woman on whom one could take revenge. Symptomatic of male defensiveness, Tatar argues, are the countless representations of butchered women in Weimar art. In their imagination, male artists inflicted on the female body the same kind of horrors that had been inflicted on their own bodies in the trenches. "[T]hose who commit murder on canvases, pages or screens," Tatar argues, "are . . . competing with the reproductive powers of women or aiming to transcend the laws of biological procreation affiliated with women's bodies."[27]

Womb-envy is a very important motive in *Metropolis*. The city in Lang's movie was built to simultaneously erase and preserve the memory of a dead woman. In the original, longer version of the movie, when the Master of Metropolis visited Rotwang in his cottage, the magician abruptly unveiled the statue of a woman he had once passionately loved. This woman, Hel, had betrayed him by becoming the beloved of Fredersen and the mother of Freder, whose birth she had not survived. Although Fredersen urges Rotwang to forget the past, he, too, has created an artifice to replace Hel and, with her, the natural world. It is because Metropolis is a substitute for Hel that it resembles the inside of a body in distress. Situated in the womb of the earth, it is a place of both gestation and death. The association with pregnancy and delivery helps explain why so much physical labor is required of the workers. As many of Lang's contemporaries pointed out, this hard physical labor bore no resemblance to what was actually required in completely mechanized factories, where work was boring and monotonous, but not physically exerting. The workers' labor resembles that of a woman in "labor"; it taxes their organisms to the extreme and leaves them utterly exhausted. All traces of distress and violence are removed, however, from the Eternal Gardens, a gift from the Masters of Metropolis to their sons. As a prime example of a male womb, the garden evokes a double set of associations. Traditionally considered a feminine space, it is an enclosed area. In the Western tradition, however, it also evokes associations with the Garden of Eden, which God the Father created for his children.

Although the Eternal Gardens remind us of Gourmenia's roof garden, Lang's enthusiasm for the alchemical dream is much less naive than that expressed in the Gourmenia brochure. No matter how hard the father-inventor tries, he never manages to create a perfectly safe and peaceful environment. What remains after nature is mastered by technology are wars, economic crises, and technological accidents. The workers of Metropolis are victimized by accidents with the same predictable regularity with which premodern society was plagued by natural catastrophes. Although Fredersen considers these accidents unavoidable, they present a challenge, even to him, for they can explode the male womb from within. Fredersen's response to the challenge is revealing: "I will send the robot to the workers to sow discord among them," he tells Rotwang. With Rotwang's help, he orchestrates a rebellion that results in a catastrophe caused by the workers but provoked by the Master. Motivated by his wish to replace workers by robots,

Metropolis (1925/26), directed by Fritz Lang.

Fredersen's actions show us the father-inventor's desire to recreate the world through technology at its most extreme. Why not protect oneself against the arbitrariness of technological disasters by provoking them, Fredersen seems to think. Like the womb-envy, this almost insane logic suggests that *Metropolis,* like many other Weimar movies, processes memories of World War I. Ernst Bloch has pointed out that modern warfare is, among other things, a conscious attempt to create technological disasters at the expense of others. Given the association with war, it is not surprising that the workers' children are the primary victims of the violence unleashed by their parents. If they had not been saved by Freder and Maria, they would have been engulfed by water, just as millions of young soldiers were swallowed by the exploding earth on the battlefields. The catastrophe is averted at the last moment. By the mid-1920s, Germany was trying to recover from the enormous bloodletting it had undergone ten years earlier. In this new climate, children became a precious possession; one hoped that they would make up for the losses one had suffered.

Since Freder helps avert the catastrophe, one could get the impression that he redeems the world created by his father. In reality, however, he delivers both the children and their parents back into the hands of the Master. His position in the plot shows again that there is something destructive about the father-inventor's alchemical dream. Linked to the father's ambitions is Freder's ultimate inability to risk being dismissed by his father—to try to replace his father as the Master of Metropolis. There is, thus, an important difference between male and female wombs. The female womb is a temporary home from which the child is expelled at the moment of birth to begin an independent existence, to a certain extent at the expense of the mother. The male womb is there to stay. I would like to argue that the adjective "eternal" applies to the father/son relationship, as well as to the space. Whereas Hel died while giving birth to Freder, Fredersen wants to be an eternal king. In a reversal of roles, he consumes the lives of others (the workers) rather than letting himself be consumed, and, in a sense, sacrifices his son. The Eternal Gardens are a world in which time stands still. Although their splendor is supposed to show how much the masters love their children, it also prevents the sons from seeing what their fathers withhold from them. Condemned to a sheltered life in an enclosed space, the young men of Metropolis are not allowed to know what their fathers need to know in order to remain masters of Metropolis. Like Marie in *The Nutcracker,* they are supposed to remain eternal children.

Should it surprise us that Freder's position resembles that of the mother in the traditional bourgeois household? Like the wife-mother, Freder is the father's Other. Whereas the father represents planning and rationality, Freder is all heart and impulse. He is, at best, a passive-reactive rebel who complements the father instead of becoming a person in his own right. He is the recipient of a world created by his father but is himself no creator. Like the wife-mother in the bourgeois household, he is the one who mediates between the father and his children (the workers). It is very much in line with Freder's passivity that his desire to see the netherworld of Metropolis is a response to the fact that he is seen by Maria's and the workers' children. His eyes are made to light up. In this episode, the actively radiating, penetrating eyes belong to Maria. The eyes that passively drink up the light (the "feminized" eyes, we could say) belong to Freder.

In all fairy tales, there is an event that brings the initial situation of (apparent) bliss and family harmony to an end. In *Metropolis,* Maria's and the children's entrance into the garden is the event that confronts Freder with the dark, uncanny side of existence and triggers a quest that will eventually lead to a "happy" ending. His first confrontation with social inequality is abrupt. Maria and the children penetrate the Eternal Gardens in very much the same way in which, according to Benjamin, the poor spilled into the quarters of the rich during the holiday season. Freder's reaction resembles that of the bourgeois child. One doubts whether he really leaves home. Like the traditional fairy-tale hero, he ends up in a kind of wilderness, the subterranean world of Metropolis. But this wilderness, although it is reminiscent of the forest, is no forest. Since it is still a world marked by the father, it is not a place where Freder will learn that he can stand on his own feet.

By following Maria, Freder seems to break a taboo. However, although Maria

Metropolis (1925/26), directed by Fritz Lang.

belongs to the working class, she remains a woman created in the image of the father, functioning as an idealized version of Hel. Whereas Hel was promiscuous, Maria evokes associations with the Virgin Mary, the mother of Christ, who made up for Eve's sexual curiosity by putting herself completely at the disposal of God the Father. She serves the status quo by preaching patience and reconciliation. By following Maria, Freder only seems to leave the realm of the father. Since there are no exits from the male womb, Freder undertakes a kind of mock journey—a motionless voyage. As the inhabitant of a completely colonized world, he has no choice but to remain dependent on the colonizer. Not without reason, the audience receives the impression that the conflict between father and workers is a setup. It is as if the father sows discord among the workers to remind them of a past conflict and to subscribe, once again, to the way it was solved.

At the end of the movie the true nature of the relationship between masters and workers is once again covered up. Like the nuts and apples on Benjamin's Christmas table, it is coated with gold paper—the gold paper of sentimentalism. The glitter of the so-called reconciliation between head and hands through the heart does not transform the relationship between masters and workers, but makes it acceptable to those who seek refuge in a fuzzy world of make-believe. A new family—the extended corporate family—is founded. By accepting the workers within the family, the Master of Metropolis blinds them to what he withholds from them, making protest almost impossible. Since they are the children of a benevolent father by whom they cannot afford to be dismissed, they have to be grateful. In the same way in which the Master of Metropolis had once colonized the workers' bodies, he now colonizes their minds.

IV

Although one might be tempted to dismiss the ending of *Metropolis* as escapist, one has to admit that Lang and von Harbou have a finger on the pulse of their times. The ending of *Metropolis* reflects the centralizing tendencies at work during the mid-1920s in both America and Germany. One of the major sites of centralization was the department store. In America, it was through the department stores that the carnivalesque aspects of Christmas were appropriated and turned into the glue that keeps the corporate family together. By the mid-1920s, the "ragamuffin parades," which had enjoyed such popularity around the turn of the century," were fully appropriated by the owners of department stores such as Macy's:

> They kept the carnival aspect of the older ragamuffin tradition but took complete managerial control over who or what marched, thereby preventing the parade from becoming spontaneous or democratic. To be sure, the store's immigrant employees marched in the parade, and in the first year, many of them appeared to have worn the colorful costumes they might have used in a ragamuffin parade; but despite the claims by today's Macy management, the idea of the parade did not come from employees but from store executives, as the "minutes" to executive council meetings in 1924 make clear.[28]

These minutes of 1924 make no mention whatsoever of employees. The fact that Macy's paid its workers to march in the parade undoubtedly undercut the basis for voluntary participation on their part. The most impressive sight in the parade, which consisted mainly of standardized carnivalesque figures based on the same few fairy-tale and cartoon characters, was, not by accident, Santa Claus, "sitting on a 'huge pile of ice,' snapping his whip at his 'deer' in the direction of Macy's."[29] By the late 1920s, the cult of Santa Claus had reached almost absurd proportions.

It is in the department store owner, in fact, that we might find a real-life model for Fredersen, the Master of Metropolis. In 1928, Dwight Macdonald, a recent graduate of Yale who would later become a critic of American mass culture, described his initial contact with department store owners as follows: "The slight glimpse I had of the business machine in my contacts with the men I talked to, at first terrified me, depressed me, and yet, fascinated me. These men were so cold, so keen, so absolutely sure of themselves, and so utterly wrapped up in business that I felt like a child before them."[30] This is exactly the reaction Freder has when confronted with his father. In Thea von Harbou's novel, we read: "Whenever he entered his room he [Freder] was once more a boy of ten years old, his chief characteristic uncertainty before the great, concentrated, almighty certainty, which was called John Fredersen, and was his father."[31] Despite obvious differences, there are also striking similarities between the underground city of Metropolis and a department store. In the eyes of contemporaries, department stores "swallow" people. The following description by Leo Colze (1907) anticipates the scene in *Metropolis* in which the Pater Noster Machine becomes a gaping maw with a row of teeth at the bottom and a flight of stairs leading up to it: "Once I have seen a caricature of the modern department store as a ventilator in whose wide-open mouth young and old, men and women disappeared, which sucked up everyone."[32]

In the 1920s, department stores were considered miracles of modernity. Department store owner John Wanamaker maintained that people visited his store in Philadelphia to get "an education in what was new."[33] He himself conducted tours of the labyrinth basements of his stores where, deep below the surface of the earth, the machines were located. The capacities of these machines, which provided gigantic buildings with light and heat, were enormous. Since the machine rooms were located deep in the earth, controlling groundwater remained a major challenge, reminding one of the deluge in *Metropolis*.[34] Like amusement parks, department stores were places of leveling; everything that was once considered sacred—religion, art, history—was for sale. "[W]hen a preacher asked John Wana-maker in 1901 if he thought 'modern commercialism' had a negative 'influence on church life,' Wanamaker answered that he didn't think anything negative had occurred. In fact, he said, 'the last twenty years have been very favorable to religious life.' "[35] In his own way, Wanamaker was right. The first department store owners in America showed a remarkable interest in religion. Wanamaker himself became a successful preacher, and "[b]y 1989 he was lecturing to nearly two thousand people at his Sunday bible classes."[36] By the end of the nineteenth century, department stores and churches had begun to look alike. "Wanamaker's Bethany Presbyterian church . . . was as multifaceted as his department stores. As early as the 1800s an orchestra played at worship services; the stained-glass windows in the church mirrored the stained-glass windows in the stores; ushers acted with the same spirit of service as did Wanamaker's salespeople."[37] Given the resemblance between churches and department stores, it is not surprising that churches, too, began to expand the power of the father (in this case, the preacher) at the expense of the children (the congregation). " 'Gradually,' historian Herbert Schneider has written, 'such churches encouraged religious passivity, with people coming to church service much as they would attend a concert or theater.' " Church services became professional performances meant to showcase the power of the minister.

It is clear that commercialism did not simply leave religion (or art, or history) alone; it sucked it into its orbit and transformed it into something compatible with the new spirit of capitalism. This process contributed enormously to the creation of a world marked by the eternal repetition of the same. For in the process of appropriation and transformation, cultural symbols lost their uniqueness and became interchangeable. Granted, the process of leveling might have met with more resistance in Germany than in America. Many educated Germans were far too proud of their cultural achievements to let them be transformed into mass culture. Lang himself demonstrated some ambivalence toward Americanization. Although *Metropolis* was inspired by a visit to New York, he continued to feel the need to assert German cultural superiority, as the following quote from an essay written while he was working on *Metropolis* shows: "Germany has never had, and never will have, the gigantic human and financial reserves of the American film industry at its disposal. To its good fortune. For exactly that forces us to compensate a purely material imbalance through an intellectual superiority. . . ."[38] Lang, one could argue, needs to insist on hierarchies, for much of the plot of *Metropolis* hinges on the distinction between a "good" Maria—a woman whose physical appearance reflects her inner beauty, whose motives are pure, and who is not for sale—and her "bad" counterpart. Wittingly or unwittingly, however, Lang contributes to the process of leveling. It is ironic that he tries to distinguish between a "good" and a "bad" Maria in film, a medium that calls the possibility of such distinctions into question. Film, after all, is nothing more than a series of images. Insofar as the "good" Maria is an image on the screen, she is always already "false"—an artifice whose features resemble those of a real person, Brigitte Helms, but who is herself mere surface. In the world created by the father-inventors of the 1920s, everything is brought back to a common denominator. The good Maria conjures up associations with the Virgin Mary, but this image is as inflated as any other. In a world in which churches resemble department stores and the public goes to church to see a show, the Virgin Maria adopts the features of a movie star and the distinction between the two becomes a mere artifice. Artifices can be powerful, however.

V

One of the ways in which Weimar's entertainment industry helped control the new dangers of modernity was by strategies of miniaturization and enlargement. Both of these strategies were at work during the Christmas season. The toys sold at the Christmas markets during the 1920s carried the signature of their times. They were miniaturized versions of the merry-go-rounds, Ferris wheels, swings, and roller and mountain coasters that enjoyed such great popularity at the Lunapark. These miniatures allowed people to regain control without even having to become dizzy:

Entrusting one's life to an aerial swing might not be everyone's cup of tea. However, when the swing sits on a trolley, which only needs to be pulled to turn around, even the grateful little figures who have to fly through the air manage to keep their senses together. The ride to a mountain top, whose dizzying height is surpassed by that of a finger, and a horse-race which can be run on the palm of one's hand are equally harmless.[39]

The earth itself became a toy that one could hold in one's hand and manipulate.[40]

Enlargement, by contrast, was at work in Tony Sarg's gigantic inflatable toys which were carried around during Macy's Christmas parades:

In November 1924 the parade took on, to some extent, the character of what we think of today when we think of the Macy's parade. Sarg's giant grotesque "animals and humans" first appeared in 1927, although they were not yet helium-inflated and thus did not float lumberingly over the paradeline. Four hundred Macy's employees led the way, each wearing one of "the unusually large masks" designed by Sarg. Behind them marched a sixty-foot "smoke-breathing dinosaur" attended by several "pre-historic cave-men." A twenty-five foot dachshund went by, so did a giant float depicting Robinson Crusoe's desert island, preceded by "a forest of walking trees." Heading a "Funny Face Brigade" was a "Human Behemoth" twenty-one feet tall.[41]

Strategies of miniaturization and enlargement were also used to master the threat represented by children. In some respects, children are like miniatures. In untamed masses, however, they form a gigantic force. Whereas a single child can be cute, a gathering of children is always something riotous and chaotic, as Elke Liebs argues in her study of the Pied Piper theme.[42] Not surprisingly, the children in *Metropolis* are treated with the same kind of ambivalence as they are in, for example, *The Nutcracker.* When we first see them, they burst forward into the Eternal Gardens. Although the threat is minimalized (the crowd is kept in check by Maria) and later transferred to the deluge, this very displacement of the danger shows why children are feared. Like the water, they form an elemental force that could destroy the city of Metropolis if not contained. Centralization provided the father-inventor with new means to neutralize this threat. In America, department store owners tried to gain control over children by regulating their patterns of consumption. By the mid-1920s, Macy's toy department had become the largest section of the entire store. The management hired a veritable army of pediatricians, child psychologists, educators, economists, and entertainers to study the needs of children—ultimately, to turn them into more willing recipients of their father's world.

The oversized toys used in Macy's Christmas parades were a sign that chaos could be turned into order, and that gigantic masses could be controlled and organized by gigantic institutions such as department stores. They invited adults to join the world of the (domesticated) child, for they were toys for grown-ups. In 1915, at the Panama Pacific International Exposition, Frederic Thompson called his display of toys "Toyland Grownup."[43] The ideal customer was an eternal child who accepted residence in a fairy-kingdom for adults. Like the child in *Berliner Chronik,* this customer would interpret social reality as if it were made of the same fabric as the displays at the department stores.

Metropolis is a studio-film produced in Neubabelsberg. Like the Christmas market, Neubabelsberg, situated in the no-man's-land between the metropolis of Berlin and the small town of Potsdam, was a kind of magic space—a world set apart. The studio was a gigantic toy shop, filled with the miniaturized versions of buildings and landscapes that would become enormous on the screen.[44] Most early spectators of *Metropolis*—even those who disliked the movie—were duly impressed by its monumentalism. This monumentalism did not stand by itself, however. A film like *Metropolis* was produced in a laboratory in which reality was first miniaturized, then enlarged. This meant that dangers produced on the screen were always already dangers of a second order. After threats had been mastered by miniaturization, they were reproduced by a series of tricks. This shows again that miniaturization represented an attempt to master overwhelming forces. In *The American Replacement of Nature,* William Irwin Thompson expresses a very similar idea when he writes, with regard to amusement parks: "The central experience of a ride in a theme park is empowerment of the body through surrender to the vehicle, and empowerment of consciousness through the distancing of evil. . . . [T]he experience is one in which evil is distanced, miniaturized, and made light of."[45] The evil that is distanced in *Metropolis* is the catastrophe which would have cost the lives of the children and which, in 1927, must have conjured up memories of World War I. The redemption of the children gains an important additional dimension when we look at the way *Metropolis* was produced. In the studio, the 750 children who acted in the movie experienced the complete opposite of what they experienced on the screen (and, possibly, at home). Granted, they had to jump into rather frigid water. But in return for their efforts they were offered a magic wonderland. In her recollection of *Metropolis,* Thea von Harbou describes with great enthusiasm how some of the poorest children of Berlin were pampered at Neubabelsberg. Those children would spend entire days in the studio. Not only were they fed four meals a day, one consisting of cake and hot chocolate, they were also provided with plenty of toys and had gigantic playgrounds at their disposal.[46]

If this is the function of *Metropolis*—to divert potentially dangerous energies that only ten years earlier had found an outlet in war—how successful was the movie as a lightning rod? Before answering this question, let us return for a moment to the tradition of the fairy tale and the place of *Metropolis* within this tradition. "In a frightful ride, you may scream in the delight of a safe terror,"[47] Thompson writes. The delight of a safe terror—this is a sensation with which the nineteenth-century bourgeois child was already thoroughly familiar. By identifying with a fairy-tale hero, he or she could undertake a dangerous journey into the forest without having to leave the safety of his or her parental dwelling—a journey that distanced evil and made light of the danger of regression. Both the amusement park and the movie theater take over an important function of the bourgeois home. This might seem surprising at first, for unlike the bourgeois home—a private space par excellence—they are public sites. Yet amusement parks and movie theaters are a very special kind of public space. Like pleasure gardens and department stores, they are exteriorized interiors—wombs in which visitors remain engulfed for the duration of their stay. Whereas the *Kinder- und Hausmärchen* entered the bourgeois home at a time when the bourgeoisie was trying to solidify the split between private and public space, amusement parks, movie theaters, and department stores signal the collapse of the opposition between private and public, inside and outside. It is difficult to tell, however, whether this collapse means the end of the bourgeois cult of privacy or whether the private realm is extended beyond its previous confines. In *Metropolis,* which depicts a world marked by the differentiation between inside and outside, everything is drawn into the private realm. History itself, as characterized by the eternal repetition of the same, unfolds in an enclosed space, the dwelling of a father who has domesticated the entire world. In the same way in which (traditional) fairy tales and films are enjoyed in different but similar spaces, their audiences are different but similar. Whereas fairy tales are mainly enjoyed by children, films are mainly enjoyed by adults, but by adults who—like Freder—are eternal children. The amusement park and the movie theater are the nursery rooms of the eternal child.

The image of the movie theater as a nursery room is not a very appealing one. If *Metropolis* tries to divert potentially dangerous energies that would otherwise lead to war, why is the spectator forced into the role of an eternal child? Is the eternal child not the child of a father who would use war to remain on top? What complicates a discussion of the ideological implications of *Metropolis* is that it is a film about the alchemical dream by a filmmaker who is himself an alchemist-inventor—someone who uses technology to recreate and transform existing reality on the screen. Is the strategy proposed by Lang and the entertainment industry—to playfully submit oneself to the very dangers of which one is afraid—not suspiciously similar to that of the Master of Metropolis who tries to protect himself against accidents by provoking a catastrophe? Even Thompson, whose account of the entertainment industry is purposefully affirmative, knows that there is a dark side to the amusement park's way of distancing evil. About the pleasure rides at Disney World he writes:

> In Disney World's Pirates of the Caribbean the experience is one in which evil
> is distanced, miniaturized and made light of. "Hi ho, hi ho, it's off to rape we
> go" could almost be the song of the pirates, as we slide in our barques past

scenes of burning port, seized women, and loaded plunder. Of course, as with all levels of social technology, from hunting to space travel, there is a shadow side to Disney's distancing of evil. Just as the Mesolithic bow and arrow of the hunt became the Neolithic weapons of battle, so Disney's technique for distancing evil can become the technique for training fighter pilots in their vehicles. There now exists an electronic helmet for jet pilots that transforms the physical terrain ahead into an abstract video map; radar warns the pilot of hidden rockets fighters, or artillery, so that we can press the button in time to eliminate the threats.[48]

The very strategies developed to combat the war can be used in the service of war. In Germany, the entertainment industry managed to divert potentially dangerous energies only temporarily. By the early 1930s, the alchemical dream had regained a strong militaristic dimension.

VI

I would like to conclude by emphasizing once more that father-inventors, such as the Master of Metropolis or his real-life counterparts, created their hermetically closed environments against the backdrop of a rapidly changing world of enormous diversity. They tried desperately to regain control over a world that could not be contained. If one puts their efforts in this light, one realizes that their victories were always also defeats. That did not necessarily make them change their tactics, however. I would like to maintain that there are ways in which we still live in the shadow of the nineteenth century. Many important manifestations of American popular culture remain variations on the story lines embedded in the fairy tales and festive rituals discussed earlier. Granted, in the course of time, these story lines have undergone transformations that are, at least at first sight, every bit as radical as the ones from popular tales, carnivals, and Christmas celebrations. I have pointed out that in the nineteenth century Christmas presents became collection items. The gifts brought by the present-day American Santa Claus, in contrast, are no longer binding. On the contrary, the custom of returning unwanted Christmas gifts to stores in order to exchange them has become a holiday tradition in itself— a tradition that indicates, or so it seems, that customers' satisfaction has become more important than the intent of the giver.

There are other aspects of American popular culture that seem to turn nineteenth-century traditions upside down. While the Nutcracker's kingdom can be seen as a literary precursor of modern amusement parks, one is struck by the way the role of the mice has changed. In *The Nutcracker,* the mice, which also stand for those at the bottom of the social order, are the enemy. Marie can visit the magic wonderland only after the Nutcracker has destroyed the mouse with the seven heads. In Disneyland, by contrast, a mouse plays the role of the host. "Mickey" welcomes the visitors and encourages them to spend their money.

Do these reversals from nineteenth-century Germany to late-twentieth-century America mean that we have come full circle—that in the United States, the land of conspicuous consumption, capitalism itself has become carnivalesque? I do not believe so. For the mouse on which Disney founded an empire is not the dirty rodent that invades the bourgeois living room by night and leaves a mess behind. His mouse was a "clean" mouse from the start—a mouse robbed of its natural characteristics and transformed into an image of what its creator considered important. Its presence in the magic kingdom, rather than a break with the nineteenth century, illustrates once again the capacity of capitalism for masquerading—for blinding people by presenting things as the opposite of what they are: technology as nature, the father as mother, exclusion as inclusion. *Metropolis* captured something of the spirit of the future, but of a future that cannot seem to free itself from a dependence on past paradigms.

NOTES

1. Welford Beaton, "Metropolis," in *American Film Criticism,* ed. Stanley Kaufmann (New York: Liverright, 1972), 189.
2. Marshall Berman, *All That Is Solid Melts into Air: The Experience of Modernity* (New York: Penguin Books, 1982), 6.
3. Ibid., 17.
4. Ibid.
5. See, for example, Robert Darnton, *The Great Cat Massacre: And Other Episodes in French Cultural History* (New York: Vintage, 1985).
6. See Marcel Mauss, *The Gift: Forms and Functions of Exchange in Archaic Societies* (New York, London: Norton, 1967); Lewis Hyde, *The Gift: Imagination and the Erotic Life of Property* (New York: Vintage Books, 1983); and Jacques Godbout, *L'Esprit du Don* (Paris: Editions de la decouverte, 1992).
7. Hyde, *The Gift,* 8.
8. For the carnivalesque origins of Christmas, see Stephen Nissenbaum, *The Battle for Christmas: A Social and Cultural History of Christmas* (New York: Knopf, 1996).
9. Hyde, *The Gift,* 10.
10. For a good discussion of German Christmas rituals, see Ingeborg Weber-Kellermann, *Die deutsche Familie: Versuch einer Sozialgeschichte* (Frankfurt am Main: Suhrkamp, 1985).

11. Siegfried Kracauer, "Weihnachtlicher Budenzauber," in *Der verbotene Blick: Beobachtungen, Analysen, Kritiken,* ed. Johanna Rosenberg (Leipzig: Reclam, 1992), 74.
12. William Leach, *Land of Desire: Merchants, Power and the Rise of a New American Culture* (New York: Vintage, 1994), 331.
13. Mit ihnen [Spielzeug, Nüsse, Stroh und Baumschmuck] quoll noch etwas anderes hervor: die Armut. Wie Äpfel und Nüsse mit ein wenig Schaumgold nebem dem Marzipan sich auf dem Weihnachtsteller zeigen durften, so auch die armen Leute mit Lametta und bunten Kerzen in den bessern Vierteln" (Walter Benjamin, *Nachträge* 7, no. 1, (1989): 420; my translation.
14. "Aber Weihnachten kam und teilte mit einem Mal vor den Augen des Bürgerkindes seine Stadt in zwei gewaltige Lager. . . . Weihnachten kam und teilte die Kinder in solche, die an den Buden des Potsdamer Platz sich mit ihren Eltern entlangschoben und solche die, im Innern, allein, ihre Puppen und ihre Schäfchen für gleichaltrige Kinder zum Verkaufe boten" (Walter Benjamin, "Berliner Chronik," in *Fragmente—Autobiographische Schriften,* vol. 6, ed. Rolf Tiedemann and Hermann Schweppenhauser [Frankfurt am Main: Suhrkamp, 1991], 518). Translation from Benjamin, *Reflections: Essays, Aphorisms, Autobiographical Writings,* ed. Peter Demetz, trans. Edmund Jephcott (New York: Schocken, 1986), 59.
15. I am capitalizing "Father" to distinguish the fantasy figure, mediated through fairy tales and Christmas rituals, from any flesh-and-blood fathers.
16. "Während man ein solches Antennenschicksal erleidet, rücken die fünf Kontinente immer näher heran. Nicht wir sind es in Wahrheit, die zu ihnen ausschweifen, ihre Kulturen vielmehr nehmen in grenzenlosem Imperialismus von uns Besitz" (Siegfried Kracauer, *Der verbotene Blick: Beobachtungen, Analysen, Kritiken,* ed. Johanna Rosenberg [Leipzig: Reclam, 1992],8).
17. "Eine winzige Kugel rollt ganz aus der Ferne auf dich zu, sie wächst sich zur Großenaufnahme aus und braust zuletzt über dich her; du kannst sie nicht hemmen, noch ihr entrinnen, gefesselt liegst du da, ein ohnmächtiges Püppchen, das von einem Riesenkoloß mitgerissen wird und in seinem Umkreis vergeht" (Kracauer, *Der verbotene Blick,* 8).
18. Knud Wolfram, *Tanzdielen und Vergnügungspaläste: Berliner Nachtleben in den dreißiger und vierziger Jahren, von der Friedrichstraße bis Berlin W., von Moka Efti bis zum Delphi* (Berlin: Edition Hentrich, 1992), 43–45.
19. Ibid., 44.
20. Ibid.
21. Fedor von Zobelitz, *Ich habe so gern gelebt: Lebenserinnerungen* (Berlin: Ullstein, 1934), 168.
22. Hans Kafka, "Lunapark: Ein Stück Amerika, versuchsweise," in *Glänzender Asphalt: Berlin im Feuilleton der Weimarer Republik,* ed. Christian Jäger and Erhard Schütz (Berlin: Fannei & Walz, 1994).

23. Leach, *Land of Desire,* 336.
24. The film no longer exists, but some documents and reviews have been preserved at the Filmarchiv Gerhard Lamprecht in Berlin.
25. Maria Tatar, *Lustmord: Sexual Murder in Weimar Germany* (Princeton, N.J.: Princeton University Press, 1995).
26. Ibid., 78.
27. Ibid., 7.
28. Leach, *Land of Desire,* 334.
29. Ibid., 335.
30. Ibid., 281.
31. Thea von Harbou, *Metropolis: Fritz Lang* (London, Boston: Faber and Faber, 1989), 36.
32. Leo Colze, *Berliner Warenhäuser* (Berlin: Fannei & Walz, 1907), 12.
33. Leach, *Land of Desire,* 209.
34. Colze, *Berliner Warenhäuser,* 52.
35. Ibid., 62.
36. Leach, *Land of Desire,* 191.
37. Ibid., 63.
38. Fritz Lang, "The Future of the Feature Film in Germany," in *The Weimar Republic Sourcebook,* ed. Anton Kaes, Martin Jay, and Edward Dimendberg (Berkeley, Los Angeles, London: University of California Press, 1994), 622. First published as "Wege des großen Spielfilms in Deutschland," *Die literarische Welt* 2 (October 1, 1926): 3–6.
39. "Wahrscheinlich ist es nicht jedermanns Sache, sich einer Luftschaukel anzu-vertrauen. Wenn aber die Schaukel auf einem Rollwägelchen sitzt, das nur gezogen zu werden braucht, bleiben sogar die zierlichen Figürchen bei Besinnung, die in ihren Kabinen durch die Luft sausen müssen. Nicht minder harmlos ist die Bergfahrt zu einem Gipfel, dessen schwindelerregende Höhe von der eines Fingers übertroffen wird, oder die Veranstaltung eines Pferderennens, das auf einer Tellerfläche gelaufen werden kann. Man zieht die Schraube an und gebietet über Kräfte, die kaum zu bändigen sind und oft Katastrophen entfesseln" (Kracauer, *Der verbotene Blick,* 75).
40. "Ja, die Erdkugel selber ist uns in Gestalt als Globus ausgebildeten Kreisels unterworfen" (Kracauer, *Der verbotene Blick,* 75).
41. Leach, *Land of Desire,* 336.
42. Elke Liebs, *Kindheit und Tod: Der Rattenfänger-Mythos als Beitrag zu einer Kulturgeschichte der Kindheit* (Munich: Wilhelm Fink, 1986), 21.
43. Leach, *Land of Desire,* 332.
44. Barbel Dalichow, "Welt im Wassertropfen," in *Filmstadt Babelsberg,* ed. Axel Geiss (Potsdam: Filmmuseum Potsdam, 1994), 181.
45. William Irwin Thompson, *The American Replacement of Nature: The Everyday*

Acts and Outrageous Evolution of Economic Life (New York and London: Doubleday, 1991), 17.

46. Thea von Harbou, "Die Kinder von Metropolis" (Filmarchiv Gerhard Lamprecht Berlin).

47. Thompson, *Replacement of Nature,* 18.

48. Ibid.

6

ELLEN RISHOLM

Formations of the Chamber: A Reading of *Backstairs*

Hintertreppe (Backstairs), directed by Leopold Jessner in 1921, is the prototypical *Kammerspielfilm* of the Weimar era. The plot is readily retold: a maid's lover comes to visit her every evening in the courtyard, where their tender moments together are witnessed by the local postman, himself secretly devoted to the maid. Unaware of the postman's infatuation, the woman frantically waits for him to deliver a letter from her lover, who hasn't appeared for several days. When a message finally arrives, the woman is so overjoyed that she brings wine to the postman's basement apartment, where she discovers that he has forged the letter. The maid overcomes her grief and begins to show signs of affection for the postman, who can barely contain his delight. Shadows at the window ominously predict disaster as it becomes apparent that the lover, who had been hospitalized, has returned. The postman kills him in a frenzy, and the woman, rejected by her employers, jumps to her death from the building's roof.

This skeletal synopsis of the melodramatic story seems to confirm both Siegfried Kracauer's diagnosis of the film as "a veritable excess of simplicity" and the generic conventions associated with the *Kammerspielfilm:* minimal plot, small cast, and limited setting. Yet the simplicity to which Kracauer alludes is hardly able to mask a profound and transgressive consideration of the operation of space in the film. This, perhaps, is the "excess" that troubles Kracauer. Space no longer serves merely as an immobile vessel for the forward impetus of the plot, but instead becomes a site of contestation and reclamation embroiled in struggles for power and presence. In *Hintertreppe,* the maid fills the spaces of the bourgeois apartment she cleans; simultaneously, the owners are bodily absent from the screen. Yet, the space is theirs; they dominate it through their constant command of the maid and of the possessions that fill the rooms. As Michel Foucault has said, the mechanisms of control are insidious, everywhere present, although out of (direct) view. The way in which *Hintertreppe* mobilizes space reveals resistance to the naturalization of these mechanisms.

This mobilization does not arise in a vacuum: the *Kammer*-tradition is marked by a history of such activation. Perhaps it seems a bit surprising to speak of a history here; the term *Kammer* calls forth disparate associations which at first sight seem to share no common history. One does, to be sure, think of the chamber as a small, enclosed space, but its peculiar linguistic status—neither the German *"Kammer"* nor the English "chamber" is a part of everyday speech—denaturalizes how one thinks of the contours of this place. The etymology of the word makes it apparent that disparate objects and places are "related": to mention but one example, the photographic "camera" and the judge's "chamber" share a common genealogy. A certain if not obscure cultural history can be read from such commonalities.

The genealogical approach to studying histories, as outlined by Foucault, can serve as a provisional mode through which to consider these *Kammer*-formations. Two aspects of this approach are particularly useful for the present study: neither is it a search for origins, for a metaphysical truth, nor does it assume progress in and through history. What this means quite simply for the *Kammer* is that this approach does not send us looking for petrified cultural forms which always reveal the same *Kammer,* even as its formations evolve in sophistication. There is no murky, hidden truth; there is no telos, no ongoing refinement of its cultural manifestation. The safe haven which this small, intimate space might seem to be is not at the heart of the *Kammer*. Transformations, according to Foucault, quite simply happen; reconstitutions arise perhaps by chance encounters, perhaps by a particular confluence of events, accidents, errors, and deviations, all of which figure in the reconstitutions which make no particular claim to advancement. Not that these changes are untouched by the political, nor is Foucault's genealogist uninterested in what Rabinow and Dreyfus call "continuities of cultural practices." The shifts are approached with a flitting eye, taking in as much as possible, always anxious to read these formations alongside and through each other. Genealogy, Dreyfus and Rabinow continue, "seeks the surfaces of events, small details, minor shifts, and subtle contours."[1] Seemingly insignificant minutia come to the fore; the everyday takes on new relevance.

This cannot and need not be an exhaustive study of the *Kammer* throughout the ages. Such a project rests on the illusion that a mastery of this history is possible. Here I bring together the traditions of *Kammermusik* and *Kammerspiel* theater with the *Kammerspielfilm,* a group of films dating from the early Weimar period, in order to explore the implications of the *Kammer* for cinema. These traditions are instances in the delineation of a space that either wrestles with the mechanisms of control or becomes a part of that very apparatus. It is essential to realize that the *Kammer* is not a particular place; its associations bring together a composite in which abstract idea and concrete space emerge simultaneously, activating the interrogation of certain often unquestioned presumptions: the indivisibility of spatial parameters; the unassailability of the private sphere; the authenticity of intimacy; and the realm of the private as exterior to history.

I

Disengaged from common usage, the concept of *Kammer* is a relic of the past, a remnant or fragment which has survived in different contexts. Yet, its seeming vestigial stasis actually marks a bond that unveils the *Kammer* as a localized component in a specific cultural system. If we consider its linguistic and cultural manifestations (*Kammermusik,* for instance), we can trace the relationship of space (chamber) and culture (music).[2] *Kammermusik* is not simply music on a small scale; we cannot reduce it to an intimate piece played by a small number of musicians. This form of music has a "noble" history, one that reveals a predilection for the playing out of relations of power as well as the subversion of these very same relations. The site of this *Spiel* is of utmost importance—a place associated with the private and intimate.

During the period of its emergence, *Kammermusik,* in contrast to church and theater music, was intended for private entertainment.[3] Although the spaces of the nobility, which typically employed its own musical staff, were the predominant sites for the performance of chamber music,[4] this form was still considered nonprofessional.[5] Moreover, "every cultured person played an instrument" in the early period, and it was not until the nineteenth century that the domain of chamber music was monopolized by professionals, as the pieces became harder to learn and connoisseurship became more fashionable.[6] The burgeoning practice of chamber music in the earlier historical setting did not include performance in concert halls; every individual with the time and financial means could participate.

Precursory forms of chamber music have a rather complex and extensive history, which can be traced back at least to the Middle Ages as forms of cultural pursuit often controlled by princes and lords. With the rise of the bourgeoisie, chamber music (the term was coined in the sixteenth century) was no longer the exclusive province of the nobility. Its appearance within the sphere of the ascendant middle class may well have brought about a significant realignment of power relations, which up to that point had allowed little room for music solely associated with free expression and entertainment.

Interestingly, it is the intimacy of this music, its dependence on the privacy and closure of the domestic space, that most likely appeared threatening. Instrumental music was suppressed by the medieval church because it introduced an element of secular pleasure; it disturbed the atmosphere and unity of the service.[7] In other words, instrumental music allowed the individual some latitude in practicing his or her cultural self via, quite simply, performance. It is striking how often performance is cited as the defining feature of chamber music.[8] Theodor Adorno, in his *Introduction to the Sociology of Music,* begins his chapter on chamber music by emphasizing the importance of the players. What distinguishes Adorno from others in this respect is his emphasis on the "social" effect of the synthesis of performance and audience: the audience qua performer *produces* music anew, practices free expression with others, and thus enjoys a particular form of emancipation.

Adorno sees chamber music as the complete realization of "the Kantian definition of art as purposeless efficacy"—a form in which the "relation of social purposes is sublimated into a purposeless esthetic in-itself."[9] His emphasis on this aesthetics, and his claim that "the sole product" of chamber music is "the process itself," detracts from another important aspect, namely the production of the *Kammer.* The very constitution of the private sphere in this particular historical moment *is defined by* the performance of music, and thus there is no complete sublimation of the social interaction. The musicians not only control the instruments, perform for the sake of performance, comprise their own audience; they also constitute and reconstitute the private sphere as a space produced by a cultural act. Even as the musicians play together, they construct the *Kammer* as a transformative site where a particular community exists quite simply to practice its control—via expertise—over the space. None of the players dominates; the musicians work together to bring forth a unique performance. It was not long, however, before this chamber grew rigid.[10] Performance was eventually drawn out of the home and into the concert hall, where the space was no longer moldable and transformative.

The *Kammer* represents a private realm that ostensibly falls outside of history and thus is not subject to everyday practices, but rather is informed by the aesthetic presuppositions Adorno describes. This "purposeless esthetic" is often the underlying assumption of scholarly treatments of chamber music. One book-length study on the subject asserts that chamber music, "of course, can hardly be said to have a 'story.' As a province of music, it is one of those happy lands without a history."[11] Here we find the age-old conception of a "happy land," of a domesticated sphere, tamed and untouched. The paradox is clear: to tame and domesticate implies that a certain essence still lies at the heart of the transformed *Kammer,* and yet the desire to consider this a sacred, untouched—that is to say *untransformed, history-less*—place is also evident. The space, in fact, is mobilized by the performance; only then does it take on meaning as a historical site for the exercise of free will. It is activated by the *Spiel.*

II

No one has ventured to discuss the "heritage" of the *Kammer*-tradition, perhaps because it seems too overdetermined on its suprahistorical perch. How could anyone argue that there was once something radical about chamber music? How might such a discussion impact our understanding of space today? In light of these questions I will explore another *Kammer*-formation, turn-of-the-century intimate theater, before moving on to Weimar cinema. Keeping in mind Foucault's genealogical model, I will view the *Kammer* with an eye for the surface play of discourses in the *Kammerspiel* theater.

As pointed out previously, with the *Kammermusik* of the developing bourgeois era we find the contours of space emerging simultaneously and only through performance; its political significance as a site for the staging of free expression is apparent. *Kammermusik* extends beyond the musical notes on the page. On the other hand, the *Kammerspiel* theater offers a particularly relevant site for observing social, cultural, architectural, and economic confluences even as the private sphere is retrenched through staging (despite the *public* nature of theater); one might call this resanctification through a false aura.

Max Reinhardt coined the term "*Kammerspiel*" in the early twentieth century. This does not mean that *Kammer*-forms had vanished in the interim. If we see the *Kammer* move into the home with chamber music, it stays there through the nineteenth century as the home gains in importance. The *Kammer* is inextricably bound up with the increasing importance of the nuclear family, which comes to depend on claims to "privacy" as an important ideological maneuver. With capitalism on the rise, the establishment of this supposedly autonomous sphere marked a key moment in the *Kammer's* migration. Homes were places where intimacy supposedly operated freely, where the individual ostensibly had free reign. The shape and function of the *Kammer* is almost uniformly depoliticized throughout the nineteenth century, as the physical delineation of space also leads to its reification—the home becomes naturalized and timeless, removed from any historical context. No longer is the *Kammer* a potentially dynamic, subversive forum, but rather it is treated as a historical vacuum, protected from the "outside."

The theater had become one space for the practice of the bourgeois public sphere; it was a place in which the bourgeoisie could see itself portrayed and legitimated. In a sense, this group was securing its own public sphere, but this sphere quickly lost its dynamism and became irretrievably petrified. The preservation of interiority through the exercise of spatial control finds its culmination in the *Kammerspiel* of the fin de siècle. The dynamic impulse of bourgeois *Kammermusik* is absent from the *Kammerspiel;* the outside is rigorously excluded from both the theatrical performance and the physicality of the theater. The *Kammerspiel's* space offers a dehistoricized realm of intimacy, a mystification of the interior.

This discussion necessitates a brief survey of late-nineteenth-century theater, which began to find itself in a stage of transition.[12] The naturalist mode sought to reassess the program of the nineteenth-century stage. Industrialization, urbanization, and developments in the natural sciences were partially responsible for this reassessment; furthermore, they brought about an enhanced awareness of technology which was subsequently incorporated into the theatrical medium. The precision of photography and sound recording so impressed naturalist playwrights that they sought to imitate the capabilities of these products of modernity. "Reality" was no longer of the nineteenth-century variety, but now forced the detail. The goal was accuracy; or, as Arno Holz put it, "aus dem Theater allmählich das 'Theater' zu drängen" ("to gradually force 'theater' out of the theater").[13] The combination of naturalism and theater inevitably led to the depiction of the voiceless classes—nonexistent as far as the dominant theatrical institution was concerned—for a medium which now called upon the formal capabilities of photo- and phonographic reproduction must dutifully record the affairs of the "lower" classes.

Yet bourgeois forces were well aware of the potential threat to their power—a power that found legitimacy through cultural hegemony. Because the dominant theater was a stage for the acting out of the status quo and represented space solely controlled by the ascendant class, the implications of naturalism had to be counteracted. The stage as a site of representation for the bourgeoisie had been wrested from the hands of this class. The naturalist play, naively deterministic in its worldview, occupied theatrical space, and this set in motion a process whose repercussions were still being felt with the advent of the *Kammerspielfilm*.

Naturalism should be discussed in relationship to the "free" theater movements which sought to establish private stages in a hostile environment; their genesis and growth were inextricably intertwined. The free theater movements, beginning with Antoine's "Theatre Libre" in Paris (1887) and followed by, among others, the "Freie Bühne" in Berlin (1889), sought both to establish a stage for the contemporary modern drama and to distinguish themselves from the dominant theater, as it became apparent that the traditional theater no longer accommodated the changes that pervaded German society. A struggle to put these plays on stage ensued. As private theaters, these establishments were able to bypass police censorship.

The free theater movements became the carriers not only of the naturalist play, but also of the modern drama, often associated with the notion of intimate drama. In fact, many of the structures built to accommodate these movements were named "intimate theaters." They arose as a loosely connected movement in the late nineteenth century and can be conceived of as both a reaction to and an outgrowth of naturalism. Although the boundaries separating these two categories are blurred, the intimate drama shied away from the deterministic element in naturalist plays and focused on the "individual." The movement certainly had no clearly defined agenda, nor did it find a common voice among its adherents. Standard characteristics of the theatrical apparatus included a small stage and audience, as well as a limited number of actors and actresses (all of which are basic components of the *Kammerspiel* as well). I hesitate to reduce the subject matter to common themes or styles, such as Maeterlinck's symbolism or Hofmannsthal's neoromantic lyricism. This would isolate a particular group or drama and thus neglect staging practice.[14] My interest lies in evaluating intimate theater in a larger cultural context by looking at the realization of these plays onstage in the theater. In what ways did the stage strive to recuperate the *Kammer?*

The intimate drama no longer relies on "action," as in the dominant theater of the nineteenth century, but instead removes the story to the interior of the person, expanding upon his or her feelings and impressions.[15] Precisely this interiority becomes interesting when synchronically related to other cultural phenomena of the era; industrialization and massification would seem to demand a radical change in this sphere of representation—indeed, a direction in which Erwin Piscator's theater moved. Yet here the individual is on center stage, reconfirmed as the orderer of space. This mystification of the position of bourgeois man in society—as he loses grasp on spatial representation, he becomes more anxious to retain an alternate sphere—is affirmed onstage. Theatrical space serves as a vessel for this affirmation, as revealed in Max Reinhardt's *Kammerspiele.*

Although the notion of "intimate theater" had been assimilated into the-atrical practice by 1906, the establishment of the Berlin Kammerspiele in this year marked an important moment in contemporary conceptions of the theatrical stage: this was the first physical space, established and staked out by Reinhardt, that put into practice key concepts of the intimate theater he envisioned.[16] While this might seem to contradict the earlier statement that the free theater movements of the late nineteenth century often thought of themselves as intimate theater, these groups were not interested in developing a specific aesthetic, as was Reinhardt, but were rather obliged to work within limited spatial dimensions. As oppositional movements working under the threat of political reprisals, they were small and private at their inception—as opposed to the traditionally established structures. Their smallness was a direct corollary of their marginalized position.

Modernism's resonance in traditional theater is certainly evident in the construction and realization of Reinhardt's *Kammerspiele*—including architecture, performance, audience demography, and critical reception. The major impulse of a conservative modernism delimited by an aesthetic elitism seems to find a home in the notions of space that are evinced by Reinhardt as the pseudotheoretician of the *Kammerspiele.* Rather than eschewing traditional assumptions of culture, as we shall see, the *Kammerspiele* embraces them. Perhaps it is simply a retrenching of the old, but with increasing intensity. Envisioning a theater where the audience no longer experiences itself as spectator, and the element of immediacy rejects any contemplative moment, Reinhardt unwittingly finds an answer to one of the key concerns of modernity—space and the control of space—by erecting an edifice which strives to placate an audience bombarded with stimuli. Modernism, in the form of aesthetic elitism, truly finds a "home" in the sanctuary of Reinhardt's *Kammer.* Yet this "home" does not advance a new perspective on the everyday, nor on the technical means whereby the "home" is reproduced. It is merely a fervent attempt to find a home for the now "homeless" bourgeoisie.

The *Kammerspiel* does not encourage the spectator to reorganize the stimuli of a rapidly changing environment, engaging the audience in an examination of modernizing society. The *Kammer,* once a locus of potential political subversion and critical thought, has now acquired new importance as sanctified, intimate space where the spectators, ensconced in comfortable leather chairs, can be lulled by the interplay with the actors and actresses. The theatrical stage has been reclaimed, and as the number of seats goes down, the ticket price goes up, securing the space for a particular economic class.

In 1906 Reinhardt commissioned the first Kammerspiele in Berlin, next to the Deutsches Theater where he was the director. Henry van de Velde was the initial architect to be considered for the *Kammerspiel* project, and even designed a plan.[17] Despite widespread support, he was ultimately dismissed, and we are left to conjecture why he was found unsuitable. Van de Velde was a famous Jugendstil architect, involved in a movement that reflected contemporary trends in art. Perhaps the ornate, decorative style of this artist would have proven too distracting for the theatrical stagings, thereby conflicting with Reinhardt's conception of an intimate setting. This space was to be inconspicuous, lulling the audience into a false sense of security by focusing attention on an intensely interiorized landscape. The Jugendstil design would have drawn attention to outline, and Reinhardt was not interested in any overt expression of form. The stage was to serve as a vacuum within which the actor and audience could meld and become one. He developed a theory of the *Kammerspiel* that, although neither elaborate nor exhaustive, reflected the changing function of the theater. As early as 1901, he pondered a theater which was subsequently realized in the *Kammerspiele*. If one were to capture the essence of Reinhardt's vision in one idea it would be harmonious intimacy: "Das was mir vorschwebt ist eine Art Kammermusik des Theaters" ("What I imagine is a chamber music of the theater").[18] This allusion to *Kammermusik* did not call upon the historical function of this genre in the private sphere, but rather envisioned a fluid integration of the constituent elements of the ensemble as the musicians worked together in accord. This notion of harmony crops up repeatedly and at times seems to be Reinhardt's obsession.

The director's ideas can be reconstructed from the comments of his con-temporaries who contributed to a collection of essays from 1924.[19] Many of the contributors discuss the Kammerspiele and the integral role this stage played in Reinhardt's conception of theater. There should be no discordant moments: lighting, acting, and the architectural parameters are carefully balanced. Heinz Harald focuses on the Kammerspiele and Reinhardt's vision of a small theater, suggesting a fluid space that effaces any clear-cut boundaries between the audience and the stage: "Here is a small hall without galleries and with the stage scarcely separated from the auditorium, panelled in warm brown."[20] Hofmannsthal com-pares Reinhardt's vision to the intricacies of a musical instrument, illuminating the director's interest in the orchestration of the whole edifice: "What he dreamed of was a house resembling as closely as possible the body of a violin and, like the violin, attuned to receive and respond to the slightest vibration. That was the famous Kammerspiele. . . ."[21] The newly built theater was open for review before a drama was even staged, accentuating Reinhardt's awareness of the importance of the physical space.

The turn to the *Kammerspiel* did not mean that the *Kammer* lost its radical impulse to the needs of the bourgeoisie. Ensconced in a leather chair, the bourgeois is perhaps lost in the ritual confirmation of the individual's autonomy, which is supported by the sanctuary of a sphere that has lost its public character. Yet German silent cinema, reestablishing itself in the post–World War I period, explores the idea of the *Kammerspiel* by transforming this intimate, timeless sphere and subjecting it to critical scrutiny. The *Kammerspielfilme* of the early 1920s suggest a more sophisticated examination of space which no longer rejects the historical and material implications of this sphere. The *Kammer* has ceased to be the naturalized setting for the universal conflicts of the bourgeois. Instead it has become a dynamic space that the filmic medium can explore in a self-consciously discursive fashion.

III

The legacy of the *Kammer*-tradition is inscribed in the intersection of the *Kammerspiel* and the cinematic medium in the early Weimar period. A set of problematics, related to spatial representation, is brought about through this confluence: how do changes in the way space is represented disrupt the conception of the *Kammer* as an eternally valid, essentially transcendental given? In what ways does the nascent cinematic medium allow for a sharper criticism of the notion of "private" space? How is the decay of the home symptomatic of the crises of modernity, and how does the *Kammerspielfilm* reveal this process? What transpires at the nexus of technology and traditional institutions?

Before exploring such questions through the analysis of *Hintertreppe,* I would like to place this set of problematics in the broader context of Weimar film scholarship, where crucial questions concerning spatial transformations have been left unanswered. This is not to say that the *Kammerspielfilm* has been neglected by German film critics. On the contrary, seminal scholars have devoted substantial attention to the *Kammerspielfilm*. In this section I want to trace briefly the history of that scholarship—in terms of both the points it has raised and the issues of space it has forgotten.

Siegfried Kracauer's *From Caligari to Hitler* does recognize the importance of the *Kammerspiel* tradition in Weimar film. A keen observer, Kracauer was able to point out salient features of the *Kammerspielfilme*. Yet, given his single-minded treatment of Weimar cinema as an index of a national predisposition to surrender to tyranny, he fails to recognize how the *Kammerspielfilme* bring to the foreground other discourses, such as those closely tied to the sociohistorical condition of the *Kammer*.[22] The chapter entitled "Mute Chaos" categorizes the *Kammerspielfilm* as an "instinct film," a group of works sharing the same setting, the lower middle class. Still dumbfounded by the support Hitler was able to garner amongst the petty bourgeoisie, Kracauer can see this group only as the "meaningless remnant of a disintegrated society," a "breeding ground for stunned, oppressed creatures."[23] He finds this chaos reflected in the manner in which the films function: "a few persons, each incarnating some particular *instinct,* are involved in a *rigidly composed action* "(emphasis added).[24] Here is one instance where, despite himself, Kracauer points out a crucial aspect in the films—the composition of the text—only to smooth over it in the course of his narrative. This very contradiction is evident in the title of the chapter, for it is difficult to imagine "chaos" as "mute." Furthermore, the films were silent—even to the extent that they did not include intertitles. In fact, the organizing principles of these films were anything but chaotic.

The other seminal work on this era in German film history, Lotte Eisner's *The Haunted Screen,* acquired a status similar to that of *From Caligari to Hitler.* Although Eisner shares Kracauer's interest in the psychological component of these texts, her study focuses more on art history and the legacy of German Romanticism. She devotes two chapters to the *Kammerspielfilm,* briefly discussing its theatrical origins in order to better understand its cinematic transformation before going on to describe the style of the films. For example, in reference to *Hintertreppe* Eisner claims, "what shocks us today in this film is the violent break in tone between the styles used."[25] Eisner is a purist, uninterested in what she interprets as the clashing of intimacy and psychologism with the techniques of Expressionism. Yet precisely this mixture in styles makes the film so intriguing.[26]

These discussions of the *Kammerspielfilm* highlight the work that has defined but also delimited comprehension of these films. Moreover, traditional genre analysis, by focusing on universal components and explicating them, could hope to do little more than establish a well-defined and clearly circumscribed classification. This would only further encourage the expressionist/realist dichotomy that had long dominated the scholarship on Weimar cinema. New possibilities for reflection begin to surface as the layers of earlier scholarship, which had, at times, adhered to certain concepts and paradigms, began to peel away.

Clearly, the fact that space enjoys a sociocultural history and is not merely a derivative of nature is generally not contested. The degree to which the perception and social uses of space are controlled, however, is indicative of "deep forms of social regimentation."[27] Kristin Ross reaches this conclusion in her study *The Emergence of Social Space: Rimbaud and the Paris Commune.* She very effectively argues that a consciousness of space and the subsequent reorganization of its revolutionary potential were essential to the initial success of the uprising and establishment of the Paris Commune. She begins with the dehierarchization of a key artifact of the ancien régime; a *place* was seized and vertically dismantled as the Vendome column was brought crashing to the ground. According to Ross, this symbolic movement is matched by the interrogation of other oppositions which also are "levelled."

Boundaries become blurred as the model of the Paris Commune offers new ways of organizing space:

> The significance of the Commune is most evident in what Marx called its "working existence": in its *displacement* of the political onto seemingly peripheral areas of everyday life—the organization of space and time, changes in lived rhythms and social ambiences. The insurgents' brief mastery of their own history is perceptible, in other words, not so much on the level of governmental politics as on the level of their daily life: in concrete problems of work, leisure, housing, sexuality, and family and neighborhood relations.[28]

Ross's work on this topic not only opens up the event of the uprising and Rimbaud's contribution as a marginalized poet, it also raises the issue of political strategies that focus on the everyday—strategies that become applicable to other histories and situations. Film, so closely tied to industrialization, the avant-garde, and modernity, offered an effective challenge to the (supposed) autonomy of traditional high art. In exploring cinematic texts, the question arises as to how they make the world intelligible, exposing dormant sites of potential political practice.

IV

I choose not to begin with a generic outline of the characteristics of the *Kammerspielfilm*, but prefer to generate new ways of discussing these films by expounding on the use and construction of space in *Hintertreppe* as simultaneously a discursive and a symptomatic manifestation of the sociohistorical epoch.[29]

Cinematic space does not serve merely as a vehicle of narration in *Hintertreppe;* the film belies the accepted axiom that time dominates and supersedes space. These two variables are inextricably bound up with the cinematic medium, which indeed is both pictorial and temporal. The opening sequence in *Hintertreppe* self-consciously plays upon the traditional time-space continuum which had so long dominated epistemology. One simple act becomes an allegory of defiance. After a few shots of the backstairs of a Berlin apartment house, a medium-long shot frames a woman asleep in a claustrophobic, barren chamber. The mise-en-scène exposes the scant surroundings, telling us much about her status: the walls are bare, with the exception of a few pictures; a chair by her bed supports an alarm clock and candle; in the background a basin and towel are visible. The next shot frames the alarm clock in a close-up—it is six in the morning—followed by a medium shot of the woman and the clock. The subsequent image exposes the mechanism on the back of the clock as the dials begin to turn. The rest of the sequence follows the woman as she defiantly sets the clock back five minutes, falling asleep again. When the alarm rings once more, a close-up captures it spinning around, seemingly out of control, and she awakens.

With this simple act of defiance, the maid exerts some control over her life *and* the cinematic medium (and the clock). She rejects the ostensible inevitability of the narrative's trajectory, touching upon a key aspect of the modernist foundations of cinema. The rigidity of modern time is refused, and the place that opens up as a result of this temporal contestation cannot be subsumed into a linear narrative. An excess of space remains, space that cannot be claimed by the story. Clock time, the forward march of which is indomitable in the modern work world, becomes an allegory of the narrative.[30] Yet, the maid knows how to resist the paradox embodied in modernity as she attempts to destabilize its forward drive in a subtle way by playing with time and thereby opening up space, thus "stretching" the narrative. Ross also touches upon this excess of space and the paradox of modern times it underscores: "the sharp division between spaces of lived time and the possibility of desire are placed over against the compartmentalized clock world of the adult, work world."[31] It is the spatial interstices seeping through the narrative that defy control and allow the maid to exert her agency playfully.

With this simple sequence, "naturalized" time is recast as contestable and historical—not simply the subordinated, temporal framework within which the "story" evolves. Concomitantly, space is also recast, calling the expectations and perceptions of the audience into question. Therefore, it is essential to examine the positioning of the spectator in relationship to the text. The viewer enters the cinema with clearly defined notions of space that have been constructed by cultural practice. The spectator in the *Kammerspiel* theater was encouraged to sit back and enjoy the play on stage from a fully constituted subject position with a clearly delineated perspective augmented by a fixed point of view. The cinematic medium, on the other hand, opens up new challenges to the positioning of the spectator in relation to the text, and narration is the key interface.

Rather than go into a long discussion of narration, suffice it to quote Rimmon-Kenan, who defines it as "the act or process of production" of the story.[32] Furthermore, the assemblage of the story's elements involves "time," "causality," and "linearity" (whether uni- or multilinearity); and how they are combined is also important, whether by "enchainment," "embedding," or "joining." Rimmon-Kenan regards the text, which is not temporal but spatial or logical, as non-narrative. It is with such summary discussions that I would disagree; moments of stasis are also integral to the narrative. The mapping out of the geography of oppression in *Hintertreppe* is an important discursive act, subtly asserting itself through spatial practices, which have stories of their own to tell.

Dispassionate, objective at best, narration in *Hintertreppe* never allows the spectator to forget his or her own role in the construction and interpretation of the story. The spectator is situated outside the story in spaces that are always somehow exterior to the action but still within the narrative. In other words, narration, by being overtly spatial, counteracts the illusion of the melodramatic story. The work spaces within the apartment figure prominently in the text, spinning different

Backstairs (1921), directed by Leopold Jessner.

tales. When the maid sets about her daily tasks at the film's onset, a long shot frames the hallway as she walks through it picking up shoes, her work filling the space. Hallways commonly serve as temporal projections, announcing the passage of time as an individual moves from one room to another, dislodging the spatial with an obvious trajectory. Yet here time is not "of the essence." The maid's work intercedes as she cleans and scrubs the home of the nonvisible apartment dwellers, interrupting the forward impetus of the story. The shot begins before she enters and lingers a bit longer than expected when she exits, emphasizing stasis. Furthermore, a frame within the frame—curtains delineate either side of the image—reconfirms the spectator's position exterior to the action, not as a voyeur who is enticed by playing out fantasies, but rather as a critical observer who is encouraged to produce and not consume the text.

The space of observation is clearly established as a "space of distance," allowing a place for examination. The spectator is positioned in diegetic gaps which are predominantly spatial and are certainly not subsumed by the story; yet, these "gaps" are crucial. In other words, this film consciously positions the spectator in spaces that are neither transtextual (omniscient) nor written into the story (point of view), but somehow both. At one point in the film, the maid is in the apartment, cleaning her work space. The image is presented as a whole; the space is not dissected. This is followed by a shot of the postman gazing out his basement window. The camera is positioned in the courtyard at a studied distance, and narration cuts to a long shot of the balcony, anticipating the entrance of the maid. Clearly one would expect this to be a point-of-view shot from the postman's perspective. Yet the spectator views the balcony from a position somewhere in the courtyard; the image is not focalized through the postman. Narration does not allow the spectator to suture gaps and thereby infiltrate the story by bonding to characters.

Often the close-up shot is used in dominant cinema to underscore the protagonist's plight, focusing on the expression of emotion and encompassing the spectator within the story. Yet, when the maid sits in the kitchen, polishing each individual crystal glass as she reflects on her lover's absence while preparing a party for her employers, narration refuses the expected cut to her face. In what I term the *Kammerspiel* shot, editing is not used to elide the geography of oppression by moving from the spatial to the psychological, and thereby moving from the physical space into the melodrama of the story. Instead, narration remains suspended as the camera remains fixed, the mise-en-scène capturing her firmly situated in the household routine. The seemingly logical use of the close-up is avoided, thwarting the illusion of a wholly private dimension, and refusing the psychologically motivated narrative. The maid is not an individual whose unique story is being told; the story is not what dominates. In other words, there are other codes—for example, the spatial—at work within the film which do not advance "the story" or, for that matter, "character development"; instead, they resist the *Kammerspiel* theater effect.

Narration seems to be organizing spaces that belong to the private sphere—the chambers of the apartment—a space that traditionally has (falsely) been associated with the eternal, intimate, psychological, and transhistorical. However, something else transpires in the apartment. The real time of the maid's workday, organized around the planning and preparation of a party in the apartment, is a parallel subtext in the film. The spaces she "works" belong to the "owners," nonvisible participants exterior to the melodramatic story. She cleans and arranges these rooms when the inhabitants have vacated them, clock-time ticking as the long takes stubbornly avoid the elision of time by reverting to skillful editing, preferring the *Kammerspiel* shot. The action of the story, however, does *not* take place in the apartment, but in the back stairwell, the courtyard, or the postman's dank basement apartment. In other words, marginalized spaces, areas that are on the periphery, become the spatial vehicle of the melodramatic triangle.

When the party does finally take place, one shot underscores the contrast between the sparse, puritanical images of the maid as she communicates with the postman in his basement room and the cluttered, oppressive compositions in the bourgeois apartment. A long shot, making use of depth, is cluttered with the personal objects of the partygoers as, in the back room, shadows of the maid's employers and their friends are barely discernable through the windows of the closed door. There is no "action" in the shot, as the insidious nature of their domination is accentuated through spatial representation; only their ominous shadows come to light here, although their presence has always been apparent. This is a moment in which the spectator is confronted with his or her own position as viewer through both self-reflexive shot composition and framing, simultaneously underlining the nature of spectatorship and obscuring vision: our vision is *blocked* by the objects in the image as the framing device *foregrounds* these objects. The act of looking is folded back on itself. It would seem that everyone—the maid, the audience, the owners—is somehow on the periphery, outside of the spaces of action but implicated in the construction of the text.

Any lingering idealization of the "home" is clearly dissipated. The film is radical in the sense that it moves beyond an examination of a "mother/wife" in her bourgeois home—representations of which historically often functioned to confirm the status quo. It is a working-class woman, here essentially a "homeless" woman, who stands at the center of the film; alienated from the spaces of the apartment, she is consigned to the margins. As pointed out previously, this alienation is underscored by the dispersion of space; she must leave the apartment, exit to the periphery, to reclaim her story and sphere. The maid is able to defy the inexorability of marginalized spaces only with small acts of impudence; for instance, when she shakes her fist at the incessantly ringing bell that summons her or when she challenges the clock-time of her workday. Only in the dank basement apartment of the postman, or in the courtyard, can her story continue.

This "home" is set in the broader context of the courtyard, which is situated in the still larger sphere of the city; nevertheless, the exterior—the city life—is never so much as glimpsed, even through the courtyard doors when the maid lets in her lover. Through extreme artificiality and the control of mise-en-scène, a safe space is rigidly constructed which then paradoxically explodes. Interestingly, this is undoubtedly symptomatic of cinema's inability to encompass, through the *Kammerspielfilm,* the radical changes in society; cinema's relationship to the city— *the* object of modernity *par excellence*—has always been problematic.

In this film, the existence of the city is completely repressed although ever present, and its volatile nature is offset by the strict control of interior spaces. Yet this artifice symptomatically seeps through the societal structure in *Hintertreppe.* For instance, one might imagine a community developing amongst the inner-city courtyard dwellers. Yet claustrophobia and separation are the ruling factors, underscored by the misunderstandings and deceits practiced by the three protagonists; in fact, the interloper, who comes from the outside, is killed at the climax of the story. It is only this moment—a violent act—that brings the inhabitants from their dwellings to witness the maid's plunge from the rooftop. The cinematic device remains constant, however, by framing the group from a distance as *they watch her* plunge, not by moving into the story and following her descent or framing her dead body, but by remaining in other spaces.

Certainly the *Kammerspielfilm* would be the place to examine the micro-politics of gender and class. At the same time that it relates the spiral of the story, *Hintertreppe* focuses on the oppressive mechanisms of the everyday, a topic that Michel de Certeau has investigated extensively. He points out that his interest in the "local" is not a return to "individuality"; the individual is not a microcosm of the whole. Instead, each individual is a locus of social relations, upon and through which "an incoherent (and often contradictory) plurality of such relational determinants interact."[33] He maintains that this person is not a passive consumer caught in an authoritarian structure, but someone who struggles, subverts, and plays with the oppressive mechanism. "The tactics of consumption, the ingenious ways in which the weak make use of the strong, thus lend a political dimension to everyday practices."[34] The maid does indeed practice everyday strategies, as proposed by de Certeau. Fantasy and laughter are subversive strategies to which she is privy as she works and plays within her marginalized spheres. De Certeau's ideas perhaps inspire a bit too much optimism in the working woman's ability to overcome the structure of oppression. Tactics of subversion on a micro level—this is certainly the locus of the private and everyday—find little space. Yet, as the film exposes the parameters of oppression, it does set up spaces from which private strategies of subversion can arise. In this sense, then, the *Kammerspielfilm* does have something in common with the historical performance of *Kammermusik.*

Patrice Petro, in her provocative challenge to Weimar film scholarship and history, discusses certain films in a new light by incorporating other texts into the discussion of cinema. She moves away from the "overriding concern with male subjectivity and identity"[35] that has prevailed in Weimar cinema and goes on to explore the site of female subjectivity in both films and photojournalism, unveiling an addressed female audience. Part of Petro's study revolves around the *Kammerspielfilm*, but the *Kammerspielfilm* as melodrama. She discusses Eisner's discontent with the mixture of styles evident in *Hintertreppe,* but argues that "*Hintertreppe* is disappointing as pure *Kammerspiel* because it is more accurately understood as melodrama. The stark contrast between visual styles and gestural support not only provides *Hintertreppe* with a melodramatic 'look' but also with a contemplative mode of looking almost demanded of the spectator."[36]

The conflation of the *Kammerspielfilm* and melodrama is somewhat problematic here, as it disregards the historically specific condition of the *Kammerspiel*. For example, Petro references Altenloh's published dissertation from 1914, *Zur Soziologie des Kino: Die Kino-Unternehmung und die sozialen Schichten ihrer Besucher,* which statistically outlines the prevalence of women among moviegoers.[37] Petro uses this study to support her tenuous contention that *Hintertreppe* was a film for women and that it attracted a female audience by opening up spaces for a female spectator. In fact, the journal *Weltbühne,* always suspicious of film, found that this movie was a more sophisticated text, not as cinema but rather as filmed theater. However problematic this statement might be, the critic maintained that it was not surprising that *Hintertreppe* had a very limited audience and did not meet with success at the box office.[38] The question, then, is whether or not women did in fact participate in this film through the "contemplative mode" Petro finds it elicits.

She describes two modes of looking which are inscribed in *Hintertreppe*—"the voyeuristic, strangely sympathetic, and ultimately sadistic look of the postman and the compassionate and seemingly passive gaze of the maid"[39]—and then goes on to describe a third inscription which is implicated in providing the female spectator access to the "significance of the suffering." In this sense it would almost seem that she reads them as characters to be analyzed. In actuality, the spaces that the text opens up for viewing the film are not vantage points from which to view suffering; they explore many parameters within the text, not least of which is the positionality of the spectator. The figures that are caught up in the story are always somehow in textual motion as the excesses of space take over, revealing mechanisms of control. The dominant yet nonvisible owners bear witness to the playing out of the decentralization of the individual.

The bodily absent, although spatially dominant, owners are simultaneously central and peripheral to the text. As Foucault would say, the mechanisms of control which feed the power nexus are insidious, everywhere present, although difficult to see. They own the apartment and the objects in it, made strikingly apparent with the appearance of such articles as a baroque clock, heralded with a close-up shot. At only one moment in the film are the owners physically manifest, and then only as grotesque caricatures who evict the maid from the space which was never her space, after which she, not in a moment of hysteria and not because of the tragedy of the melodrama, slowly walks up the stairs to throw herself from the rooftop. The expressionist apparitions are the bourgeois inhabitants of the apartment who act as one to evict the woman. Their body movements are expressionist as they point in unison down the stairs, their eyes blackened by makeup. Expressionism is thought to allow the outer expression of inner feelings; yet, ironically, these figures are textually constituted as the oppressors, with no insight into their "inner" feelings, which are truly unimportant to the text. Their acting style is more reminiscent of Brecht's theory of disengaged acting, and in fact he was well aware of the promise of Expressionism—not because it liberated the individual, but because of its potential as a "revolutionary" tool.[40] The last scene in the film is also suggestive of Brechtian methods, as the courtyard dwellers hang from their balconies to witness the suicide. It is a long shot which foregrounds the inhabitants, who move in unison, following the body as it falls to the ground. We do not see the maid, but we do see the mechanism that makes this community dysfunctional. The figures can participate only as one mechanized mass in this moment of crisis.

Perhaps it seems rather odd to have discussed the film at length without mentioning Expressionism other than in passing. To initiate this discussion it would seem appropriate to return to *Hintertreppe*'s beginning. The film opens with a few shots of a back stairwell—normally one of the hidden places or spaces— of a bourgeois Berlin apartment house. One might expect these images to be establishing shots and anticipate the initiation of the story. Yet the space stands by itself, motivated merely by its physical presence before narration shifts to the maid's chamber. The stairwell is clearly expressionist in style, a motif encountered in numerous films from the period. The awkward curves of the rail, the shadows painted on the wall, and the misshapen staircase attest to this legacy, reminding us of recurring images in other Weimar films, images that are often associated with the uncanny. Although Elsaesser maintains that such uncanny motifs are commonly employed in Weimar film to "cover up a potential class difference,"[41] in *Hintertreppe* composition and editing techniques reject any such cover-up. It is a dark, unpleasant space that signifies the real divisions within the microcosm of the city courtyard, rather than a displaced cover-up of class difference.

Other so-called expressionist elements in the story serve a similar function. For instance, the stilted, infantile behavior of the postman is organized around his inability to function within the community. He is also a conduit to the exterior: serving as a channel of communication, he delivers messages from the outside world. Unable to fulfill his function—he cannot deliver a message to the maid— he is emblematic of the difficulties of adapting to the modern world. Whereas the maid is playfully defiant of encroaching modernity, the postman can only appear

Backstairs (1921), directed by Leopold Jessner.

trapped and helpless as he is caught between two worlds. Peeling back the obvious oedipal scenario—infantile son (postman) kills absent father (lover) over mother (maid)—reveals the spatially and historically contextualized discourses of diverse concerns such as gender and class that are at work in the film.

It should be evident from the preceding discussion that the *Kammer*-forms have a rich and varied genealogy that interacts with cultural, political, private, and social structures. Even though I have been able to trace only the surface of a series of variations, the *Kammer*'s impact is evident: from the dynamic and constantly shifting space which arises from the performance of *Kammermusik;* to the petrified sphere of the *Kammerspiel* theater, where the patriarchal bourgeois compulsively sits and watches the repeated mirroring on stage of his long lost presence; and then on to the *Kammerspielfilm,* where cinema throws into question the validity of the private sphere and its spatial boundaries by highlighting the antichamber, the marginal spaces in *Hintertreppe,* where a struggle ensues.

NOTES

1. Hubert L. Dreyfus and Paul Rabinow, *Michel Foucault: Beyond Structuralism and Hermeneutics* (Chicago: University of Chicago Press, 1983), 106.
2. Needless to say, there is extensive musicological scholarship on chamber music and its history, form, and performance. Any comprehensive discussion of this material is beyond the scope of this article.
3. Ruth Halle Rowen, *Early Chamber Music* (1949; reprint, New York: Da Capo Press, 1974), 5.
4. Rowan pulls together material from various contemporary sources and summarizes: "The furnishings of the room set aside for chamber music varied, of course, with the taste, the income, and the social status of its owner. But while the academic burgher often furnished his own relatively modest chamber music room, and even the ordinary citizen had access to small instrumental ensembles in the coffee house, the majority of theorists make it clear that chamber music was envisioned amid aristocratic, not middle-class surroundings . . . . The word 'chamber' itself referred generally to the men responsible for the administration of a princely residence. Musical affairs at the court were in the hands of a director who had under him a body of chamber musicians, both performers and composers. The director was entrusted with choosing the music to be performed, although it was generally assumed that he would favor his own work. His position in chamber music was a strategic one; yet his status in the aristocratic household was that of a domestic" (6).

5. Homer Ulrich, *Chamber Music* (New York: Columbia University Press, 1966), 2–3.

6. Ibid.

7. Ernst H. Meyer, *Early English Chamber Music: From the Middle Ages to Purcell* (Boston: Marion Boyars, 1982).

8. N. Kilburn, *Chamber Music and Its Masters in the Past and in the Present*, ed. G. E. H. Abraham (New York: Scribner, 1932), 21.

9. Theodor W. Adorno, *Introduction to the Sociology of Music*, trans. E. B. Ashton (New York: Seabury Press, 1976), 86–87.

10. Indeed, one could argue that, coupled with the cultural production of the *Kammer*, the nonlinguistic aspect of the music made it all the more radical (words at least can be monitored).

11. Kilburn, *Chamber Music*, preface.

12. As has been well documented, the drama of nineteenth-century Germany can be located within the restorative tendencies that followed 1848, an era in which the theater was dominated by the sociocultural expression of these tendencies. For instance, the closed structure of the classical drama was considered the sole legitimate form, while anything "revolutionary"—that is, aesthetically innovative—was summarily dismissed.

13. Quoted in *Geschichte der deutschen Literatur vom 18. Jahrhundert bis zur Gegenwart. Band II/I: 1848–1918*, ed. Victor Zmegac (Königstein: Athenäum, 1980), 201.

14. Peter Szondi, *Das lyrische Drama des Fin de siècle*, ed. Henriette Beese (Frankfurt am Main: Suhrkamp, 1975), 21. Szondi's monumental study of the lyrical drama at the turn of the century begins by pointing out how difficult it is to situate this drama in a historical continuum that relies on some notion of a history of genres. The coordinates are too complex. He sees late nineteenth-century intimate drama as a reaction to contemporary drama, and not merely as a function of the development of a transepochal genre. A process is certainly at work, but it cannot be subsumed in a historical continuum. This is precisely what is at stake here: the coordinates include conceptions of space that seek to recuperate the lost *Kammer* onstage.

15. Ibid., 21.

16. See Hugo Fetting, ed., *Max Reinhardt. Schriften. Briefe, Reden, Aufsätze, Interviews, Gespräche, Auszüge aus Regiebüchern* (Berlin: Henschel, 1974).

17. Alfred Dreifus, *Deutsches Theater Berlin. Schumannstrasse 13a. Fünf Kapitel aus der Geschichte einer Schauspielbühne* (Berlin: Henschel Verlag, 1987), 156.

18. Fetting, *Max Reinhardt*, 66.

19. Olivier Sayler, ed., *Max Reinhardt and His Theatre*, trans. Mariele S. Gudernatsch (New York: Benjamin Blom, 1968). First published in 1924.

20. Ibid., 148.

21. Ibid., 24–25.
22. By calling his position reductive, I merely wish to point out that there is a radical process of elision at work which cuts out other aspects and avenues of exploration. For example, in a letter to Carl Mayer (May 29, 1944, in the archives of the Stiftung Deutsche Kinemathek), Kracauer inquires about the *Kammerspielfilm* in a very leading way: "I feel terribly worried about intruding upon your precious time; but would it be possible that you give me some inside information with regard to these films? I mean information not included in the printed material. Did you plan SHATTERED, NEW YEAR'S EVE and THE LAST LAUGH as a sort of trilogy? To what extent did you yourself participate in the directing of these films? How did it happen that you so insistently concentrated upon lower middle class people? Did you consciously portray in all these films the doom of a world governed by despotism and greed? Or how else would you like to formulate the significance of your work? Did you feel indebted to any great writer or poet (Hebbel, for instance or Kafka)? What are your personal impressions of Jessner, Lupu Pick, Murnau? Would you mind telling me the inside story of THE LAST LAUGH: how it came to this film and its concluding sequence, and why Pick was superseded by Murnau? Were you anyhow connected with Karl Grune's film THE STREET?"
23. Siegfried Kracauer, *From Caligari to Hitler. A Psychological History of the German Film* (Princeton, N.J.: Princeton University Press, 1947), 96.
24. Ibid., 97.
25. Lotte H. Eisner, *The Haunted Screen: Expressionism in the German Cinema and the Influence of Max Reinhardt,* trans. Roger Greaves (Berkeley: University of California Press, 1969), 178.
26. These studies of Weimar film were often appropriated in toto by others interested in the period, and one such "imitation" is John D. Barlow's discussion of the *Kammerspielfilm* in *German Expressionist Film* (Boston: Twayne Publishers, 1982). In a chapter called "The Tyranny of Objects," he claims that these works "differ from more consistently expressionist films in their *emphasis on impulse and obsession,* on the psychology of their characters" (137, emphasis added). He thus rather pedantically calls to mind Kracauer's argument as to the psychological "predisposition" that leads to Hitler. Objects, for instance, are acknowledged as figuring prominently in the text. However, they are brought in line with the narrative's trajectory as they once again become the personified vessels of the "predisposed" players: "In *Kammerspiel* films objects take on a life of their own as tokens and reflections of the intensely driven internal lives of the characters" (138). Spatial practices are all but ignored.
27. Kristin Ross, *The Emergence of Social Space: Rimbaud and the Paris Commune* (Minneapolis: University of Minnesota Press, 1988), 5.

28. Ibid., 33.
29. This is the first film that was extensively advertised as a *Kammerspielfilm* in the trade journals. Interestingly, when the discussion first arose about a *Kammerspiel* film, virtually all writers seemed to be holding out for a filmed *Kammerspiel* play—in other words, they saw cinema as another medium for Reinhardt's form, for small audiences and intimate theaters.
30. This is very artfully parodied in such films as Charlie Chaplin's *Modern Times,* where the workers are completely mechanized by the factory stopwatch.
31. Ross, *Social Space,* 53.
32. Shlomith Rimmon-Kenan, *Narrative Fiction: Contemporary Poetics* (London: Methuen, 1983), 3.
33. Michel de Certeau, *The Practice of Everyday Life,* trans. Steven Rendall (Berkeley: University of California Press, 1984), xi.
34. Ibid., xx.
35. Patrice Petro, *Joyless Streets: Women and Melodramatic Representation in Weimar Germany* (Princeton, N.J.: Princeton University Press, 1989), 224.
36. Ibid., 175.
37. See ibid., 18–19.
38. Hans Siemsen, "Die lehrreiche 'Hintertreppe,'" *Weltbühne* 3 (19 January 1922): 71.
39. Petro, *Joyless Streets,* 183.
40. Bertolt Brecht, "Against Georg Lukács," trans. Stuart Hood, in *Aesthetics and Politics,* trans. and ed. Ronald Taylor (New York: Verso, 1977), 73–74.
41. Thomas Elsaesser, "Film History and Visual Pleasure: Weimar Cinema," in *Cinema Histories, Cinema Practices,* ed. Patricia Mellencamp and Philip Rosen (Frederick, Md.: University Publications of America, 1984), 66.

7

KENNETH S. CALHOON

Horror vacui

DER PANTHER

Sein Blick ist vom Vorübergehen der Stäbe
so müd geworden, daß er nichts mehr hält.
Ihm ist, als ob es tausend Stäbe gäbe
und hinter tausend Stäben keine Welt.

Der weiche Gang geschmeidig starker Schritte,
der sich im allerkleinsten Kreise dreht,
ist wie ein Tanz von Kraft um eine Mitte,
in der betäubt ein großer Wille steht.

Nur manchmal schiebt der Vorhang der Pupille
sich lautlos auf—. Dann geht ein Bild hinein,
geht durch der Glieder angespannte Stille—
und hört im Herzen auf zu sein.

THE PANTHER

The passing bars have left his gaze so worn,
that nothing it receives it long retains.
A thousand bars do seem to pass before him,
and behind a thousand bars no world remains.

The padding gait of strides both strong and supple,
in tiny circles turning tightly round,
is like a dance of force about a middle,
in which, benumbed, a mighty will is bound.

But seldom does the curtain of his pupils
draw up—. An image steals past,
goes through the waiting sinews taut with silence,
Goes to the heart and, finally, is lost.[1]

First published in 1903, Rilke's "Panther" is a contemporary of such cinematic sensations as *The Great Train Robbery.* The connection may not be immediately clear. The panther, however, circling wearily in its cage and unable to see beyond the bars that pass before its eyes, is marred by the historical impulses that led to the modern disintegration of perspective, of which both cinema and railroad were constituents. The import of this impairment (and of the cage) can be specified in the context of the post-Enlightenment dramatic tradition, which in the interest of aesthetic autonomy made of visual reciprocity an explicit and systematic taboo: actors were not to jeopardize the illusion by looking directly at the audience. This tradition, which arose with Diderot and Lessing and culminated in the works of Ibsen and Chekhov, exhibits a disaffection with the chaos, voluptuousness, and spatial fluidity of Baroque festival and theater. Lessing's *Laokoon* (named for a figure itself synonymous with entanglement) formulates this rejection in terms of a law that works to disengage the body of the spectator by enforcing a division between spectator and spectacle. This aesthetic distance is replicated in the structure of domestic drama, in which the parameters of the stage coincide with the limits of an intimate interior that is by definition disembodied. It is hardly by chance that technological and artistic modernity, which brought an end to this tradition (as well as to the autonomy of that interior), and to which early cinema also belongs, witnessed a reappraisal of the Baroque. Heinrich Wölfflin's seminal *Renaissance und Barock* appeared in 1888; the arrival of motion pictures seven years later (1895) constituted a provisional return of the reciprocated gaze, undermining the spatial boundaries defended arduously by an aesthetics struggling with a fear of the void.

The Baroque identity of world and stage is summoned by Rilke himself in a poem that figures the portal of a cathedral, yawning a vast and dark emptiness, as a proscenium arch that openly contradicts the closure, intimacy, and gentle illumination of the modern interior and its theatrical counterpart:

Sehr viele Weite ist gemeint damit:
so wie mit den Kulissen einer Szene
die Welt gemeint ist; und so wie durch jene
der Held im Mantel seiner Handlung tritt:—

so tritt das Dunkel dieses Tores handelnd
auf seiner Tiefe tragisches Theater. . . .

A great expanse is here implied:
just as the scenery on stage
implies the world; and just as the hero
bestrides the scene in the mantle of his role:—

so the darkness of this portal performs
tragic theater over its depth. . . .
        "DAS PORTAL," 1905/06

This opening is the passage through which theater migrates, from the passion performed within as part of a sacred rite (the historical origins of European theater) to the street outside, where the savior's only remaining representatives are the blind beggars, madmen, and other outcasts who serve as his collective dramatic vehicle ("wie ein einziger Akteur"). They, like the fool, are the descendants of a ritual dimension they have the power to restore, the inversion of sacred and profane values being the achievement of both the carnival and *theatrum mundi*.[2] The child's riddle that challenges one to name an invention for seeing through walls draws wit from the mundanity of its answer: the window. Admitting light, the window is the mundane counterpart to the cathedral's portal (emitting darkness), a threshold that became sacred again in an age in which the theater itself became a device for seeing through walls. At the dawn of this age a play straddling the divide between popular and exalted drama also straddles that threshold, which even the devil, who in the guise of Mephistopheles is the most urbane of tricksters, is compelled to respect. A darkness born of light, Goethe's Lucifer dramatizes Baroque chiaroscuro,[3] which recurs in Expressionist cinema, where phantoms personify an ambivalence toward those apertures that threaten to expose the interior to the outside. The window per se is one of these, as are the stage and movie screen. The window of a moving railway car is a specifically modern example—one that lends the spectacle the impermanence and immateriality of the phantom and suggests a connection between the visual dissipation of Rilke's panther and film itself.

From Lessing to Lumière

Rilke's arch has a precursor in Goethe. Reveling in the Easter thaw that figures his own reconciliation with the earth, Faust turns his gaze from the melting streams to the townfolk, who, themselves reborn, emerge from the city gate as if from the womb: "Aus dem hohlen finstern Tor/ Dringt ein buntes Gewimmel hervor" ("Through that cavelike gloomy gate/ Pours a motley human spate").[4] Dark and hollow, the gate is at once birth canal and proscenium. This conflation of bodily cavity and theater is consistent with a popular dramatic tradition that understood the stage as an opening rather than a wall, and as such located player and spectator along a continuous and fluid spatial axis. Modern theater broke this continuum, enforcing a division between inside and out that defined the former as a disembodied interior, and Faust, his doggerel notwithstanding, already inhabits a world in which the theater connotes mediacy, distance, and an isolation of the spirit. The tension between modern (i.e., illusionist or naturalistic) drama and the popular tradition in the theater is reflected in the difference between the *absorption* of Faust on the brink of suicide and the *theatricality*[5] of the Easter processional that restores him to circulation ("Die Träne quillt, die Erde hat mich wieder" [A tear falls, the earth now has me back] 784).[6] Proclaiming his own resurrection, Faust is transported to the spectacle unfolding before the city gate, where theater and festival converge on a scene in which the social classes intermingle and to which the phrase "buntes Gewimmel" ("motley spate") is altogether appropriate.[7]

This return of an embodied outside runs contrary to the program of domestic drama, in which the growing autonomy of the intimate sphere coincides with the increased self-containment of theatrical space. The gradual confinement of the audience to a darkened area invisible from the stage is commensurate with Diderot's insistence that the spectacle not evince an awareness of being watched.[8] Standing in the dark, incidentally, is the condition for being able to see through a window into a house, which illustrates the degree to which domestic drama helps define a privacy predicated on (self-)surveillance.[9] For Lessing, the need for detached observation dictated an enmity toward the opening into the body potentially represented by the mouth of the famous Laocoön figure.[10] The sculptor, so Lessing maintained, captured his subject in the moment prior to the agonized cry, leaving the scream itself—and the gaping mouth—to the imagination, exemplifying a classical restraint that allowed for a corresponding composure on the part of the beholder. At stake here is the autonomy that is eroded whenever the work of art provokes disgust, nausea, or any other response that summons the spectator's *body*. The modern theatergoer, like Foucault's clinical observer, sits silent and motionless (*muet et sans geste*) in the presence of a self-absorbed tableau.[11]

The placement of spectators in a darkened room before a spectacle that, for all intents and purposes, was two-dimensional (domestic dramas were often referred to as "family paintings" [*Familiengemälde*]) would seem to anticipate the cinema, in which the illusionist thrust of modern theater is total, and which reinforces the decorum—the distance—that eighteenth-century drama helped institute. It should be added, however, that this distance had to be cultivated and was in no way endemic to the early cinema, whose original settings—in markets, fairs, and exhibitions—bordered on the carnivalesque. Today's cinemagoer who finds it necessary to "hush" a fellow viewer renews the residual tension between the illusionist aims of film production and a popular tradition in which spectators were as much participants as recipients. The development of cinema thus repeats the transitional history of the theater here summarized by Robert Weimann: "Actors did not perform in the midst of an audience but against a localized scene which the spectators watched but which their presence did not help constitute. . . . No longer the creator of the scene, the performer needed only to adapt himself to it. Scenic conventions of locality achieved a greater autonomy, and the beginning of the 'fourth wall' . . . was set up between audience and play."[12]

As a barrier, the fourth wall creates a safety zone for the audience. If the development, in both drama and film, from embodiment to representation can be seen as part of the civilizing process described by Freud, Elias, or even Lévi-Strauss, then the advent of the cinema seems to have induced a regression, in which the wall suddenly becomes an opening all over again. Let us imagine that the "cavelike gloomy gate" Faust describes is a tunnel from which issues not a throng of people but a locomotive. Such, roughly, was the spectacle beheld by visitors to the Grand Café in Paris in 1895 when Louis Lumière screened his *L'arrivée d'un train à la Ciotat,* in which a slowing locomotive pulls toward the camera, even passing it partially before drawing to a halt. It has frequently been claimed that the spectators, growing apprehensive at the train's approach, rose from their seats and fled for fear of being struck. The veracity of this account tends to be doubted even by those who mobilize it.[13] The residual value of the anecdote lies in the way it implicates both railroad and cinema as part of the common anxiety that is the modern age. The train seems a particular expression of the formula $E=MC^2$, not only through its conjunction of unprecedented velocity and mass, but also because it tethers the human subject to the moving object so as to make speed an attribute not of the train but of the landscape racing past. Like a cat in a moving automobile, the early railway passenger could only wince at the vistas that flashed by his or her window, and the difficult adjustment to the rapid succession of sights, an adjustment that took years and entailed the conversion of the view into a tableau devoid of depth, helped condition the possibility of cinematic perception.[14] Train travel and moviegoing thus represent two kindred experiences of visual speed, and for decades following Lumière's demonstration, the cinema continued to project the railroad as its unique mechanical double.[15]

The origins of cinema thus appear traumatic, though one hastens to add that the very concept of "trauma" was at this time being assimilated to a framework that made origins as such ever more indeterminate. That framework was psychoanalysis, which described the power of an *anxiety* to project—as memory—the anticipated *event* whose impact the anxiety is there to mitigate. In *Beyond the Pleasure Principle* (1920), Freud cites the railway disaster as prototypical of the kind of "severe mechanical concussion" to which traumatic neuroses may be attributed.[16] It is a moment in Freud's thinking at which he returns, though briefly and with some trepidation, to what he calls the "old, naive theory of shock," which would ascribe greater etiological importance to the immediate disturbance than to experiences reactivated from childhood.[17] This juncture is pivotal in the now familiar discussion by Wolfgang Schivelbusch, for whom the reinstatement of a more historical, less psychological understanding of trauma is reason for locating the railroad within the realm of "actual cause." Schivelbusch argues that the advent of the railroad, with its real potential for sensational disaster, constitutes the kind of unalloyed fright that, according to Freud, gives rise to traumatic neurosis.[18] Inspired in part by Walter Benjamin, various recent studies have incorporated this argument, extrapolating that cinema emerged as a strategy for repeating the shock, a neurosis as it were, its function being to master the stimulus retroactively by creating the anxiety whose absence enabled the initial trauma.[19] So understood, cinema effects a hypercathexis, much like the tensing of the body in expectation of a blow.

Two signatures common to these studies are revealing. First, under the aegis of "better history," they reinstate a decidedly mechanical explanation, invoking Freud at the very point where he seems most prone to determinism,[20] and lending the train the status of instigator of an original shock. Second, they focus more on the nature of the train than of the *space* it threatens to invade—this despite their acknowledgment of the train compartment and the movie house as cognate interiors: both are enclosed spaces within which one views a rapid sequence of moving images. This is not to say that the historical novelty of the invention was negligible, but rather that its encroachment on existing parameters had been anticipated by an aesthetic tradition that had been bracing itself against modernity well before the modern came to be embodied by an engine spewing smoke and chasing the horizon. As a machine for penetrating, conquering, and traversing space, the train has a unique capacity for investing the surface of the movie screen with a semblance of depth. Furthermore, the recognition of this depth as an illusory space is a crucial step in reestablishing the autonomy of the interior, in which everything, including space, is mere appearance. As a place where nothing exists except as *Schein,* the interior was a product of a tradition that had defined the aesthetic in terms of an immunity to the instincts of self-preservation. This aesthetics, whose preoccupation with unpleasurable objects had already led "beyond the pleasure principle," itself displays the symptoms of an anxiety. Not unlike the compulsion to repeat identified by Freud, it makes mimesis the guarantor of a distance that deprives frightening phenomena of their immediacy. The achievement of the aesthetic is thus a neutralization of the defensive impulses that allegedly sent spectators running into the aisles of the Grand Café in 1895.

More than a century before Lumière's train arrived, and well before the arrival of the railroad itself, a philosophical vocabulary was in place that named *fright* as the explicit antonym of aesthetic experience. The prerequisite of such experience was the very incredulity threatened by the locomotive bearing down on the cranking camera. The taboo hereby violated had in fact been described by Lessing in his attempt to explain the restraint exhibited by the Laocoön statue: the failure of the marble man to cry out in pain was consistent with a prohibition against any artistic rendering in which *imitation* would pass itself off as *nature.* The theory of the sublime, which admitted the *illusion* of fear but not fear itself, marked the outer boundary of a more general aesthetics that never wanted anything other than semblance, verisimilitude—*Schein.*[21] In a passage that acquires a fresh resonance when read with an eye to Lumière's film, Lessing warns against the artistic incursion of internal responses that have no aesthetic counterpart:

> "Representations of fear," [a perceptive critic] says, "of melancholy, terror, compassion, etc., can arouse our dislike [*Unlust*] only insofar as we believe the evil to be real. Hence, these feelings can be transformed into pleasant ones by recalling that it is an artificial illusion. But whether or not we believe the object to be real, the disagreeable sensation of disgust [*des Ekels*] results, by virtue of the law of our imagination, from the mere mental image. Is the fact that the artistic imitation is ever so recognizable sufficient to reconcile the offended sensibilities? Our dislike did not arise from the supposition that the evil was real, but from the mere mental image of it, which is indeed real. Feelings of disgust are therefore always real [*allezeit Natur*] and never imitations."[22]

Lessing's preoccupation with nausea as a response the spectacle should not induce betrays the markedly anti-Baroque sensibility of *Laokoon*—a persistent concern for maintaining clear and distinct boundaries of which nausea represents a transgression. It is worth noting that vomiting, in the Baroque, was both sign and object of wonderment,[23] a fact that links wonder with the delimitation of the self and suggests a form of aesthetic reception which the law of beauty works to interdict. This law is not simply a proscription against the open mouth of the statue, but against a public that stares agape—open-mouthed—at the spectacle before it.

To "gape" (*gaffen*), and to "cleave" (*klaffen*), words that describe the mouth of the hypothetically screaming Laocoön figure, render the Ancient Greek *cháskein,* from which we derive "chaos," and also "gas."[24] The second derivation helps explain the first, for "chaos" (especially as it came to be defined by Newton) does not denote sheer anarchy, but the decentering process of entropy—the increase with time of the distance between bodies or particles in space. Among Newton's concerns was the way physical bodies act upon other bodies even at great distances and across a void (i.e., in the absence of any intermediary material). This is the *actio in distans* to which the absolute monarch aspires—the ability to exercise power over distant satellites with which he has lost direct contact. The king who names himself after the sun envies not only the brilliance of that heavenly body, but also its gravitational pull.[25] The principle of *actio in distans,* which underscores the link between distance and disembodiment, is applicable to a model of dramatic reception, such as Lessing's, from which the body has been banished: the modern spectator may be *moved,* but not *touched.* The chaotic opening, such as the gaping mouth of a screaming Laocoön would represent, does not simply mark a delimitation of the subject, but also of the disembodied, and as such autonomous, interior in which modern subjectivity is constituted.[26] An aesthetics that valorizes distance is intent on reinforcing the closure of this interior against the delimited excess of an expanding universe. The revulsion at the yawning cavity parallels, then, a *horror vacui,* a fear that, prompted by the suggestion of a vast and empty space, sends the modern bourgeois subject in search of an interior both closed and filled.[27]

The arrival of Lumière's train constitutes a violation whose nature is given emblematic form in René Magritte's painting *La Durée poignardée,* which depicts a sleek locomotive trailing smoke and emerging, as if from a tunnel, out of a living room fireplace. The fireplace, especially in the Anglo-American tradition, is the point of entry for Santa Claus, who, in knowing which children have behaved badly, imports a panoptical omniscience into a domestic interior so closed that he has to squeeze in through the flue. The sight of the chubby dwarf tumbling out of the chimney evokes a comical birth (tethered, significantly, to the bearing of gifts) that makes the hearth both womb and stage—a scene watched furtively by children themselves intent on not being seen.[28] Like Father Christmas, the spectator of modern drama is a benign intruder. In the fictional preface meant to explain the history of Diderot's *Le Fils naturel* (1757), the author recalls how, with the contrivance of an insider, he became privy to a play performed in a private home and exclusively for members of the family in which the events dramatized had occurred: "I climbed through the window into the salon . . . where I, without being seen, could see and hear what followed."[29]

These examples represent moments in a history of the interior in which Magritte's painting implicates Lumière's film. The film, in turn—at least in its mythological dimension as "primal scene"—provokes an acute agoraphobia already voiced by the "poet" of the *Vorspiel* to Goethe's *Faust,* whose opposition of spirit and marketplace (*agora*)[30] follows an aversion to visual overload:

> O sprich mir nicht von jener bunten Menge,
> Bei deren Anblick uns der Geist entflieht.
> Verhülle mir das wogende Gedränge,
> Das wider Willen uns zum Strudel zieht.
> (*Faust,* ll. 59–62)

> Speak not to me of that rank motley swarm,
> At very sight of which one's spirit shrinks.
> O, spare me from this gurging human storm
> That gulfs us and in whirlpool sinks.

The marketplace, here the site of a dramatic production with all the earmarkings of popular theater (Harlequin included), resembles also the kind of location that was to furnish the cinema with its first setting, and the poet's retreat blazes a trail for those Parisians who supposedly fled the approach of Lumière's "train." Yet the poet's desire for a veiled view ("Verhülle mir . . .") anticipates something more mundane, namely the introduction in the nineteenth century of window drapes into not only the private home but also the railroad car, required by passengers who found the

René Magritte, *Time Transfixed* (*La Dureé poignardeé*), oil on canvas, 1938, 147 x 98.7 cm,
Joseph Winterbotham Collection. Photograph @1995, The Art Institute of Chicago. All
Rights reserved.

view from the moving train simply intolerable.[31] The gradual adjustment of these passengers (over the course of a decade) to the rapid succession of visual stimuli created a cinematic audience *avant le lettre*. The cinema adopted certain technical features of the railroad—for example, the mounting of cameras on tracks, the basis of the standard "tracking shot," as well as an early cinematic genre meant to simulate railroad journeys.[32] More importantly, perhaps, is the role played by the railroad in creating a culture of speed and in enabling us to describe the effects of speed on the visual apparatus. In 1825 Peter Mark Roget observed how the spoked wheels of a moving train seen through the vertical bars of a fence appeared either to stand still or to turn backward—an illusion made possible by the retina's momentary retention of optical impressions after the object seen is gone from view.[33] This "persistence of vision" is the principle behind such devices as the zoetrope, and eventually the film projector, which interrupt the beam of light between frames in order to provide a dark background against which the persisting image of the previous frame combines with the subsequent image to create the illusion of a continuous movement. American inventor Albert E. Smith, who helped perfect the projector, described how, during a railroad journey, he noticed that the speed of the train made the upright pickets of the fence beside the tracks virtually invisible, making him realize that he could reduce the flicker effect of film by increasing its frequency.[34]

The observations of Roget and Smith help shape a context within which to place Rilke's panther, which also perceives the world through (passing) vertical bars, and which finds refuge from the onslaught of visual stimuli behind the "curtain of the pupil" ("Vorhang der Pupille"). This metaphorization of the eye as window suggests, too, the shutter and aperture of a camera, emphasizing what is mechanical about a subject beyond stimulation. The poem also stresses the immaterial nature of the surface, and the taming of the beast corresponds to a complete two-dimensionality—a flickering, shimmering simulacrum behind which there is nothing:

> Sein Blick ist vom Vorübergehen der Stäbe
> so müd geworden, daß er nichts mehr hält.
> Ihm ist, als ob es tausend Stäbe gäbe
> und hinter tausend Stäben keine Welt.

> The passing bars have left his gaze so worn,
> that nothing it receives it long retains.
> A thousand bars do seem to pass before him,
> and behind a thousand bars no world remains.

Mechanical in movement and empty inside, the panther represents the same uncanny hybrid of animation and lifelessness typical of those monsters the cinema

154

would later use to turn the camera on itself. The animal's denatured gaze anticipates the dull and vacant eyes of Dr. Frankenstein's famous creation. A Kaspar Hauser of sorts ("I've kept him in darkness until now"),[35] the disfigured creature is a monument to a process of modernization—of "enlightenment"—in which the domination of nature is indelibly inscribed.

The Woman at the Window, or *Nosferatu the Sailor*

The association of train and panther makes vivid the mythicizing function of the anecdote of Lumière's frightened spectators. Treating this account as a fabrication, Christian Metz explains its origin in terms of a paradox: while no moviegoer ever really mistakes the cinematic illusion for reality, narrative films are nonetheless constructed *as if* such a viewer existed. This implied viewer, whose naive expectations furnish the standards of verisimilitude, represents a primitive part of the self that provides the viewer with a phylogenetic foil against which his or her composed incredulity is affirmed. The memory of spectators so gullible they felt physically endangered by the image on the screen is thus literally a "screen memory" (*Deckerinnerung*), the projection of a residual anxiety as external past event.[36] Metz draws an anthropological analogy, comparing the "sophisticated" cinemagoer to a tribal community in which rituals using masks are performed, and although the performers no longer ascribe magical powers to the masks, they can tell of a remote past in which their ancestors truly *believed*.[37] The comparison is relevant in that it locates the Lumière episode within the process of disenchantment that informs the history of the theater, in which myth gives way to realism, (magical) reenactment to acting, and in which masks, drained of their power, survive in the form of burlesque parody or baroque masquerade.[38] Theatrical descendants of ritual such as the fool and trickster (suggested by not only the *lustige Person* at the beginning of Goethe's *Faust* but also Mephisto himself) continue, like Lumière's train, to threaten the "fourth wall," and with it the internality that modern aesthetics strives to maintain. The aim of this aesthetics is not magic, but substitution. Schivelbusch's histories, whether of the railway or of artificial lighting, attest to a process of reenchantment in which technological progress is tempered through aesthetic intervention; just as the train compartment was converted into a salon in which the industrial origins of the railroad could be comfortably forgotten, so too the increased efficiency of lighting was resisted by a bourgeoisie that preferred the warm flicker and soft shadows of the candle and oil lamp to the unerring brilliance produced by gas and electricity. These innovations were countered with strategies for shading and refracting that gave the illusion of something preindustrial, even mythical, anchoring the lamp, along with the fireplace and stove, at the social and spiritual center of the inhabited space. Certain of Mörike's poems treat the lamp and hearth (*Herd*) as guarantors of memory and introspection,[39] and Rilke's "Apollo" likens the gaze of the sightless

155

statue, which is ultimately the self-directed gaze of the beholder, to a lamp that has been dimmed:

> sein Torso glüht noch wie ein Kandelaber,
> in dem sein Schauen, nur zurückgeschraubt,
>
> sich hält und glänzt.

> his torso keeps on glowing like a lamp,
> in which his gaze, now only turned to low,
>
> abides and glimmers.

This diminished brightness represents a disinterestedness, which in the nineteenth century found its spatial articulation in the middle-class interior, the locus of an autonomy that depended on the exclusion of all functional relations. The "Selig scheint es in ihm selbst," the aphorism with which Mörike circumscribed his famous lamp, is brilliant in its isolation of *Schein,* which it both localizes within the private chamber and splits off from the literal radiance that is the lamp's instrumental function.[40] To see the aesthetic object as an object unto itself is to recognize a self-sufficiency guaranteed by the ambient space it occupies, in the case of Mörike's poem a "Lustgemach,"[41] and generally an enclosure from which all the exigencies of survival have been locked out. The compound "Lustgemach" carries into the bourgeois interior an echo of the classical *locus amoenus,*[42] designating as *utopia* a region in which self-preservation has ceased to be a concern. The interior and the work of art, as domains in which appearance prevails, present the common possibility that one can experience shock without reverting to the insular posture of the organism struggling simply to stay alive. This, at least, is what Adorno contended, holding that aesthetic shock (*Erschütterung*) enabled one to transcend the confines of one's individual ego by entering into a kind of self-annihilation—a surrender to the almost abject realization that the work of art is something radically not of the self.[43] It is the state of being overwhelmed by the knowledge that the artwork does not exist for us and does not depend on us for its truth. The train that seems on the verge of leaving the movie screen manifests the indifference already intimated by Mörike: "But whatever is beautiful / Shines blissfully in itself." In keeping with Adorno's particular antihistoricism, the truth of the lamp is not immanent in its historical context; rather, its truth is released through the very disintegration of that context[44]—a moment emblematically deferred onto Lumière's film, in which the train undoes the integrity of an enclosed space that extends the formal closure celebrated by the poem. That moment, and this film rather specifically, was for Adorno the telos of an aesthetic tradition whose doctrine of disinterestedness had to delay its confirmation until modernism avowed the radical Otherness of art—something that doctrine had intimated yet which its formalism suppressed. Laocoön, whose restraint represented a triumph of appearance over expression—of *Schein* over *Ausdruck*—would wait more than a century to scream. Scream he did, however, even if the dreaded moment of temporalized animation took the form of a train unfrozen from the stasis of still photography: "Das Verhältnis zur Kunst war keines von Einverleibung, sondern umgekehrt verschwand der Betrachter in der Sache; erst recht ist das der Fall in modernen Gebilden, die auf [den Betrachter] zufahren wie zuweilen Lokomotiven im Film." ("The relationship to art was not one of incorporation, but on the contrary the viewer disappeared into the object; this is only truly the case in modern constructions, which approach [the viewer] like locomotives in film.")[45]

The dialectics Adorno describes is one by means of which images that try to present history as nature eventually falter to expose nature's own historicity—the fact that nature is always *Bild*. The view of the countryside from the window of the speeding train, like landscape painting earlier, was one in a long succession of historical mediations of the natural world. When Ralph Waldo Emerson reported what he saw from the window of his Pullman car in 1834, his words suggested that the experience deprived nature of any semblance of stability: "The very permanence of matter seems compromised and trees, fields, hills, hitherto esteemed symbols of stability, do absolutely dance by you."[46] In Murnau's *Nosferatu* (1922), in which the impermanence of matter takes the form of a phantom characterized as "bodiless" (*körperlos*), the disorientation noted by Emerson acquires a decidedly demonic tone. Abandoned by the guides leading him up Dracula's mountain, Jonathan Harker (Hutter) mounts a horse-drawn carriage, driven by the vampire himself, which travels at a velocity so blinding that the effect required trick photography. This is a speed more appropriate to the railroad, and Harker resembles those early train passengers as he peers from behind the curtain of his carriage, staring wide-eyed and open-mouthed at the forest racing by.

Murnau's apparent quotation of a discourse on railway travel may be said to efface technology by replacing the train with an object of superstition, preserving reason by displacing the irrational from the machine; or by virtue of the aforementioned dialectic, it unmasks the machine as truly demonic by reviving the primitive agon of which rationality was born.[47] One might also argue that *Nosferatu* isolates the spatial dimension of train travel as the salient component of horror, and this is my more limited claim: the vampire film clarifies what was at stake in the film of the approaching locomotive, namely the illusory space of the movie screen and the implications of that illusion for the "interior" it occupies. Kracauer's association of this illusory space with a precipitous vertical depth (*das Bodenlose*)[48] evokes the sublime, the importance of which is again apparent in *Nosferatu*. During his second night in the vampire's castle, Harker opens his chamber door and peers down the long corridor, at the end of which he spies his host standing as if frozen. This shot, which has the feel of a still photograph, is then repeated at closer range, in a manner not to suggest movement but to scrutinize more closely what has already been seen. Seized with fear, Harker shuts his door and runs to a window in search of an escape route, finding instead a deep and craggy crevasse below. As he cowers in the corner, his chamber door swings open, and Nosferatu emerges from the darkness into the lighted room. The shot from the window into the abyss below has the simple, structural function of representing the corridor out of which Nosferatu appears as a corresponding and equivalent depth. The formal introduction of depth has the effect of bringing the monster to life, a process of animation that repeats the supersession of photography by motion pictures, which Lumière's work was meant to demonstrate.

The two scenes from *Nosferatu* described thus far—the first in which Harker stares agape from the window of the speeding carriage, the second in which he peers into the chasm below his bedchamber—point to a pattern in the film that reveals the historical saturation of the window per se. The second example in particular conflates window and abyss; the first, in which the terrified passenger takes refuge behind a heavy curtain, inflects the history of window covering with the dialectics of fear. Sunlight pouring in through an uncovered window is what finally destroys the vampire, who as fiend duplicates the window as "source of disquiet" ("Quelle der Beunruhigung").[49] This climactic moment repeats the framing of the earlier scene in which Ellen, in a gesture of self-sacrifice, throws open the same window to expose herself to the vampire watching from the abandoned house opposite hers (a doubling of the facade without a soul).

The shot composition that frames Ellen, seen from behind, against a window suddenly flung open, reproduces a generic constellation found in a painting that predates *Nosferatu* by exactly one hundred years—Caspar David Friedrich's *Frau am Fenster* (*Woman at the Window,* 1822). Depicted is the full-length figure of a woman (thought to be the artist's wife), her back to the beholder, contemplating the placid diurnal spectacle beyond a large window (presumably of their apartment overlooking the Elbe canal in Dresden). The lower portion of the window consists not of glass but of wooden shutters, the center panel of which has been opened to frame the subject's head against a faint background of distant poplars. Rising in the middle ground is the mast of a ship, its tip visible through the leaded glass that begins where the shutters end. This horizontal division between transparency and opaqueness occurs just above head level, manifesting an ambivalence toward an opening that cannot admit a voluminous light without also compromising the privacy of those within. The transcendence alluded to by the mast (being like a church spire) goes beyond the iconography of Romantic allegory;[50] it is a sign of sustained interiority, "an inside without an outside."[51] There is a consistency between the diaphanous immateriality of background and sky and the absence from view of the ship's hull—its "belly." The frigate, after all, represents the avenue of transportation and commerce that bore Nosferatu, who literally "hatches" out of the ship's hold, from the Balkans to Northern Europe.

Nosferatu—Symphony of Terror (1922), directed by F. W. Murnau.

As a remainder of what might be seen as the historical unconscious of Friedrich's painting, the bit of exposed mast hints at the "wide world," which is absent from an interior to which the outside is available as mere view. In place of the seafaring vessel beheld by the "woman at the window," Ellen spies a phantom who by nature is indifferent to walls and whom Murnau's film expressly names as the captain of a ship. The vampire's role is, however, most ambiguous. If he represents bloodthirsty capital moving insipidly and ruthlessly across Europe (and following herein the migration of Eastern European Jews),[52] he is also the aesthete who shuns the light of day, his bodilessness true to the renunciation that precludes participation among the living. This apparent contradiction gives shape to the tension between an ideology, which finds freedom in self-denial, and the social practices this ideology at once undergirds and falsifies. Straining against the fetters that bind him to the mast of the ship he commands, Odysseus enacts the process of self-discipline that divides the spirit from the body and projects this division as that between inside and out.[53] The struggle that wrests art from the realm of necessity also brands the oarsmen with what for the nineteenth century was the height of

159

Caspar David Friedrich, *Woman at the Window* (*Frau am Fenster*), 1822, oil on canvas, 44 x 37 cm, Staatliche Museen zu Berlin, Nationalgalerie.

uncouthness—insensitivity to music.[54] After a life of self-denial, Nosferatu (with the ears of a bat) succumbs to the Sirens' song and is destroyed. It is a transgression that resurrects the outside as presence and thus, appropriately, concentrates fear on the window itself.

We know that German Expressionist filmmakers (directors and cinematographers) borrowed consciously from Friedrich and other Romantics, due in part to a common investment in the fantastic.[55] Of still greater importance is the multiplication of framings by means of which Friedrich ironizes and violates spatial conventions. His *Frau am Fenster* exemplifies a telescoping of progressively smaller apertures (niche, window, shutter panel) that draws the eye rapidly into a depth of field reinforced by the reverse chiaroscuro and the axis of the floorboards. A similar succession of complementary framings occurs in *Nosferatu* when Harker passes through the outer gate of the vampire's castle and follows a path that takes him through other portals, bringing him face to face with his host, who emerges ominously from the tunnel-like blackness of an opposing arch. "Aus dem hohlen finstern Tor"—Faust's words, so accurately do they describe the vampire's emergence, reveal the theatrical ramifications of the Romantic pictorial constellation from which the film borrows.

Woman at the Window is an instance of Friedrich's signature unorthodoxy, namely the figure whose back is turned squarely toward the beholder. *Der Wanderer über dem Nebelmeer* (*The Wanderer above the Sea of Mist*, 1818), which in placing the subject before an abyss suggests the vertiginous latency of the window, is a more famous example. This turning of the back is a genuinely dramatic gesture, and from the standpoint of modern theater (à la Diderot), no less an affront to spectatorial autonomy than looking directly at the audience (or into the camera).[56] Friedrich's paintings commonly tether the eye of the beholder to unstable subject positions—on a mountaintop or in a boat—for which the aforementioned human figures are but "diegetic" extensions. At a time when the tableau had come to be the model for the theater, Friedrich was ignoring precisely those conventions of landscape composition, as established by Poussin and Claude Lorrain, which worked to disentangle the beholder from the pictorial space. These conventions dictated that the material closure of the composition be reinforced by framing strategies within the scene—for example, the placement of a dark cypress or a marble column at the painting's left or right edge. The technique of darkening the lower foreground to the point of invisibility, which had the effect of both "grounding" the beholder and setting him or her apart from the spectacle, was contemporaneous with the confinement of the theatergoer to a darkened area invisible from the stage.[57]

A need for self-disentanglement was identified by Wilhelm Worringer (1907) as the anthropological impetus behind the abstraction—the lack of spatial perspective—characterizing so-called primitive and non-Western art (and eventually European modernism). The practice of isolating objects in space expressed a

Nosferatu—Symphony of Terror (1922), directed by F. W. Murnau.

desire for clear boundaries in the face of a luxuriant and enchanted natural world whose boundless undifferentiation threatened the borders of the self.[58] This linkage between abstraction and distantiation was confirmed by Horkheimer and Adorno, for whom enlightenment was a process of spiraling abstraction that began with the "savage" shuddering at the cry of nature reverberating through his innermost soul.[59] Freud had already addressed the mechanism through which internal disturbances are relocated outward, external dangers being easier to flee from than "inner demons."[60] Nausea represents the most basic impulse to project outward, and Lessing's aesthetic interdiction against a shrieking Laocoön targets a visceral nature whose return would bind subject to object. The Siren episode projects nature's cry as distant singing, but it also recalls what ultimately is at risk: the fettered Odysseus, the quintessence of the immobilized spectator, commemorates the primordial struggle every hint of which bourgeois interiority had systematically erased.

Decades before Horkheimer and Adorno used the Siren episode to demonstrate the paradoxes of liberation, but exactly contemporaneous with Worringer's claim that modern art exhibited signs of a "primitive" agoraphobia (*Raumscheu*), Rilke composed his "Island of the Sirens" (1907), delivering a chilling account of how the fear of the unknown evolves a heightened sense of self (and of isolation). The poem tells of Odysseus trying to recreate in words the terror that derived not from the Sirens' song but from an expansive calm that eerily proclaimed the *possibility* of their singing. This apprehension has no external source, and the crew's desperate flight effectively makes anxiety revert to fear by giving it an object once again; they created the object in the very act of running from it. Goethe's "Erlkönig" tells a similar tale, and the attempt by Odysseus's oarsmen to escape by rowing blindly ("blindlings") evokes the response of children seeking refuge behind their eyelids, as if one were not threatened by what one cannot see. Regression is the price of progress, however. A society that abolishes superstition, thought Freud, becomes increasingly neurotic. The interior (psyche), purged of everything immediate, creaturely, and agonic, develops into an echo chamber in which the call of the wild, which the civilizing process has pushed beyond earshot, reawakens as inner voice. Grown wholly introspective, the *horror vacui* reveals that there is no greater fear than the fear of nothing whatsoever:

Die Insel der Sirenen

Wenn er denen, die ihm gastlich waren,
spät, nach ihrem Tage noch, da sie
fragten nach den Fahrten und Gefahren,
still berichtete: er wußte nie

wie sie schrecken und mit welchem jähen
Wort sie wenden, daß sie so wie er
in dem blau gestillten Inselmeer
die Vergoldung jener Inseln sähen,

deren Anblick macht, daß die Gefahr
umschlägt; denn nun ist sie nicht im Tosen
und im Wüten, wo sie immer war.
Lautlos kommt sie über die Matrosen,

welche wissen, daß es dort auf jenen
goldnen Inseln manchmal singt—,
und sich blindlings in die Ruder lehnen,
wie umringt

von der Stille, die die ganze Weite
in sich hat und an die Ohren weht,
so als wäre ihre andre Seite
der Gesang, dem keiner widersteht.

Island of the Sirens

Whenever those who took him in,
late, after their day was done,
inquired about the voyages and adventures,
he grew still: he never knew

how to frighten them and with which bold
word to grip them so that they, like he,
in the hushed blue of that island-sea,
would envision islands shimmering like gold,

whose very sight makes danger veer
around: for it is not the pounding
now and rage, which always summoned fear.
Without a sound it overtakes the sailors,

who know that on those distant
golden isles there is sometimes singing—
and blindly lean into the oars,
as if surrounded

164

by the calm that has a vastness
all its own and is heard upon the wind,
As if its other aspect
were the song that pulls you in.

The quiet that strikes fear into the hearts of Odysseus's crew lends a certain gravity to the noiselessness with which the panther's eyes open. This constellation of terror is confirmed by the horror film, in which an absolute, all-encompassing silence is the surest sign that one is not alone. The horror film makes explicit, in other words, what is generally the case: the particular power of those early motion pictures arises in part from their inability to speak to us. After the advent of sound in cinema around 1930, the muteness of the silent era lived on in the form of monsters, such as Frankenstein's creature or the Mummy, which could seldom speak and were all the more uncanny for it. Karl Freund, who directed *The Mummy* (Hollywood, 1932), was director of photography on *Der Golem* (1920), in which the creature's stony silence is foregrounded as a constituent of horror. When the hulking man of clay first appears before the terrified citizens of Prague's ghetto, the words with which he is presented imply a contradiction between his muteness and his supposed harmlessness: "He cannot speak, but he will not hurt you." *The Golem,* whose creation gives phantasmagoric shape to the act of cinematic animation, embodies what is monstrous about film as such, and the above words of assurance address whichever anxieties or fears the projected spectacle activates.

This figural doubling of film within film occurs literally when Rabbi Loew takes his new servant to the imperial palace to urge the emperor to rescind a decree expelling the Jews from the city.[61] A festival is in progress, and the emperor bids the rabbi entertain the assembled guests with a display of the magical powers for which he is renowned. The rabbi agrees to "show" the history of his people and their patriarchs, but with a proviso: "Let no one laugh or even speak if they value their lives." Then, with a wave of his arm, he produces a moving image on the palace wall, one we recognize as cinematic, which shows Moses leading the Exodus out of Egypt. The very solemnity of the scene triggers irreverence, and it is not long before the audience explodes with laughter. In response, a wrathful Moses, looking directly at the howling spectators, moves aggressively toward the camera until his fierce scowl covers the entire wall. At this point, the image dissolves, whereupon the palace begins to collapse. Significantly, the fateful laughter is prompted by a court jester dressed as Harlequin, a denizen of the carnivalesque tradition, the embodied topsy-turvydom of which is at odds with the cultic regimen that, for safety's sake, imposes on the public the muteness of the spectacle (a de-*monstration*). Operating outside of ritual conventions, the fool offends the fourth wall, which is broken through by Moses himself with the force and consequence of a locomotive.

165

Notes

1. All translations of Rilke's poetry are mine, except "Archaischer Torso Apollos," which is by Stephen J. Mitchell.
2. Robert Weimann, *Shakespeare and the Popular Tradition in the Theater,* ed. Robert Schwartz (Baltimore: Johns Hopkins University Press, 1978), 11.
3. Jean Starobinski, *1789: The Emblems of Reason,* trans. Barbara Bray (Cambridge: MIT Press, 1982), 175–76.
4. Goethe, *Faust: Part One,* trans. Bertram Jessup (New York: Philosophical Library, 1958), ll. 918–19. Subsequent references to *Faust* are found in the text.
5. Cf. Michael Fried, *Absorption and Theatricality: Painting and the Beholder in the Age of Diderot* (Berkeley: University of California Press, 1980).
6. The "choirs" at the end of the first monologue scene (*Chor der Engel, Chor der Weiber,* etc.) are taken almost verbatim from medieval mystery cycles. Cf. *English Mystery Plays,* ed. Peter Happé (London: Penguin, 1985), 580–81; Jane K. Brown, *Goethe's Faust: The German Tragedy* (Ithaca, N.Y.: Cornell University Press, 1986), 15ff.
7. Cf. Richard Alewyn, *Das große Welttheater: Die Epoche der höfischen Feste* (Munich: Beck, 1989).
8. See Fried's discussion (*Absorption and Theatricality,* 94) of Diderot's instruction (*Discours de la poésie dramatique*) to both author and actor that they "forget the beholder," an enjoinder tantamount to that of disregarding the opinions of one's neighbors ("Eh! laissez là les voisons"). Concerning the darkening of the theater beyond the stage, see Wolfgang Schivelbusch, *Lichtblicke: Zur Geschichte der künstlichen Helligkeit im 19. Jahrhundert* (Frankfurt am Main: Fischer, 1986), 193–201.
9. Jürgen Habermas discusses a privacy oriented toward an audience. *The Structural Transformation of the Public Sphere,* trans. Thomas Burger and Frederick Lawrence (Cambridge, Mass.: MIT Press, 1991), 43ff.
10. David E. Wellbery, "Das Gesetz der Schönheit: Lessings Ästhetik der Repräsentation," in *Was heißt "Darstellen"?* ed. Christian L. Hart-Nibbrig (Frankfurt am Main: Suhrkamp, 1994), 192ff.
11. Michel Foucault, *Naissance de la clinique* (Paris: Presses Universitaires de France, 1963), 108.
12. Weimann, *Shakespeare,* 9.
13. Tom Gunning, "An Aesthetics of Astonishment: Early Film and the (In)credulous Spectator," *Art and Text* 34 (1989): 31–36.
14. Wolfgang Schivelbusch, *Geschichte der Eisenbahnreise: Zur Industrialisierung von Raum und Zeit im 19. Jahrhundert* (Frankfurt am Main: Fischer, 1989), 61; John Stilgoe, *Metropolitan Corridor: Railroads and the American Scene* (New Haven, Conn.: Yale University Press, 1983), 249ff; Anne Friedberg,

"*Les Flaneurs du Mal(l)*: Cinema and the Postmodern Condition," *Publications of the Modern Language Association* 106 (1991): 419–31.

15. Lynne Kirby, "Male Hysteria and Early Cinema," *Camera Obscura* 17 (1988): 113–14.

16. Sigmund Freud, *Studienausgabe,* ed. Alexander Mitscherlich, Angela Richards, and James Strachey (Frankfurt am Main: Fischer, 1982), 3:222, 241–42.

17. Ibid., 3:231.

18. Schivelbusch, *Geschichte der Eisenbahnreise,* 131.

19. Freud, *Studienausgabe,* 3:241–42. Schivelbusch's study figures prominently in the essays by Gunning and Kirby (and somewhat less so in the essay by Friedberg), who in turn cite Miriam Hansen's more general discussion of "shock" as a strategy, implemented by film, for adapting to industrial modes of production. "Benjamin, Cinema and Experience: 'The Blue Flower in the Land of Technology,' " *New German Critique* 40 (1987): 179–224.

20. Paul Ricoeur speaks of a "positivistic transposition" in Freud's later thought. *Freud and Philosophy,* trans. Denis Savage (New Haven, Conn.: Yale University Press, 1970), 209.

21. Christian Begemann, *Furcht und Angst im Prozeß der Aufklärung* (Frankfurt am Main: Athenäum, 1987), 128–29.

22. Gotthold Ephraim Lessing, *Werke,* ed. Jost Perfahl (Munich: Winkler, 1974), 3:136; *Laocoön,* trans. Edward Allen McCormick (New York: Bobbs-Merrill, 1962), 126.

23. Lynne Tatlock, "Quixotic Marvel: Emesis and the Miscarriage of Subjectivity in Christian Reuter's *Schelmuffsky,*" in "*Der Buchstab tödt—der Geist macht lebendig*" (Festschrift zum 60. Geburtstag von Hans-Gert Roloff), ed. James Hardin and Jörg Jungmayr (Bern: Peter Lang, 1994), 297–319.

24. *Duden "Etymologie": Herkunftswörterbuch der deutschen Sprache,* 2d ed., ed. Günther Drosdowski (Mannheim: Dudenverlag, 1989), 214.

25. Jeannot Simmen, *Vertigo: Schwindel der modernen Kunst* (Munich: Klinkhardt & Biermann, 1990), 34ff.

26. Wellbery, "Das Gesetz der Schönheit," 199.

27. Dolf Sternberger, *Panorama oder Ansichten vom 19. Jahrhundert* (1938; reprint, Frankfurt am Main: Suhrkamp, 1974), 166ff. Jonathan Crary's discussion of the popularity of the stereoscope in the nineteenth century addresses a similar *horror vacui:* "the most intense experience of the stereoscopic image coincides with an object-filled space, with a material plenitude that bespeaks a nineteenth-century bourgeois horror of the void; and there are endless quantities of stereocards showing interiors crammed with bric-a-brac, densely filled museum sculpture galleries, and congested city views" (*Techniques of the Observer: On Vision and Modernity in the Nineteenth Century* [Cambridge, Mass.: MIT Press, 1990], 124).

28. Cf. Anne Leblans: "What is more surprising is that the celebration of the father

is grafted onto a celebration of the mother and that, as a consequence, things that are purchased with money are presented as if they belonged to the realm of the gifts offered by the mother: life itself, nurturance, care (things that remained more or less outside of the market). Christmas represented . . . an attempt by the father to assert his power over the domestic sphere by suggesting that the domain of the mother—including her capacity to give birth—is really his." See chapter 5 of the present volume.

29. Denis Diderot, *Le Fils naturel* (Paris: Librairie Larousse, 1988), 27.
30. Cf. Habermas, *Structural Transformation,* 3.
31. Schivelbusch, *Geschichte der Eisenbahnreise,* 60–61, and *Lichtblicke,* 161ff; also Sternberger, *Panorama,* 156–58.
32. Noel Burch, *Life to Those Shadows,* trans. Ben Brewster (Berkeley: University of California Press, 1990), 36–39.
33. Crary, *Techniques of the Observer,* 106.
34. Albert E. Smith, *Two Wheels and a Crank* (Garden City, N.Y.: Doubleday, 1952), 36.
35. Quoted from James Whale's *Frankenstein* (Hollywood, 1931).
36. Cf. Freud's essay entitled *Über Deckerinnerungen* (1899).
37. Christian Metz, *The Imaginary Signifier,* trans. Celia Britton et al. (Bloomington: Indiana University Press, 1982), 71–73.
38. Weimann, *Shakespeare,* 5, 12.
39. In addition to the famous "Auf eine Lampe," there is also "Das verlassene Mägdelein," which mimes the words of a servant girl who rises early to light the stove and finds temporary solace in the flames and sparks of the nascent fire.
40. Eduard Mörike, "Auf eine Lampe," in *Sämtliche Werke,* ed. Jost Perfahl (Munich: Winkler, 1976), 1:735. See Kenneth S. Calhoon, "The Urn and the Lamp: Disinterest and the Aesthetic Object in Mörike and Keats," *Studies in Romanticism* 26 (1987): 3–25.
41. "Noch unverrückt, o schöne Lampe, schmückest du, / An leichten Ketten zierlich aufgehangen hier, / Die Decke des nun fast vergeßnen Lustgemachs."
42. Leo Spitzer, "The 'Ode on a Grecian Urn'; or Content vs. Metagrammar," in *Essays on English and American Literature* (Princeton, N.J.: Princeton University Press, 1962), 92–93.
43. Theodor W. Adorno, *Ästhetische Theorie* (Frankfurt am Main: Suhrkamp, 1970), 364. See Fredric Jameson, *Late Marxism: Adorno, or, The Persistence of the Dialectic* (London: Verso, 1990), 216–17.
44. See Robert Hullot-Kentor's forward to his translation of Adorno's *Kierkegaard: Construction of the Aesthetic* (Minneapolis: University of Minnesota Press, 1989), xv.
45. Adorno, *Ästhetische Theorie,* 27.
46. Quoted in Stilgoe, *Metropolitan Corridor,* 250.

47. Jameson's summary is especially lucid when he states that, for Adorno, the presence of nature is at the heart of all historical contradictions, "since the domination of nature is deeply inscribed within them as their ultimate dynamic" (*Late Marxism*, 215).

48. Siegfried Kracauer, "Kult der Zerstreuung: Über die Berliner Lichtspielhäuser," in *Das Ornament der Masse* (Frankfurt am Main: Suhrkamp, 1977), 314.

49. Sternberger, *Panorama*, 156.

50. Helmut Börsch-Supan, *Caspar David Friedrich* (Munich: Prestel, 1980), 128.

51. Gilles Deleuze, *The Fold: Leibniz and the Baroque*, trans. Tom Conley (Minneapolis: University of Minnesota Press, 1993), 28–29.

52. Regarding Dracula as an allegory of capitalism, see Franco Moretti, *Signs Taken for Wonders: Readings in the Sociology of Literary Form*, trans. John and Ann Tedeschi (London: Verso, 1984), 90ff. The Nazi propaganda film *Der ewige Jude* (1942), which likens the migratory patterns of Jews to those of rats, has been offered as evidence of how *Nosferatu* (1922), whether or not its intentions were anti-Semitic, codifies the fear of infestation and creates a visual vocabulary that would facilitate explicit associations between Jews, vermin, contagion, and the like. On vampirism and anti-Semitism, see Linda Schulte-Sasse's discussion of Veit Harlan's *Jud Süß* (*Entertaining the Third Reich: The Illusion of Wholeness in Nazi Cinema* [Durham, N.C.: Duke University Press, 1996], 62–67).

53. Max Horkheimer and Theodor Adorno, *Dialektik der Aufklärung* (Frankfurt am Main: Fischer, 1985), 32ff.

54. Pierre Bourdieu, *Distinction: A Social Critique of the Judgement of Taste*, trans. Richard Nice (Cambridge: Harvard University Press, 1988), 19, 54.

55. Norbert M. Schmitz suggests that the appeal Romantic painting held for such directors as Murnau represented a denial of the truly modern, industrial character of photography and as such repeated the pictorialist movement within photography proper, which sought to make painting the model for the photographic art. While this by itself does not account for the specific importance of Romanticism, it does confirm the same aesthetic sensibility that caused the nineteenth-century bourgeoisie to avert its eyes from the train window or to intervene aesthetically in the industrialized glare of interior lighting. Only in the 1920s, Schmitz maintains, did film liberate itself from the hegemony of pictorialism and realize its potential as a truly technological medium ("Zwischen 'Neuem Sehen' und 'Neuer Sachlichkeit': Der Einfluß der Kunstphotographie auf den Film der zwanziger Jahre," in *Gleißende Schatten: Kamerapioniere der zwanziger Jahre*, ed. Cinema Quadrat e. V., Mannheim [Berlin: Henschel, 1994], 92–93. With respect to the chiaroscuro of Murnau's *Faust*, Jacques Aumont contends that Murnau deploys lighting with the precise intention of consigning to oblivion the electrical source

of light (" 'Mehr Licht!'—Zu Murnaus *Faust,*" in *Literaturverfilmungen,* ed. Franz-Josef Albersmeier und Volker Roloff [Frankfurt am Main: Suhrkamp, 1989], 70–71). For a discussion of Murnau's citations of C. D. Friedrich, see Ursula von Keitz, "Der Blick ins Imaginäre: Über Erzählen und Sehen bei Murnau," in *Die Metaphysik des Dekors: Raum, Architektur und Licht im klassischen deutschen Stummfilm,* ed. Klaus Kreimeier (Marburg: Schüren, 1994), 98–99.

56. See Goethe's "Regeln für Schauspieler" in *Hamburger Ausgabe,* vol.12, ed. Erich Trunz, 8th ed. (Munich: Beck, 1978), 256–57.

57. E. H. Gombrich, *Art and Illusion* (Princeton, N.J.: Princeton University Press, 1972), 44–49. See also August Langen, *Anschauungsformen in der deutschen Dichtung des 18. Jahrhunderts: Rahmenschau und Rationalismus* (Darmstadt: Wissenschaftliche Buchgesellschaft, 1965).

58. Wilhelm Worringer, *Abstraktion und Einfühlung* (Munich: Piper, 1976), 36.

59. Horkheimer and Adorno, *Dialektik der Aufklärung,* 17.

60. Sigmund Freud, "Triebe und Triebschicksale" (Instincts and Their Vicissitudes), in *Studienausgabe,* 3:82–83, 98.

61. Friedrich Kittler, *Draculas Vermächtnis* (Leipzig: Reclam, 1993), 99–100; Lawrence Rickels, *Aberrations of Mourning: Writing on German Crypts* (Detroit: Wayne State University Press, 1988), 329.

CARSTEN STRATHAUSEN

8 The Image as Abyss: The Mountain Film and the Cinematic Sublime

A photograph from 1939 shows the interior of Adolf Hitler's Alpine retreat near Berchtesgaden. A window of regal proportions frames hills that rise to meet snow-capped peaks. At center foreground stands a table with a pot of flowers; further to the right a comparatively small human figure, Hitler himself, is seen from behind. More than a photograph, the image presents nature itself as a painting, framed on all four sides by the window that furnishes this grandiose view. The entire scene is reminiscent of Caspar David Friedrich's famous *Wanderer above the Sea of Mist* (1818). Yet there are differences. Friedrich's wanderer stands imperiously at the center of the painting, high above the majestic scene. His back to the spectator, the figure mediates between representation and reality, inviting the onlooker to "enter" into the image. In contrast to the three-dimensionality of Friedrich's painting, the photograph of the Untersberg appears flat, lacking frontage and thus devoid of depth, while the inserted spectator—Hitler—is located on the periphery and thus outside the spectacle he is contemplating. Like Friedrich's wanderer, Hitler shares his view with the onlookers, but he reserves the privilege of experiencing its grandeur: twice removed from the mountain presented as a photograph of a "painting," the spectator capitulates before a scene to which he or she is refused access. A transference takes place: one senses that the divine experience is Hitler's and his alone. He seems to apprehend what we merely watch, to feel as we remain obtuse.

If the photograph thus converts the communal experience of the sublime granted by Friedrich's painting into Hitler's personal affair, it nonetheless renders the transference itself public. The photograph, which could be purchased in the form of a postcard, contributed to the attempt to mythologize Hitler's private life at the Obersalzberg and to inspire fantasies about his clandestine genius.[1] Contained within the photograph we find some of the major characteristics of Nazi aesthetics: while it remains the privilege of the genius to experience the metaphysical quality of life in the form of art, the masses are merely granted the right to witness the spectacle of divine revelation. Not the experience itself, but its imagined essence transferred upon the genius's eye, is all that survives of Friedrich's painting. The photograph presents the imaginary experience of the sublime as real while reducing the benefactor of that experience—nature—to its mere representation.

The following essay attempts to reexamine the connection between romantic imagery and Nazi aesthetics via the analysis of the Weimar mountain film. Arnold Fanck's *Der heilige Berg* provides a scene similar to the one discussed above, picturing the dancer sitting on a vast windowsill as she contemplates the mountains outside. (The image is reproduced in the introduction to this volume, page 11.) Yet, by alluding to the similarity between the "pictures" and their obvious concern for the representation of the (artistic or political) genius vis-à-vis the grandiose sight of nature, I do not intend to equate the mountain film with protofascism.[2] Rather, I want to suggest a theoretical framework that allows us to discern how Nazism exploited an aesthetics already prominent in eighteenth- and nineteenth-century Germany. The discourse on the sublime, which focused on the traditional mode of representation in the realm of art, reappeared in the fascist attempt to aestheticize politics—that is, to revive traditionally elitist concepts within the political realm of mass culture. The Weimar mountain film functioned as an intermediary agent before and during the proclamation of the arrival of the "aesthetic state."

The Construction of Cinematic Space in the Mountain Film

The postwar condemnation of the mountain film generally focuses on the glorification of myth, nature, and heroic sacrifice—that is, on the study of thematic codes—and thus repeats a diegetic analysis that continues to be reworked.[3] However, Fanck's first films, such as *Die Wunder des Schneeschuhs* (1919) and *Im Kampf mit dem Berge* (1921), generally lack succinct plot or character development; they consist of little more than spectacular photography of glaciers, mountain peaks, and acrobatic ski races. Typical of all of Fanck's films, including his later dramas, is his radical accentuation of "offscreen" space: while the location of the camera remains fixed, the skiers suddenly emerge out of nowhere, rush by the camera, and disappear again into the "offscreen," often without being pursued by the camera. Fanck's interest in film focused less on the consecutive movement of images than on the depth of field achieved within the single shot.[4] This quality is still apparent in Fanck's later comedies such as *Der große Sprung* (1927) and *Der weiße Rausch* (1930/31), which present a plethora of landscape images held loosely together by an abstract plot, usually a "fox hunt on skies" (*Fuchsjagd auf Skiern*).

Yet, in spite of the pacified landscape they depict, these comedies also emphasize continuous movement directly toward or away from the camera; in *Der weiße Rausch*, Fanck produces "dangerous" images by blocking off parts of the frame, increasing the dynamics of the skiers racing by. On occasion he even has cameras mounted on top of skis speeding downhill.[5] In order to achieve a higher "reality-effect" in his films, Fanck refused to stage scenes in the studio, and insisted on the original cast performing "live" on location, a practice that often put the lives of the entire film crew at risk.

One might say that Fanck's mountain films were among the first action films and thus clearly continued the tradition of the "cinema of attractions." This term was coined by Tom Gunning to refer to films preceding the dominance of narrative (up to 1903/1904)—films meant to shock and thrill the audience through the sudden movement of images rather than absorb the spectator into a fictional or dramatic sequence. Early cinema, in which plot functioned as a mere vehicle to demonstrate the magical power of cinema for an enthralled audience, was little concerned with narrative closure. Referring to examples of oncoming trains or performers gesticulating toward the camera, Gunning remarks that the "images of the cinema of attraction rush forward to meet their viewers."[6] In other words, early cinema dwelled on the illusion of depth as it frightened or thrilled the spectator with potentially dangerous images. Although film viewers knew that the images were harmless, they were nonetheless stunned by the abyss opening up before their very eyes.

Contrary to this "primitive cinema,"[7] later narrative films tried to flatten the pictorial surface and thus replace the chaotic disorder of images with a linear and spectator-centered presentation of reality, which became indispensable for the fictional narration of events.[8] Contrary to early film, which relocated the epistemological abyss between subject (spectator) and object (i.e., its cinematic representation on the screen) within its own representation such that the image itself became the abyss, classical narrative film diminished the threatening effect of spatial depth by placing emphasis on the rapid succession of single images. Early film deliberately highlighted the artificiality of its visual projection; later films attempted to hide this mechanism through specific forms of editing and mise-en-scène.

This suturing of the film's diegesis into a coherent whole repeats on the textual level the constitutive mechanism of the medium itself, which is based on the denial of difference in favor of the impression of continuity.[9] In other words, the technical suppression of the black space that separates the single images on the film roll reappears as the suppression of the offscreen space in the film's diegesis—that is, the abyss that yawns between two shots.[10] The movement-image requires the subject to bridge this gap by functioning as a stand-in, thus keeping the "whole" from breaking apart.[11] The despatialization of film was supported by the whole design of the Weimar movie palaces, whose revue-like programs and lush decor, according to Kracauer, "served one sole purpose: to bind the public to the periphery in order that it not sink into the abyss."[12]

The connection between Fanck's films and the "cinema of attractions" was noted by critics as early as 1924: "Put bluntly: our best culture-film is not a path

173

to the heart of nature, but a means of tickling the nerves, an accumulation of sensations."[13] The exciting and thrilling effect of Fanck's films was enhanced by their mode of presentation: his first films were, incidentally, not shown in movie theaters, but in modified lecture halls. Since this environment lacked the lush interiors of the Berlin movie palaces, the aforementioned despatialization of film by means of accentuating the flat surface of the surroundings was necessarily absent. To paraphrase Kracauer, one might say that Fanck intended for the spectator to indeed "sink into the abyss."

Given their almost documentary style, it seems questionable to ascribe the appeal of early mountain films solely to the propagation of protofascist sentiments: thematic codes like sacrifice, heroism, and male bonding were not yet a major concern of these films. Furthermore, one must regard Balács's apologia toward the mountain film as indicative of the genre's success also among leftist intellectuals in Weimar Germany, who were certainly less prone to be "taken in" by its purportedly conservative values.[14] If we want to understand the success of the mountain film, it seems prudent to supplement the thematic analysis with a heightened concern for the working of cinematic codes within the genre. Focusing particularly on the portrayal of mountains and the notion of the sublime—that is, the representation of the abyss—I hope to expose the psychological mechanisms already at work before the Nazi ascent to power. Nazi aesthetics mainly capitalized on preexisting perceptual patterns in order to fascinate the masses.

Financial considerations forced Fanck to change his initial documentary approach and begin to include a melodramatic plot in his films, typically the rivalry of two men over a woman.[15] This shift seems to recuperate the mountain film for classical narrative cinema. In fact, one might argue that the internal development of the genre mirrors the broader history of film as such, presenting a condensed version of the medium's transition from a "cinema of attractions" toward the preoccupation with narrative closure of later films. However, the mountain film proved yet again to be maladapted to the demands of the market. While applauding the film's depiction of nature, critics at the time generally lamented what Kracauer called the "stupidity of the plot" prevalent in these films.[16] Unanimously shared by film critics even today, this broad condemnation of the narrative elements of the mountain film is certainly justified: the plot line often leaps between crucial developments and subsequently tries to conceal the ensuing ruptures with the help of intertitles; the fictional characters remain underdeveloped, their actions seem unmotivated, the story unconvincing.[17] As a consequence, these films "do not attain the usual narrative closure, and the spectator must . . . constantly re-define the story in order to follow its course."[18]

Equally important, however, is Fanck's refusal to set up a coherent cinematic space for his audience. The joint effort of most Weimar films to eliminate the spatial depth of the image, a process which culminates in the completely flat prop-stage used for Robert Wiene's *The Cabinet of Doctor Caligari,*[19] remains foreign to the mountain film even after its adoption of narrative plot. Fanck's films continue to exploit the threatening three-dimensionality of film by providing a great depth of field as the camera enters crevasses and penetrates the inside of mountains; often, the daring photography of thundering avalanches literally swallows the "I" of the camera.

Due to Fanck's cinematic technique, the images gain spatial depth and are literally transformed into the precipitous chasms they depict. In Fanck's dramas, the spectator is continuously threatened with sinking into the abyss, a scenario meticulously illustrated in Fanck's film *Der heilige Berg* (1925/26): Recognizing his friend Vigo as the rival and destroyer of his love, Robert menacingly steps forward toward the camera (i.e., Vigo) until his face fills and exceeds the entire screen, causing Vigo to retreat and fall off the cliff. Reminiscent of similar scenes in Georges Méliès's *L'homme à la Tête en Caoutchouc* (1901/2) and Fritz Lang's *Dr. Mabuse, der Spieler* (1922), Robert's anger seems to be directed less toward Vigo than at the spectators themselves as he threatens to transgress the fictional realm and materialize out of the screen. The subsequent shot, showing Vigo dangling on a rope secured by Robert, briskly relocates the action into the cinematic space and thus recuperates the scene for the voyeuristic pleasure of the film audience.

Die weiße Hölle von Piz Palu provides another example of an extreme point-of-view shot that blurs the lines between fictional space and reality. Maria's husband is preparing a birthday cake for his wife, while she secretly follows the scene by peeking through the fingers that cover her eyes. Her "eyes," however, have been replaced by the camera lens itself, so that Maria's hands function like a veil in front of the spectator's "eyes." Gradually extending her hands as she walks toward her husband, Maria moves away from the camera and enters the scene that slowly takes shape. While Robert's transgression in *Der heilige Berg* posits a confrontational threat directed against the audience, Maria's maneuver reverses that movement and gently leads the spectator into the "picture" of an intimate domestic space thus created. Both scenes, however, clearly contemplate and actually stage the "shocking" implosion of fictional into real space.

In most of his films, Fanck sets up a contrast between long shots with a great depth of field that emphasize perspective and its subsequent annihilation in times of natural catastrophes that destroy any sense of spatial organization.[20] Fanck's use of the "vertical" camera, meant to impose upon his audience the grandiosity of the mountain region, as well as the continued "experience" of drifting clouds, roaring storms, thundering avalanches, and vast ice fields, often renders spatial orientation impossible, not only for the fictional characters and the acting cast on location, but for the audience as well.

Fanck occasionally mitigates this disorientation by inserting human bodies into the picture, as, for example, in *Stürme über dem Montblanc* or *S.O.S. Eisberg*. While these figures serve as the only comparative markers to highlight the grandiosity of the scenery, they often remain barely discernable to the spectator's eye as they vanish into the storm or dissolve into the vastness of space. In *Die weiße Hölle von Piz Palu*, Udet's plane is reduced to a small black spot against the background of moving clouds and snow-covered mountain peaks melted together into a vast, amorphous field of white. Udet's ceaseless caprioles and loopings signify the loss of direction in a space that can no longer be quantified nor measured in terms of up and down, left or right: "Although the stranded couple provides a center for the cinematic space and the entire action taking place therein, the scene nonetheless remains a space without a center, without structure."[21]

The destruction of cinematic space in Fanck's films is usually "framed" by coherent narrative elements meant to reassure the audience of an organizing principle working to shape landscape into tableaus, a practice that naturally highlights the subsequent shock of losing "perspective" as nature destroys the space provided by the camera. Fanck employs this technique not only to emphasize the contrast between the different genres, such that the idyllic landscape in his comedies "prepares the ground which will then be shattered in his dramas";[22] rather, Fanck also prepares this shock-reaction within the individual films themselves. *Die weiße Hölle von Piz Palu*, for example, contrasts the calm opening scenes in the alpine cabin with Krafft's agitated recollection of the fatal accident that led to the death of his wife. Structured primarily along the shot/countershot paradigm, the cabin scenes create a coherent cinematic space, the subsequent destruction of which once again centers around the classic plunge into the abyss. This fall is characterized by the excessive use of montage (more than twenty cuts during the sequence of the accident proper, comprising about thirty seconds), the direct juxtaposition of extreme close-up (Krafft's face) and extreme long shot (the approaching avalanche) responsible for a complete loss of dimensionality for the audience, and the radical exploitation of offscreen space: if the take lasts more than three seconds, it usually shows first a picture devoid of movement in which an external element suddenly intrudes and vanishes again; for example, the body of Krafft's wife falling into the crevasse.[23] Krafft's recollection of the accident ends with a long-lasting medium shot on Krafft as he stares at the torn rope in his hands, thus returning to the coherent presentation of distinct images.

In spite of the attempts of later mountain films to adhere to the rules of narrative film, the genre nonetheless continues to exhibit explicit traces of its origins. In Fanck's films, the "cinema of attractions" has literally gone underground: it hides in the deep crevasses that suddenly give way beneath a character's feet or within the windy storms that surprise mountaineers and spectators alike, seeming to annihilate the space they inhabit. Thus, the sustained ruptures of fictional space in Fanck's presentation of landscape do not merely result in the audience's loss of orientation, as recent studies have stressed, but activate the thrill of the primitive, exhibitionist cinema that seemed all but forgotten at the time.[24] The mountain film's failure to achieve narrative closure is mirrored by its inability to provide the coherent cinematic space needed for such a narrative to unfold. The two aspects are interconnected; not only the fictional characters, but the diegesis itself seems to get lost in the turmoil caused by nature gone rampant.

The Romantic Tradition in the Mountain Film

The mountain film deliberately attempts to revive Romantic motifs within the realm of modern mass culture, often by means of direct citations of famous paintings by Friedrich and other artists celebrating the beauty of the mountains.[25] Yet, similar to Romantic imagery in literature and painting, the status of nature in the mountain film remains ambiguous, for the praise of scenic beauty is balanced by depictions of nature's destructive power. The film's aesthetics of shock, its exploration of deep crevasses and mountain caverns mirror the thematic concern in Romanticism with the relationship between surface and depth: the minute description of surface in Romantic painting and nature-poetry is usually accompanied by the allegorization of nature's interior, particularly obvious in the case of the mountain, which often represents the unconscious or the dark side of human nature the hero has to explore, frequently with devastating consequences.

The resurfacing of Romantic codes in the mountain film seems hardly surprising, given the intimate relationship discernable between Romanticism and Weimar film in general. As early as 1952, Lotte Eisner thought it "reasonable to argue that German cinema is a development of German Romanticism, and that modern technique merely lends visible form to Romantic fantasies."[26] The specificity of the mountain film, however, belies such generality, for while the genre indeed promotes antimodern sentiments, it also introduces technology into its stories (airplanes, cars, observatories, radios) and employs the most sophisticated equipment (cameras, wind generators, dynamite) in order to produce its "romantic" effect.[27] The construction and subsequent annihilation of cinematic space in the mountain film seems inextricably linked to modern technology: the self-referential exploration and organization of space in *Stürme über dem Mont Blanc* through scopic devices is eradicated by Udet's chaotic vision, provided by the "flying" camera. Fanck's films constantly oscillate between affirming and eradicating perspective through the use of modern technology.

Two conclusions might be drawn from this assessment. The seamless reconciliation between romantic nature and modern technology within the mountain film could be regarded as a perfect illustration of Weimar's "reactionary modernism," characterized by Jeffrey Herf as an attempt to "incorporate modern technology into the cultural system of modern German nationalism, without diminishing the latter's romantic and antirational aspects."[28] According to Herf, the appeal of reactionary modernism for Nazi ideology lay precisely in its peculiar fusion of rationality and sentimentality, expressed strikingly in Goebbels's call to create a new era of "steel-like romanticism" ("stählerne Romantik"). The mountain film thus appears once again as a paradigm for protofascist sentiments in Weimar

177

culture and provides additional evidence for the fatal entanglement between German romanticism and the rise of fascism.[29] The escapist nature of the genre lends this reading further support. Faced with the social problems caused by modernity, Fanck's heros tend to escape from the crowded metropolis into the alpine regions only to find nature itself even more uninhabitable and alien to mankind than the "flatland" they fled. "Beautiful, tough and dangerous," the hero in *Der heilige Berg* tersely says of his life in the mountains, a statement that indeed functions as the guiding motto for all of Fanck's mountain films as they ceaselessly try to transform these words into the imagery they evoke. Fanck's *Der König des Montblanc* provides a rare example in which the hero actually succeeds in "resocializing" the mountain region and thus sustains the romantic idyll as a counterparadigm of social life in the city below.[30] In general, however, whenever the (male) hero attempts to live his life alone in the heights, he either dies, usually sacrificing his life to rescue others (*Der heilige Berg, S.O.S. Eisberg, Die weiße Hölle von Piz Palu*), or he is rescued and forced to return to civilization (*Stürme über dem Montblanc*). By destroying the romantic utopia of an inhabitable space outside of civilization, the mountain film truly functions as the double of the social disillusionment portrayed in the Weimar street film:[31] both expose the impotence of the (bourgeois) individual to sustain himself against superior powers, be they of social or natural origin. The diegesis of the mountain film hence does not provide an answer to the problems of modernity, but instead promotes a defeatist attitude toward the world.[32]

A second, less denunciatory reading might link the genre with an attempt to expose the complicity between primitive nature and the industrialized metropolis. In Louis Trenker's *Der verlorene Sohn,* for example, the image of two mountain peaks is superimposed over two skyscrapers in New York, identifying the metropolis as the primeval "jungle" of civilization. In Benjaminian terms, the mountain film provides yet another opportunity for the "industrialized consciousness" of the masses to rehearse the modern mode of perception.[33] Fanck's mountain films provide "shocking" imagery of the alpine region as the equivalent to the social upheaval the audience witnesses in real life, enabling spectators to adapt to a technological world they experience as second nature.

Yet both readings are reductive: as I have argued previously, it seems highly questionable to implicate the mountain film within the ideological framework of Nazi aesthetics without considering the specific formal structure that distinguishes Fanck's films from other examples of Weimar cinema. It is crucial to examine how the defeat of the individual on the textual level echoes in the mountain film's regression toward an earlier stage of cinema that does not allow the spectators to suture the film into a coherent whole, but rather presents a dialectical movement oscillating between voyeurism and exhibitionism, pleasure and frightening thrill. Yet, the Benjaminian reading of the mountain film equally lacks specificity, as it merely addresses the role of the medium of film in general without giving consideration to the decisive differences between various genres in Weimar cinema. One reading lacks comparative breadth, the other analytical depth.

By examining the films' exploration of the "cinematic sublime," I hope to ascertain more precisely both the way in which the mountain film participated in the Benjaminian shock-rehearsal of modernity as well as its implication in the framework of a fascist aesthetics. Although it seems obvious that the romanticized content of the mountain film, as well as the audience's ambivalent reaction of both fright and pleasure, link these films to the pre-Romantic notion of the sublime, critics have not yet examined how this aesthetics, on a structural or aesthetic level, relates to the medium of film in general and the mountain film in particular.[34] The following, then, is not a lengthy treatise on the history of the sublime; rather, it is a reading of specific authors, concentrating on what I believe to be the essential psychological quality of the sublime, its "subjectivity effect."

Cinema and the Sublime

For Longinus, the sublime in language involves a sort of "transport" on the part of the listener (reader): "the effect of elevated language is not to persuade the hearers, but to entrance them; and at all times, and in every way, what transports us is more telling than what merely persuades or gratifies us."[35] Recent studies on Longinus have characterized this transport as a "fictive identification with the speaker"[36] in order to appropriate the text as one's own and thus merge with the grandiosity of the sublime utterance—a practice that characterizes Longinus's own approach. As he argues with regard to a poem by Sappho, the relief offered by the sublime consists in the masterful "skill" with which the poem, describing a process of fragmentation on the textual level, ultimately succeeds in suturing the various parts "into a single whole" through its formal structure.[37] Sappho's poem, then, describes the imaginary—that is, artistic—process of self-constituting subjectivity and offers the reader the possibility of identifying with the subject-position thus created. If this reading of Longinus may seem too literal an interpretation, guided by Lacanian psychoanalysis and its invocation of the "Mirror-Stage," Longinus's comments nonetheless point to the essential mechanism at work in the sublime, a mode of "transport" by means of which the listener partakes of the imaginary wholeness achieved in the medium of art to combat the prevailing fear of death and demise.[38]

This aesthetic fortification of the subject is more readily accessible in Kant, who identifies the (dynamic) sublime with man's feeling of moral superiority vis-à-vis devastating power of nature.[39] It follows that the sublime is not to be found in nature as such, but rather refers to an act of human self-recognition, called forth most efficiently in the realm of art: "Sublimity, therefore, does not reside in any of the things of nature, but only in our mind, in so far as we may become conscious of our superiority over nature within, and thus also over nature without us."[40] The category of the sublime here functions as the last refuge of the mind against the superior forces reigning in the world outside. If the process of enlightenment is nothing but "mythical fear turned radical," as Horkheimer and Adorno have claimed, then the category of the sublime appears as the last stronghold against the recognition of the powerlessness of reason to dissipate those fears, an effort to establish absolute human sovereignty by means of aesthetic projections that promote the harmless presence of an otherwise dangerous nature.[41] In other words, since destructive nature around 1800 "epitomizes all of those unsolved problems whose attempted dissipation caused reasonable history to resign," as Odo Marquard has argued,[42] the continuous evocation of such a nature in the realm of art signifies the compulsion to repeat and reverse the traumatic experience of reason's own impotence.[43]

From Longinus to eighteenth- and nineteenth-century aesthetics in Kant and Schiller, the concept of sublimity shifts from the description of a sublime "exterior" (nature, divinity, God) to a recognition of a sublime "interior" located within human consciousness.[44] The discourse of the sublime speaks to the mobilization of regressive tendencies at the moment of social crisis, activating illusions of grandeur to dissipate the narcissistic predicament of modern man by bridging the abyss between inside and outside, mind and world, subject and object. It is precisely the function of Kant's third *Critique* to provide a passage or a "bridge over the abyss" that separates theoretical from practical reason. The image of the abyss in particular provides an essential metaphor for Kant's aesthetic reflections, which repeatedly evoke it to illustrate the dangers dissipated by the sublime: Kant explicitly refers to the infinite as the abyss for human "sensibility,"[45] and later portrays the wild ocean as the "threatening abyss which we find sublime after all,"[46] while Schiller pictures the sublime as the strong arm that "carries us [humans] over the dizzying depth" of human existence.[47]

The concept of the sublime hence comprises both the evocation and subsequent surmounting of the abyss. The sublime is the very abyss it bridges.[48] This dialectic is strikingly articulated by Thomas Weiskel, who proposes that we redefine the sublime moment as a process consisting of three consecutive phases: a harmonious, preconscious relationship between mind and object collapses due to an excess of external stimuli and is subsequently reconstituted by erecting a conscious metarelation between mind and image. The essential function of the sublime in nineteenth-century aesthetics is to guarantee the survival of meaning vis-à-vis superior outside forces.

Although his study refers to literary texts exclusively, Weiskel's insights prove extremely useful when applied to the analysis of cinematic imagery. Within his framework, one might regard the excess of external stimuli caused by industrialization and urbanization as a "sublime" crisis of meaning that demanded and achieved its immediate resolution with the arrival of film. The impression of continuity within the "movement-image" results from the syntagmatic flow of images, which the spectator's imaginary attempts to suture into a coherent whole. Weiskel's account of the working of the sublime reads like an illustration of the very process of suture: the sublime recovers meaning "through the insertion of a substituted term into the chain, i.e., through metaphor. The absence of a signified itself assumes the status of a signifier, disposing us to feel that behind this newly significant absence lurks a newly discovered presence, the latent referent, as it were, mediated by the new sign."[49] The newly discovered presence masking the significant absence is nothing but the subject itself. For Lacan, the subject merely covers the void between two signifiers, meaning that "the definition of the subject comes down to the possibility of one signifier more," as Miller phrases it. The sublime moment might be conceptualized as the constitutive element of ideological interpellation at work in film-aesthetics. Suture is the "cinematic sublime." Because of the "reality effect" achieved through the use of monocular perspective and the illusion of spatial depth, film in general seems superior to all other art-media in replicating an awe-inspiring object (the mountain), without, however, actually frightening the spectator. This, according to Kant, would destroy the sublime moment altogether.

Aligning the "subjectivity effect" produced by the sublime with the process of primary cinematic identification strikingly reveals that the narcissistic regression exemplified in the mountain film is not primarily located at the diegetic level, that is, in the protagonist's return to untamed nature or in the frequent image of the male hero seeking refuge from the world in the lap of his beloved—a scene that, according to Kracauer, is typical for Weimar film in general. Rather, it is built into its formal structure. The genre's established preference for the spatial illusion of depth presents a deliberate attempt to revive the history of early cinema and its aesthetics of shock within the realm of natural landscape. The "high and exalted" point of view stipulated by the sublime is precisely the perspective provided by Fanck's portrayal of icy glaciers and mountaintops from which the protagonist peers down onto the world below.[50] Moreover, Fanck's oscillation between peaceful and dangerous images—that is, the dialectics between the destruction and confirmation of cinematic space in the mountain films—works along the mechanism of Weiskel's romantic sublime, producing an imaginary subject-position with which the audience can identify. If the sublime is the abyss, then the frequent portrayal of crevasses and mountain ridges in the mountain film serves the purpose of evoking the sublime danger and its subsequent apotheosis in order to redeem the spectator from the threatening experience of "sinking into the abyss."

Nazi Aesthetics and the Sublime

It would be naive not to acknowledge the political implications of the sublime for Nazi aesthetics in general, and yet research on the topic is sparse.

Given the obvious megalomania of fascist architecture and sculpture, investigations occasionally allude to the Kantian sublime, though without further considering the aesthetic implications of this nexus.[51] Instead, critics have focused more generally on the explicit parallel between art and politics at work in Nazi ideology, arguing that the fascist aestheticization of politics presents a perverted redemption of eighteenth- and nineteenth-century aesthetic ideals.[52] In his novel *Michael,* Goebbels explicitly acknowledges the similarity between art and politics as the founding principle of Nazi ideology: "The statesman is also an artist. For him, the nation is exactly what the stone is for the sculptor. Führer and masses, that is as little of a problem as, say, painter and color."[53] Nazi propaganda efficiently mobilizes the Romantic concept of the ingenious artist transforming chaos into the timeless harmony of true art as a means of legitimizing the absolute power of the political "genius" Adolf Hitler.

Within this context, the notion of the "cinematic sublime" I have tried to develop with reference to the mountain film helps to provide further insight into the psychological mechanism at work in Nazi aesthetics. The current prevalence of the sublime in postmodern aesthetic discourse functions as a reminder that prominent philosophical problems of the past do not simply vanish, but undergo a series of transformations in order to adapt to recent sociohistorical developments. When Hitler addressed throngs of people during Nazi mass rallies and rituals, he was confronted with an "ocean" of human bodies that facilitated his own self-presentation as the romantic genius commanding nature itself. In other words, the continuous restaging of the sublime during these rallies recast the original confrontation between human subject and terrifying nature as that between political leader and national masses. Both experiences activated a "subjectivity effect" that disseminated from its center to the periphery, from the genius to the masses: just "as a result of the Kantian esthetics [of the sublime], every artistically inclined citizen could aspire towards the status of genius,"[54] so the "sublime" aestheticization of politics during German fascism allowed every individual in the mass to identify with the leader and thus regain the ego-ideal he had seemingly lost.[55] The grandiose mass spectacles and party rallies not only celebrated Hitler as the spiritual genius who had established contact with the transcendental "beyond," but also fostered what Wolfgang Haug calls the process of "rendering the subject fascist" by calling upon the masses to aspire to the status of the leader.[56]

The influence of the mountain film on Nazi aesthetics becomes apparent in the comment by the British ambassador Henderson on Albert Speer's cathedral of lights ("Lichtdom") in Nürnberg: "Solemn and beautiful at the same time, as if one stood in an overwhelming cathedral of pure ice."[57] It was Fanck's *Der heilige Berg* that first provided the material prototype of Henderson's image: hallucinating the final reunion with his beloved in a gigantic "cathedral of pure ice," Robert fatally steps forward as he tries to "enter" the mirage, and plunges to his death. Nazi aesthetics renders Robert's private fantasy public, except that it disregards the tragic ending, instead leaving the "realization" of the subsequent "fall into the abyss" to history itself. The sublime, originally offered by the artistic genius as the last consolation for the anxious bourgeois subject in crisis, is radicalized by German fascism into a form of mass hysteria proclaiming the absolute superiority of an entire population over the rest of the world, including nature and death itself.

Christine Pries rightly observes that the sublime appears in its most reified form during German fascism; it suppresses all the negativity from which it originates and thus becomes indistinguishable from the beautiful or what the capitalist fetishization of the commodity form had left of it.[58] The Benjaminian aura is thus transformed into its own simulacrum, while the romantic sublime reemerges as mere kitsch.[59] Contrary to Pries, however, I would argue that this regression of the sublime was already motivated by Kant's insistence on aesthetic disinterestedness and his prohibition on the evocation of real danger in the realm of art: with actual fear being reduced to an aesthetic experience, the critical potential of the sublime is dissipated; its negativity has always been, from its very beginning, nothing but a ghost—mere "shadows on the wall." Fascism continues this aesthetic tradition as it renders the sublime devoid of any fear of death and begins mass-producing it— brutally imposed for some, joyfully embraced by others. To paraphrase Friedländer, one might say that fascism turns death into one more commodity. Death becomes kitsch, one banality among many, and thus the source of an aesthetic *jouissance*. Yet, it was also Kant who foresaw the dangers inherent in this form of excessive aestheticism, a "fanaticism" ("Schwärmerei") that he defines "as a form of madness that wants to see something beyond all limits of reasonable sensuousness."[60] Such visionalism ends in the abyss, not only for the unfortunate mountaineer in film, but also for the German people in reality.

NOTES

1. Cf. Wolfgang W. Weiß, "Spurensuche am Obersalzberg: NS-Geschichte(n) zwischen Vermarktung und Verdrängung," in *Faszination der Macht,* ed. Wolfgang W. Weiß et al. (Nuremberg: Tummels, 1992), 267–82.
2. "Es gibt einen Fall 'Dr. Fanck,' denn man regt sich auf über ihn. Dr. Fanck wird nicht gelobt, sondern geliebt, nicht kritisiert, sondern angegriffen." This comment, made in 1931 by the renowned Marxist film-critic Béla Baláz in reference to the creator of the Weimar "mountain film," proved to be more prophetic than Balázs himself could have anticipated. Ever since Siegfried Kracauer asserted that "these mountain climbers were devotees performing the rites of a cult," their heroism "rooted in a mentality kindred to Nazi spirit" (*From Caligari to Hitler: A Psychological History of the German Film*

[Princeton, N.J.: Princeton University Press, 1947], 111), postwar critics have identified the mountain film with protofascism and sparked a debate that has continued up to the present. Susan Sontag, for example, regards the mountain film as "an anthology of proto-Nazi sentiments" ("Fascinating Fascism," in *Under the Sign of Saturn* [New York: Farrar, 1976], 76), whereas Andrew Sarris remains suspicious of both Kracauer and Sontag's analysis: "[Sontag] quotes from the very few film historians who support her position, and ignores or insults the rest. Siegfried Kracauer's very questionable *From Caligari to Hitler* is trotted out as if it were holy writ . . . ." (Andrew Sarris, "Notes on the Fascination of Fascism," *Village Voice*, 30 January 1978, 33).

3. The postwar criticism of the mountain film has been summarized by Renata Berg-Pan, *Leni Riefenstahl* (Boston: Twayne, 1980), 68. For a comprehensive overview regarding the reception of the genre before and after World War II, see Klaus Kreimeier, *Fanck-Trenker-Riefenstahl: Der Deutsche Bergfilm und seine Folgen* (Berlin: Stiftung Deutsche Kinemathek, 1972), and Eric Rentschler, "Mountains and Modernity: Relocating the Bergfilm," *New German Critique* 51 (fall 1990): 137–63.

4. Fanck's knowledge of cinematic editing was in fact minimal. According to Fanck himself, the reason why he first visited a movie theater in 1920 was to get some idea about how to edit his first film. Cf. Arnold Fanck, *Er führte Regie mit Gletschern, Stürmen und Lawinen: Ein Filmpionier erzählt* (Munich: Nymphenburger, 1973).

5. Cf. Thomas Jacobs, "Visuelle Traditionen des Bergfilms: Von Fidus zu Friedrich oder Das Ende bürgerlicher Fluchtbewegungen im Faschismus," *Film und Kritik* 1 (June 1992): 37.

6. Tom Gunning, "An Aesthetics of Astonishment: Early Film and the (In)credulous Spectator," *Art and Text* 34 (1989): 36.

7. Gunning's "cinema of attractions" roughly corresponds to what Noel Burch called the "Primitive Mode of Representation" (pre-1909), as opposed to the "Institutional Mode of Representation." According to Burch, the former is characterized by the "autarchy of the tableau (even after the introduction of the syntagm of succession), horizontal and frontal camera placement, maintenance of long shot and 'centrifugality.'" Thus, "primitive cinema" unwittingly highlighted the artificiality of its own projection, which was "non-closed as a whole" (*Life to Those Shadows* [Berkeley: University of California Press, 1990], 188).

8. Ibid., 34, 40.

9. Jean-Louis Baudry argues that film "lives on the denial of difference: difference is necessary for it to live, yet it lives on its negation" ("Ideological Effects of the Basic Cinematic Apparatus," in *Film Theory and Criticism*, ed. Gerald Mast et al. [New York: Oxford University Press, 1992], 306). Christian Metz states similarly with regard to mainstream narrative film: "The rule of the

'story' is so powerful that the image, which is said to be the major constituent of film, vanished behind the plot it has woven . . . so that the cinema is only in theory the art of images. . . . The sequence does not string the individual shots; it suppresses them" (*Film Language* [New York: Oxford University Press, 1974], 45).

10. Metz addresses this process as follows: "Indeed, the equipment is not just physical . . . ; it also has its discursive imprints, its extensions in the very text of the film" (*The Imaginary Signifier: Psychoanalysis and the Cinema* [Bloomington: Indiana University Press, 1982] 76).

11. The concept of suture, introduced by Jacques Alan Miller, describes the relationship between subject and language in Lacanian psychoanalysis ("Suture," *Screen* 18 [1977/78]: 24–34). Suture, according to Miller, "names the relation of the subject to the chain of its discourse; . . . it figures there as the element which is lacking." The subject "is not purely and simply absent," but takes the "form of a stand-in" (25f). Thus, suture names the process by which the subject identifies with itself as the nonidentical; it identifies with the lack as the result of its failed representation. As such, the subject is built on the denial of the process that constitutes it.

12. Siegfried Kracauer, "Kult der Zerstreuung," in *Das Ornament der Masse* (Frankfurt: Suhrkamp, 1977), 314.

13. Quoted in Jürgen Keiper, "Alpträume in Weiß," *Film und Kritik* 1 (1992): 57.

14. Cf. Rentschler, "Mountains and Modernity," 143.

15. Fanck specifies his reasoning in his interview with Hermann Weigel (*Filmhefte* 2 [1976]: 5f.) and in his autobiography, *Er führte Regie mit Gletschern, Stürmen und Lawinen* (Munich: Nymphenburger Verlagsbuchhandling, 1973), 310ff.

16. Kracauer, *Caligari,* 400. For a comprehensive overview of similar comments on Fanck's films, see Rentschler, "Mountains and Modernity," 148.

17. Ben Gabel provides various examples in his essay "Der ewige Traum," *Film und Kritik* 1 (1992): 41–45.

18. Ibid., 41.

19. Cf. Burch, *Shadows.* There exist, of course, counterexamples to this tendency; for example, the films of Friedrich Murnau.

20. This technique sometimes even produces the unwanted effect of a montage within the shot, as, for example, in *Der weiße Rausch,* where the image presents Riefenstahl and Schneider in the foreground peering at the pursuers from the top of a hill.

21. Martin Seel, "Arnold Fanck oder die Verfilmbarkeit von Landschaft," *Film und Kritik* 1 (1992): 74.

22. Keiper, "Alpträume," 64.

23. Fanck also experiments with shots completely out of focus, as in the case of

the students being buried underneath the avalanche in *Die weiße Hölle von Piz Palu.*

24. Cf. Gabel, "Der ewige Traum," 41; Keiper, "Alpträume," 63f; Seel, "Arnold Fanck," 73.

25. For a discussion of Friedrich's paintings with respect to German cinema, see Brigitte Peucker, *Incorporating Images: Film and the Rival Arts* (Princeton, N.J.: Princeton University Press, 1995), 39–41, 91–93. Also see Jacobs, "Visuelle Traditionen," 28f.

26. Lotte Eisner, *The Haunted Screen,* trans. Roger Greaves (Berkeley: University of California Press, 1973), 113.

27. For a comprehensive overview regarding the debate on the "modernity" of the mountain film, see Rentschler, "Mountains and Modernity," 145.

28. Jeffrey Herf, *Reactionary Modernism: Technology, Culture, and Politics in Weimar and the Third Reich* (Cambridge: Cambridge University Press, 1984), 2.

29. In 1930, Thomas Mann was among the first to address the connection between Romanticism and German fascism; see Peter Reichel, *Der schöne Schein des Dritten Reiches: Faszination und Gewalt des Faschismus* (Munich: Hanser, 1991).

30. Riefenstahl's *Tiefland,* as well as Luis Trenker's *Der verlorene Sohn,* provide further examples of a successful synthesis of social order and mountain utopia.

31. Cf. Rentschler, "Mountains and Modernity," 152.

32. Likewise Jacobs, "Visuelle Traditionen," 36. I hence disagree with Keiper, who argues that "Fanck asserts the realm of the mountains and its people against the reigning society" ("Alpträume," 61). Certainly, the mountain people appear to be stronger and more "humane" than the urban bourgeoisie (cf. *Der heilige Berg,* where none of the theater visitors is ready to risk his or her life trying to rescue the two friends in danger), but the films nonetheless unveil any attempt to sustain the simple life in the mountains as illusory, given the superior power of nature. Most of Fanck's films do not, as Keiper claims, "portray nature as a social form of organization that provide models of organic structure and natural hierarchic order" (58).

33. Cf. Walter Benjamin, "The Work of Art in the Age of Mechanical Reproduction," and "On Some Motifs in Baudelaire," in *Illuminations,* ed. Hannah Arendt (New York: Schocken, 1969), 217–52, 155–200. In both texts, Benjamin appropriates Freud's concept of shock and traumatic neurosis for the analysis of the psychological effects of film on the metropolitan masses.

34. Commentators have repeatedly referred to the presence of the sublime in the mountain films, often charging the genre with mobilizing the sublime in preparation for fascist aesthetics. Rentschler, for example, insinuates Herf's

comments on fascism's "reactionary modernism," arguing that "modern tools . . . produce the sublime" in the mountain film ("Mountains and Modernity," 146), while Jacobs focuses on Fanck's mystification of the sublime (cf. Thomas Jacobs, "Der Bergfilm als Heimatfilm," *Augen-Blick* 5 [1988]: 30). Dieter Bartetzko establishes an explicit connection between the mountain film and Nazi aesthetics via the sublime without, however, giving specific consideration to film: "Friedrich's picturesque world found a macabre successor in the extraordinarily successful genre of the mountain film. . . . The art of the Third Reich continued all of this in a consequent fashion" (Dieter Bartetzko, "Zwischen Todesschwärmerei und Empfindelei: Erhabenheitsmotive in NS-Staatsarchitektur und postmodernen Bauten," in *Das Erhabene nach dem Nationalsozialismus,* (special issue) ed. Karl-Heinz Bohrer, Sonderheft *Merkur* 43, 9/10 [1989]: 835).
35. Longinus, "On the Sublime," *Classical Literary Criticism,* trans. T. S. Dorsch (Baltimore, n.d.), 100.
36. Suzanne Guerlac, "Longinus and the Subject of the Sublime," *New Literary History* 16 (1985): 275.
37. The entire passage reads: "Are you not astonished at the way in which, as though they were gone from her and belonged to another, she at one and the same time calls up soul and body, ears, tongue, eyes, and colour; how, uniting opposites, she freezes while she burns, is both out of her senses and in her right mind? . . . but it is, as I said, the selection of them [emotions] in their most extreme forms and their fusion into a single whole that have given the poem its distinction" (114f).
38. Cf. Michel Deguy, "The Discourse of Exaltation," in *Of the Sublime: Presence in Question,* trans. Jeffrey S. Librett (New York: State University of New York Press, 1993). For a more detailed account of how the sublime produces a "subjectivity effect" within its audience, see Frances Ferguson's "A Commentary on Suzanne Guerlac's 'Longinus and the Subject of the Sublime,'" *New Literary History* 16 (1985): 291–97.
39. "Now in just the same way the irresistibility of the might of nature forces upon us the recognition of our physical helplessness as beings of nature, but at the same time reveals a faculty of estimating ourselves as independent of nature, and discovers a pre-eminence above nature that is the foundation of a self-preservation of quite another kind from that which may be assailed and brought into danger by external nature. This saves humanity in our own person from humiliation, even though as mortal men we have to submit to external violence" (Immanuel Kant, *The Critique of Judgement,* trans. James Creed Meredith [Oxford: Clarendon Press, 1952], 111).
40. Kant, *Critique,* 114. For similar passages, see also Kant, *Critique,* 92, 98, 104. Similarly, Friedrich Schiller, in his essay "On the Sublime," simply

defines the sublime as "the absolute great within us." "Über das Erhabene," in *Theoretische Schriften,* ed. Rolf-Peter Janz (Frankfurt: Deutscher Klassiker Verlag, 1992), 827.

41. Odo Marquard, "Zur Bedeutung der Theorie des Unbewußten für eine Theorie der nicht mehr schönen Künste," in *Die nicht mehr schönen Künste: Grenzphänomene des Ästhetischen,* ed. H. R. Jauß (Munich: Fink, 1968), 375–92.

42. Odo Marquard, "Ästhetik und Therapeutik," *Literatur und Gesellschaft,* ed. H. J. Schrimpf (Bonn: Bouvier, 1963), 34.

43. Rejecting this argument as reductive, Christine Pries recently proposed that one regard the sublime as the irreducible experience of oscillation between the destruction and reconstitution of subjectivity. For her, even the rationally constructed subject forged by the Kantian sublime still remembers and remains bound to the sensation of fragmentation and "Unlust" from which it springs forth. The sublime hence represents the margin both separating and aligning the two paradigms; its inherent ambivalence is its main characteristic. See Christine Pries (ed.), *Das Erhabene: Zwischen Grenzerfahrung und Größenwahn* (Weinberg: VCH, 1989), 1–30. While Pries's normative understanding of the sublime may be both accurate and provocative, it remains imperative to realize that, historically speaking, the metaphysical trajectory of the sublime toward harmony and the resolution of conflicts remained far more influential than the possible exploitation of any of its critical potential—a fact Pries herself readily admits (24–25).

44. Andrew Wilton (*Turner and the Sublime* [London: British Museum Publication, 1980], 37–41) provides a detailed description of the historical shift leading from the concept of sublime objects to the idea of sublime moods.

45. Kant, *Critique,* 115.

46. Immanuel Kant, *Kritik der Urteilskraft,* ed. Wilhelm Weischedel (Frankfurt: Suhrkamp, 1974), 196; my translation.

47. Friedrich Schiller, "Über das Erhabene," 826.

48. Several scholars have pointed to the connection between the sublime and the abyss; for example, Thomas Weiskel: "The sublime moment establishes depth because the presentation of the unattainability is phenomenologically a negation, a falling away from what might be seized, perceived, known. As an image, it is the abyss" (*The Romantic Sublime: Studies in the Structure and Psychology of Transcendence* [Baltimore: Johns Hopkins University Press, 1976], 24). Also see Henry Sussman, *Psyche and Text: The Sublime and the Grandiose in Literature, Psychopathology and Culture* (Albany: State University of New York Press, 1993), 37.

49. Weiskel, *Romantic Sublime,* 28.

50. For Andrew Wilton, "the word sublime, both according to its use and etymology, must signify high and exalted" (*Turner and the Sublime,* 27), a view

188

augmented in Michel Deguy's "The Discourse of Exaltation": "To elevate oneself to this *high* which was translated as the sublime is to carry oneself to the place from which one can get a view of the 'mortal condition,' to this perspective that is *like* the divine" (9).

51. The articles by Bartetzko, "Todesschwärmerei," and Claus-E. Bärsch, "Das Erhabene und der Nationalsozialismus" (in *Das Erhabene nach dem Faschismus* 777–90) are certainly exceptions to the rule.

52. See, for example, Rainer Stollmann, *Ästhetisierung der Politik* (Stuttgart: Metzler, 1978) and Martin Jürgens, "Der Staat als Kunstwerk," *Kursbuch* 20 (1970): 123–55.

53. Joseph Goebbels, *Michael: A Novel,* trans. Joachim Neugroschel (New York: Amok, 1987), 14. See also Goebbels's letter to Furtwängler: "Art is politics, too; maybe the highest and most comprehensive there is, and we, who are governing modern German politics, regard ourselves as artistic people, having the responsible task to transform the raw material of the masses into the firm and clear contours of the people." Letter to Wilhelm Furtwängler, 1 April 1933, quoted in Rainer Stollmann, "Faschistische Politik als Gesamtkunstwerk: Tendenzen der Ästhetisierung des politischen Lebens im Nationalsozialismus," in *Die Deutsche Literatur im Dritten Reich,* ed. Hans Denkler et al. (Stuttgart: Metzler, 1976), 87f.

54. Sussman, *Psyche and Text,* 29f.

55. According to Freud, individuals dissolved into a mass (i.e., individuals who identify with each other) nonetheless entertain strong libidinal ties with the leader of the group, who possesses a narcissistic nature of which the crowd longs to partake (*Group Psychology and the Analysis of the Ego,* trans. James Strachey [New York: Norton, 1975]). See also Serge Moscovici, *The Age of the Crowd: A Historical Treatise on Mass Psychology* (Cambridge: Cambridge University Press, 1985).

56. Cf. Wolfgang Fritz Haug, *Faschisierung des Subjekts: Die Ideologie der gesunden Normalität und die Ausrottungspolitiken im deutschen Faschismus* (Hamburg: Argument, 1987). See also Louis Althusser's theory on ideological interpellation in "Ideology and Ideological State Apparatuses: Notes towards an Investigation," in *Essays on Ideology* (London: Verso, 1984), 1–60.

57. Quoted in Bartetzko, "Todesschwärmerei," 841.

58. Cf. Pries, *Das Erhabene,* 30.

59. Cf. Saul Friedländer, *Reflections on Nazism: An Essay on Kitsch and Death* (Bloomington: Indiana University Press, 1993).

60. Quoted in Bartetzko, "Todesschwärmerei," 841.

CONTRIBUTORS

MARY BRODNAX has taught at the University of Missouri-Columbia, Penn State, and Middlebury College. She is now an adjunct professor in the Humanities and Philosophy Department of the University of Central Oklahoma in Edmond.

KENNETH S. CALHOON, professor of German and comparative literature at the University of Oregon, is author of *Fatherland: Novalis, Freud, and the Discipline of Romance* (1992). Recent publications include "Emil Jannings, Falstaff, and the Spectacle of the Body Natural," "Blind Gestures: Chaplin, Diderot, Lessing," and "The Eye of the Panther: Rilke and the Machine of Cinema."

COURTNEY FEDERLE has taught at Mills College, the University of California at Santa Cruz, and was most recently assistant professor of German at the University of Chicago. He currently resides in Chicago, where his urban surroundings remind him of an academic career devoted to the study of architectural modernity. In addition to essays on Siegfried Kracauer and Hannah Höch, he has published on eighteenth-century anthropology and pedagogy.

SABINE HAKE is professor of German at the University of Pittsburgh. In addition to numerous essays on Weimar cinema, she is author of *Passions and Deceptions: The Early Films of Ernst Lubitsch* (1992), *The Cinema's Third Machine: Writing on Film in Germany 1907–1933* (1993), *Excursions: Weimar Berlin and the Writing of Urban Experience* (forthcoming), and *German National Cinema* (with Katie Trumpener, forthcoming).

ANNE LEBLANS is associate professor of German at St. Mary's College of Maryland. She has published essays on the Brothers Grimm, Grimmelshausen, Kafka, Foucault, and Bakhtin.

ELLEN RISHOLM teaches German literature, film, and American studies at the University of Dortmund. She has published on cinema, contemporary German literature, and children's culture. She is currently completing a book on Weimar cinema called *Technologies of Space.*

CARSTEN STRATHAUSEN, assistant professor of German at the University of Missouri-Columbia, has published articles on Louis Althusser, Ernst Jünger, and Walter Benjamin. He is completing a book-length study entitled *The Look of Things: Word, Image, and the Art of Reading around 1900.*

JANET WARD is associate professor of German Studies at the University of Colorado at Boulder. She is author of *Weimar Surfaces: Urban Visual Culture in 1920s Germany* (2001). She is co-editor of *Agonistics: Arenas of Creative Contest* (1997) and *German Studies in the Post-Holocaust Age: The Politics of Memory, Identity, and Ethnicity* (2000). She is currently writing a book entitled *Berlin Borders: Architectural Reformations of a Millennium Metropolis.*

INDEX

INDEX OF FILMS

197

Heads or Tails: The Poetics of Money, by Jochen Hörisch, trans. by Amy Horning Marschall, 2000

Dialectics of the Will: Freedom, Power, and Understanding in Modern French and German Thought, by John H. Smith, 2000

The Bonds of Labor: German Journeys to the Working World, 1890–1990, by Carol Poore, 2000

Schiller's Wound: The Theater of Trauma from Crisis to Commodity, by Stephanie Hammer, 2001

Peripheral Visions: The Hidden Stages of Weimar Cinema, edited by Kenneth S. Calhoon, 2001